FUNCTIONAL CATEGORIES

In every language there are descriptive lexical elements, such as *evening* and *whisper*, as well as grammatical elements, such as *the* and *-ing*. The distinction between these two elements has proven useful in a number of domains, but what is covered by the terms 'lexical' and 'grammatical', and the basis on which the distinction is made, appear to vary according to the domain involved. This book analyses the grammatical elements ('functional categories') in language, a topic that has drawn considerable attention in linguistics, but has never been approached from an integrated, cross-disciplinary perspective. Muysken considers functional categories from the perspective of grammar, language history, language contact, and psychology (including child language and aphasia). Empirically based, the book examines the available converging evidence from these various disciplines, and draws on comparative data from a wide range of different languages.

PIETER MUYSKEN is Professor of Linguistics at the Radboud University Nijmegen, The Netherlands. His previous publications include *One Speaker, Two Languages* (with Lesley Milroy, 1995), *Bilingual Speech. A Typology of Code-Mixing* (2000), and *The Languages of the Andes* (with Willem Adelaar, 2004).

In this series

Earlier issues not listed are also available

CAMBRIDGE STUDIES IN LINGUISTICS

General editors: P. AUSTIN, J. BRESNAN, B. COMRIE,
S. CRAIN, W. DRESSLER, C. J. EWEN, R. LASS,
D. LIGHTFOOT, K. RICE, I. ROBERTS, S. ROMAINE,
N. V. SMITH

Functional Categories

FUNCTIONAL CATEGORIES

PIETER MUYSKEN

Radboud Universiteit Nijmegen

CAMBRIDGE
UNIVERSITY PRESS

CAMBRIDGE UNIVERSITY PRESS
Cambridge, New York, Melbourne, Madrid, Cape Town, Singapore, São Paulo, Delhi

Cambridge University Press
The Edinburgh Building, Cambridge CB2 8RU, UK

Published in the United States of America by Cambridge University Press, New York

www.cambridge.org
Information on this title: www.cambridge.org/9780521619981

First published 2008

Printed in the United Kingdom at the University Press, Cambridge

A catalogue record for this publication is available from the British Library

Library of Congress Cataloging-in-Publication data
Muysken, Pieter.
Functional categories / Pieter Muysken.
  p.   cm.   – (Cambridge studies in linguistics ; 117)
Includes bibliographical references and index.
ISBN 978-0-521-61998-1 (hardback)
1. Grammar, Comparative and general–Grammatical categories.   I. Title.   II. Series.
P240.5.M896 2008
415–dc22   2007050653

ISBN 978-0-521-85385-9 hardback
ISBN 978-0-521-61998-1 paperback

Contents

CONCLUSIONS

Tables

Figures

Preface

This book grew out of an earlier paper, 'Accessing the lexicon in language contact', and took a long time in getting conceived. Once I had realised that all the material I wanted to cover could not conceivably be crammed into a single paper the actual planning became much easier, and then it was just a question of keeping the manuscript to a manageable size. Countless people commented on earlier versions of the material presented here, at conferences, summer schools, and seminars at Szeged, Groningen, Amsterdam, Utrecht, Nijmegen, Düsseldorf, and Girona, and at a lecture at the Royal Netherlands Academy of Sciences in Amsterdam. Given my own research background, it should come as no surprise that the topic of language contact figures quite prominently in this book.

Much of the material for this book grew out of the research that I could do with the support of the Spinoza Prize 1998 of the Netherlands Organization for Scientific Research NWO. In particular I am grateful to the people in the research team in Nijmegen on the languages of Bolivia and Rondonia, Mily Crevels, Swintha Danielsen, Rik van Gijn, Katja Hannss, Katharina Haude, and Hein van der Voort, and to Simon Musgrave and Marian Klamer who worked on the SCALA typology database. Margot van den Berg and Adrienne Bruyn commented on the pidgin and creole chapter, and Anna Fenyvesi commented extensively on an earlier draft of the article version. Helena Halmari helped with the Finnish Foreigner Talk examples. When writing this book, exploring various corners of linguistics, I realise that some of the ideas grew out of work together with colleagues over a long time. I want to mention a few people in particular, although the list is actually much longer. Henk van Riemsdijk taught me much of what I know about syntactic categories, and with Catherine Snow I worked on issues of simplification and Foreigner Talk. I also would like to acknowledge the invaluable advice of Peter Bakker on the issue of mixed languages, and of Roeland van Hout in our work together on borrowing. Neil Smith gave insightful comments on the pre-final draft on behalf of Cambridge University Press, but his work and that of his students also helped me in the writing of several of the chapters. Similarly, Adrian Stenton, working on behalf of the Press, also helped to improve the quality of the manuscript considerably.

I am grateful to the Netherlands Institute for Advanced Studies (NIAS) in Wassenaar for hosting me while I wrote the final text in the Spring semester of 2006, and to their editorial staff, particularly Anne Simpson. At NIAS my colleagues in the Nucleus on Restricted Linguistic Systems as Windows on Language Genesis, in particular Anne Baker, Sandra Benazzo, Rudi Botha, Adrienne Bruyn, Bernd Heine, Tania Kouteva, Henriette de Swart, and Christa Vogel also were very helpful in commenting on chapters, as were our visitors, among them Gertjan Postma, Riny Huijbregts, Tonjes Veenstra, and Arie Verhagen. Monique Lamers commented on the neurolinguistic material, and made helpful suggestions. At a presentation of some of the material here in Nijmegen, Melissa Bowerman pointed out to me the importance of Roger Brown's *A first language*, which turned out to be most helpful. It takes a perspective on functional categories similar to that of Ray Jackendoff's *Foundations of language*, another important source of inspiration for the present work.

Needless to say, the misrepresentations and errors in interpretation in this work are all my sole responsibility.

Abbreviations

1...	first ... person
4	fourth person, i.e. first person inclusive
2D	two-dimensional
exc	exclusive
f	feminine
in	inanimate
inc	inclusive
m	masculine
n	neuter
ob	object
p	plural
s	singular
ABL	ablative case
ABS	absolutive
AC	accusative case
ADV	adverbial marker
AF	affirmative
AFO	affected object
AGR	agreement
AM	adjectival marker
AN	animate
ART	article
ASP	aspect
ASS	associative
AU	augmentative
BEN	benefactive
C	class marker
CAS	case marker

CAU	causative
CIS	cislocative
CL	classifier
CL1, 1a	noun class 1, 1a marker
CLI	clitic
COMP	complementiser
CON	connector pronoun
COND	conditional
CONF	confirmative
DA	dative case
DEF	definite
DEL	delimiter ('just')
DEM	demonstrative
DET	determiner
DIM	diminutive
DIR	directional
DIS	discourse marker
DR	bivalent direct marker
DS	different subject subordinator
DSC	discontinuity marker
DUB	dubitative
DUR	durative
ELAT	elative
EMPH	emphasis marker
ERG	ergative
EXH	exhortative
FOC	focaliser
FU	future tense
FV	final vowel
G	Pfau
GE	genitive
GM	general class marker
HES	hesitation marker
IL	illative
IM	imperative
IMP	impressive
IMPF	imperfective
IMPP	imperfect past

IND	indefinite
INE	inessive
INF	infinitive
INS	inessive
ITN	intentional
LOC	locative
MEA	measure
M.LOC	locative case in modal function
M.PROP	proprietive case in modal function
NEG	negative
NFU	non-future
NOM	nominaliser
NOMI	nominative
NPST	non-past
OB	oblique
OBV	obviative
P	adposition
PASS	passive
Part	particle
PERF	perfective aspect
PERL	perlative
PM	predicate marker
PN	pronoun
PO	possessive
POT	potential
PR	progressive aspect
PRC	process verbalisation
PRE	present tense
PRO	pronoun
PROX	proximity to speaker
PST	past tense
Q	question marker
QA	quantifier
RC	relative clause
RE	relator
REC	recent past
REF	reflexive
REL	relative marker

REP	reportative
SD	sudden discovery tense or evidential
SM	specific class marker
SOC	sociative
SS	same subject subordinator
SU	subject
SUB	subordinator
SUPER	superessive
TA	transitive animate verb
TF	transformative
TO	topic marker
TR	transitiviser
VBL	verbaliser
Wh	Wh-type question word
WI	with

A	adjective
AP	adjective phrase
Adv	adverb
ADVP	adverbial phrase
AgrP	agreement phrase
AgrS	subject agreement
C	complementiser
CP	complementiser phrase
Comp	complement
D	determiner
Deg	degree marker
DegP	degree phrase
DP	determiner phrase
I, INFL	inflection
IP	inflection phrase
MP	measure phrase
N	noun
NP	noun phrase
PP	prepositional phrase
QP	quantifier phrase
S	sentence
Spec	specifier

T	tense
V	verb
VP	verb phrase
TMA	tense-mood-aspect
Ar	Arabic
Du	Dutch
E	English
F	Fongbe
Fr	French
It	Italian
Lat	Latin
ML	Media Lengua
Pap	Papiamentu
Port	Portuguese
Q	Quechua
Sc	Sicilian
Sp	Spanish

1 Introduction

This book is concerned with the well-known but not unproblematic distinction between lexical and grammatical or functional categories, as it manifests itself in a number of areas of linguistics. It is fairly obvious to most observers that in the following English dialogue lexical elements like *ask, money* and *parents* have a status different from functional elements like *the, you* and *am*:

(1)   (a) Where will you get the money from?
       (b) I am going to ask my parents.

The distinction between the two classes has proven useful in a number of domains of linguistic research (such as child language, grammaticalisation, creoles), but what is covered by the two terms – lexical and functional – and on the basis of which criteria the distinction is made, appears to vary according to the domain involved.

Also, some elements appear to have an intermediate status. The preposition *from* is often termed grammatical, but is also somewhat concrete in its meaning. Similarly, *going* functions as an auxiliary, but has developed out of a main verb, and *get* has acquired some auxiliary qualities, as in *Let's get started* and *He got hit by a car*. Altogether, three groups can be listed, where group (2b) has an intermediate status:

(2)   (a) *functional*   (b) *intermediate*   (c) *lexical*
           where   from   money
           will   get   ask
           you   go-ing   parent-s
           the
           I
           am
           to
           my

The sheer number of functional categories present underlines their fundamental role in structuring the clause. Notice, however, that none of the groups is homogeneous in terms of syntactic category. For instance, the verb/non-verb distinction cuts across the three groups.

Furthermore, there is a second way of looking at these categories, besides the word-based one, namely in terms of the grammatical categories expressed. Thus *I*, *am*, and *my* all contain the grammatical notion of 'first person singular', but in addition to other grammatical notions, yielding different word forms. *Parent-s* and *go-ing* contain separate affixes to indicate 'plural' and 'progressive', respectively. Thus functional categories can also be seen as combinations, 'bundles' as they are sometimes called, of grammatical categories or features. Sometimes the term *phi*-features is used to refer to the relevant set. In the next chapters this set is further characterised.

Yet a third way is in terms of certain syntactic positions, like the auxiliary position of *will* in utterance (1a); this auxiliary position has always played an important role in the development of generative grammar (Chomsky 1957 and much later work). Hudson (2000: 8) distinguishes three kinds of category: Word Category, Subword Category, and Position Category, corresponding to the three perspectives mentioned, and presents insightful discussion of some of the background issues treated here, in particular the tension between the diffuse lexical features that may characterise functional categories and the fairly rigid absolute distinction drawn in theoretical syntax.

Given its important status in many sub-domains of linguistics, yet its unclear theoretical basis, there is good reason to consider the distinction more closely. This book is meant to provide an analytic survey of this topic, which has drawn considerable attention in a number of sub-disciplines of linguistics but which, as far as I am aware, has rarely been systematically approached from an integrated, cross-disciplinary perspective. The disciplines discussed are:

- Grammar
- Historical linguistics
- Psycholinguistics
- Language contact and bilingual speech.

The book is empirically based: it aims to take a hard look at the available converging evidence from various disciplines. It also is based on comparative evidence from different languages and language families.

Theoretically, the book constitutes a plea for a differentiated, multi-factorial view of functional categories. Two papers should be mentioned which have attempted a similar, if less complete, integrative perspective: Cann (2000) tries to link the theoretical discussion of functional categories to evidence from language processing, acquisition, and breakdown. Myers-Scotton and Jake (2000) adduce evidence from aphasia, code-switching, and second language acquisition for a differentiated view of the lexical/functional distinction, which has led to their 4-M model (see chapter 13).

Before concluding this introductory section, I should try to justify my terminology. I use the term 'functional category' in this book rather than 'function word' (often used in contrast to 'content word') or 'functor' because not all elements discussed (and in some languages very few of them) are actual words. The term 'grammatical category' could be used, in contrast to 'lexical category', but is a bit vague by itself, and can refer to lexical categories as well. Bybee and Dahl (1989) have introduced the term 'gram'; I will not use this term because it carries a number of additional theoretical assumptions associated with it, particular to a specific theoretical framework. Sapir's (1921) terms 'radical' (= lexical) and 'relational' (= functional) concepts likewise are a bit confusing (particularly 'radical'). Finally, the term 'system morpheme' coined by Myers-Scotton (1993) has the right touch as far as the first part of the compound is concerned, but the term 'morpheme' is generally used to designate a particular part of a word, rather than a notional category. Cann (2000) distinguishes the abstract underlying functional 'categories' from concrete functional 'expressions'. In itself this is useful, but somewhat cumbersome, and it is a distinction closely linked to his theoretical assumptions.

Theoretical perspectives on categorisation

Grammatically, functional categories can be viewed from the perspective of lexical classes (e.g. function words) and morphological endings (e.g. inflections), but they can also be seen from the perspective of the system of syntactic projections. Similarly, they can be seen as the dependent elements in phonological phrases, and as the carriers of abstract information. All these perspectives – lexical, syntactic, phonological, semantic – may lead to a different internal classification, or the different classificatory criteria may coincide in establishing the same types and sub-types. The coexistence of these different dimensions may lead to the perception of gradience. This gradience has also been argued to extend to lexical categories. Ross (1972: 325) notes that 'all [categories] manifest the same "funnel direction": nouns are more inert, syntactically, than adjectives and adjectives more than verbs'. From this perspective, verbs may be seen as more 'functional' than nouns, and thus it may be that there are more general underlying categorisations cutting across the supposed lexical/functional distinction, in addition to this distinction being a gradient one.

There is fairly widespread recognition, already hinted at above, that not all elements are equal among the functional categories. Some adpositions are more clearly 'functional' than others (compare French *de* 'of' to *dessus* 'on top'), clitic pronouns show special behaviour compared to strong pronouns (compare *le* '3s.m.ob' to *lui* 'him'), copulas are more restricted than aspectual auxiliaries. In order to properly deal with this, several models can be envisaged, which correspond to different approaches to grammatical categories. Currently there are at least four main models for categorisation (some of which, to be sure, have not yet been given very precise definitions, and may be better labelled 'views' or 'perspectives'):

- Prototype models
- Scale and Hierarchy models
- Mono-dimensional models
- Multi-dimensional models, including Multi-level and Chain models.

The **Prototype** model (e.g. Croft 1991) assumes that each category has a typical meaning or use (e.g. nouns are typically used to refer), expressed by core members of the category, while other words may belong to a category without expressing this core meaning. A typical noun would be *table*, a less typical one *size*. Thus, one could envisage a proto-typical functional category such as *the* at the centre of the definition (highly specific morpho-lexical properties, specialised syntax, reduced phonological shape, abstract meaning) and other elements more or less distant from this prototype.

The **Scale** model (Ross 1972; Sasse 2001a) likewise assumes that the boundaries of a category may be fuzzy, but makes the additional assumption that categories can be arranged on a linear scale, there being no 'core' category. There is a large literature on gradience in grammatical categories (cf. the summary in Sasse 2001a), e.g. the adverb ... preposition cline or the noun ... verb cline. The **Hierarchy** model (cf. e.g. Comrie 2001: 34, who makes this relevant distinction) is a scale model which has a high/low dimension. This asymmetry could be due to historical change, as in grammaticalisation theory, to cognitive development (from simple to complex), language evolution, etc. Thus adpositions could be on a scale with adverbs on the lexical end and case markers on the functional end. Modals could be on a scale with auxiliaries on the functional end and full verbs on the lexical end, etc.

The **Mono-dimensional** model (e.g. Baker 2003) assumes that categories are not squishy and that they consist of one-to-one pairings of forms and meanings. Possible disparities between form and meaning are solved through special adjustment rules at either the syntax/phonology or the syntax/semantics interfaces. With respect to the issue at hand, this model would assume that there is a true set of functional categories, and a number of other elements which might share features of functional categories but which are really lexical in nature. The discussion then would be whether a certain class is 'truly' functional or not.

The **Multi-dimensional** model (Plank 1984; Sadock 1991; Jackendoff 2002; Francis and Matthews 2005) assumes that categories lie at the interface of different representations – morpho-lexical, syntactic, phonological, and semantic. A sub-type, the **Multi-level** model (Cann 2000: 58) would assume that functional categories can be distinguished, in absolute terms, at one level of analysis, in this case E-language (external language, at the level of the speech community), but not at another level, I-language (internal language, at the level of the individual cognitive system). The **Chain** model assumes that various categories may be part of a chain of some kind, as in the T-chain proposal (Guéron and Hoekstra, 1988), where the Verb, Tense, the Inflection, and the Complementiser nodes may be part of a syntactically coherent sub-system. Conceptually, it can be seen as a type of multi-dimensional model, since the feature determining the chain represents only one dimension.

The perspective taken in this book

In this book a multi-dimensional, modular approach is taken to the human language faculty, and subsequently, to grammatical categories, including functional categories. This approach implies that several capacities are assumed to cooperate conjointly in what appears to be a single phenomenon: the human language capacity. These capacities include syntactic computation, interactive communication, sign building (semiotics), and cognition. This modular perspective implies that functional elements can and should be viewed as multi-dimensional. Not only do they have a form and a meaning (the traditional Saussurean notion of sign), but they may or may not play a separate role in syntactic computation (through their feature content), and they may have an interactive function. This multi-dimensional character is also responsible for the fact that categories are often perceived as gradient. However, we can also perceive the distinction between lexical and functional as non-gradient but discrete, since different distinctions are made on different dimensions. An early example of this approach appears in a study by Friederici *et al.* (1982: 526), reporting on earlier work by Garrett and associates on speech errors: 'for speech error patterns which implicate the syntactic and logical structure of sentences, prepositions show error behavior which is comparable to that of other major grammatical classes, but for error patterns which implicate the sound structure of sentences, prepositions behave not with the major classes (content words), but with the minor class items (function words)'.

Newmeyer (1998) and Baker (2003) attempt to compare formal and functional approaches to linguistics. I should make clear at some point where I stand in this domain. My own background is in formal linguistics, and I guess this is where I feel most comfortable. However, I find the generative literature on functional categories rather vague. Even though the notion is assumed to have great theoretical importance for various researchers, it is not very well defined and delineated. The same remarks that Baker (2003: 1–3) makes in his introduction about syntactic categories in general could as well be made about functional categories.

To illustrate the multi-dimensional perspective, as well as the problems it raises, take the case of *pe* 'where' from the Surinam creole language Sranan. An example of one of the contemporary uses of *pe* would be a fragment of a poem by Trefossa (from *Trotji*, 1957):

(3)   *Bro* 'breath, rest'
      na kriki-sei dren kondre mi sa si,   'at the creek side the dream land I shall see'
      pe alasani moro swit' lek dya   '**where** everything is sweeter than here'
      èn skreki-tori no sa trobi mi.   'and scary stories shall not trouble me'

In (4), the development through grammaticalisation is presented of Sranan *pe* 'where' out of English *which place*, from the seventeenth century onwards (Bruyn 1995):

(4)   which place > uch presi > o presi > o pe > pe

The development involves independent semantic, syntactic, morphological, and phonological changes. Semantically and pragmatically, there was a progressive abstraction of the meaning from 'which place' to simply 'where', and a shift from a focalising use of the question word to an ordinary fronted form without necessarily focal meaning. Morphologically, there is a shift from a complex phrase to a simple element. This parallels the phonological reduction to a mono-syllabic CV (consonant vowel) particle. Syntactically, there is a change from a phrase, often in focus position, to a question word which can then also be used as a conjunction.

The interesting thing is that these conceptually very different changes all co-occur, and move in the same direction. It is this parallelism between apparently separate dimensions of lexical items, holding at least in an overall statistical sense, which calls for an explanation. Without going into this further, I will assume bi-directional optimality checking (Blutner, de Hoop, and Hendriks 2006) as the mechanism which ensures parallel development. In this perspective the relation between forms and meanings (e.g. a complex form and a complex meaning, and a simple form and a basic meaning) is subject to optimality ranking. There is no absolute condition but this matching holds if there are no other overriding constraints. The different dimensions along which we may classify an element as functional or not may be quite independent, in some cases, and the optimality checking mechanism allows for that possibility.

I will argue here, following researchers like Hudson (2000) cited above, that two definitions of functional categories should be kept apart: functional categories as words, subject to processes of grammaticalisation, and functional categories as structural positions in a syntactic skeleton. Sentence structure is syntacticised to various degrees in various languages. In some languages, both clauses and noun phrases are heavily syntacticised, and clearly articulated in terms of functional positions, and in other languages it is largely clauses that are heavily syntacticised, but not noun phrases. Exceptionally, even the clause may show little evidence of strong functional projections internally.

Even though the concept of functional category is multi-dimensional, it is clear that its roots lie in morpho-syntax. Elements are functional because of the particular role they play in the organisation of the sentence. Other dimensions are to some extent independent from this, leading to a complex set of relations between them. This said, let me briefly recapitulate some of the main points in the book:

- A multi-dimensional conception of functional categories
- An impression of overall gradience, since dimensions are logically independent
- Optimal matching between the positioning of categories on the different dimensions, driven by processing
- Focus on different aspects of categories, and on different definitions of what is or is not a functional category.

Disclaimers

A few disclaimers are in order. First of all, as I started on the research for the individual chapters, I discovered that the amount of material available which threw light on the role of functional categories in each domain tended to be vast, and much larger than I had originally realised. This book manuscript grew out of a single article manuscript, but easily could give birth to seventeen monographs. Thus the coverage is incomplete; I hope it inspires specialists on individual subjects to pursue the exploration of functional categories in their area of expertise.

Second, the topic of numerals, which share many of their features with functional categories, is not touched upon. Numerals may be part of tightly organised lexical sub-systems, often show special morphology, have a specific abstract meaning, tend to be historically stable, etc. However, I think that their special characteristics result from the fact that the numeral system is used in, and interacts with, a special highly organised area of human cognition and communication: counting and calculus. Functional categories are special because they interact with syntax, with the grammatical system. Thus functional categories are cousins of numerals rather than siblings. Only in the lower range, and then particularly with the element 'one', do numerals and functional categories intersect.

Third, discourse markers, those lexical elements that also play a role in, and interact with, the system of human interaction and discourse organisation, are treated in only a few chapters in this book. Like numerals, they are of a different kind than true functional categories, but syntax and discourse interact more closely, and hence discourse markers are often very close to functional categories proper.

The organisation of this book

In the first section, *Grammar*, a number of theoretical approaches are presented. To broaden the empirical range beyond what has been found in languages like English, I start with the perspective of **language description and typology** in chapter 2. Going from representatives of structuralist work on typology like Edward Sapir and Roman Jakobson, I consider the still expanding range of functional categories in language description, and the classifications of these categories in recent work in linguistic typology. Chapter 3 deals with the **lexical, morphological, and phonological** dimensions of functional categories. How are these categories realized lexically and morphologically? What are their derivational possibilities? Does morphological suppletion play a privileged role in the creation of functional categories? Can they be distinguished by the tightness of paradigmatic organisation? Do we find compounding in category innovation? As to the phonological properties of functional categories, topics discussed include phonological weight, cliticisation, and stress. In chapter 4 I turn to the **semantic and pragmatic** dimensions of functional categories.

Does the lexical/functional distinction coincide with that between concrete versus abstract meanings? Can we usefully analyse the special status of discourse markers and particles in terms of a model of functional categories? The perspective of Chomskyan **theoretical syntax** is the topic of chapter 5. After a brief excursus on earlier generative approaches, I turn to the work of scholars like Abney and Cinque, who heralded the renewed interest in functional categories within this tradition. Van Riemsdijk and Grimshaw formulated models in which the relation between lexical and functional categories was stressed, while Baker has tried to shift the typological debate about differences in the lexical categories between different languages to functional category differences. I then turn to the position of functional categories in Minimalism, before discussing two interface issues: functional categories and the phonology/syntax interface, and the syntax/semantics interface and interpretability of features.

In the second section of the book, ***Historical linguistics***, two topics are central. First, in chapter 6 I discuss the link between functional categories and **grammaticalisation** theory. After presenting an overview of developments and debates in this theory, I turn to a number of components of the process: semantic bleaching, phonological reduction, and constructional tightening. Finally I evaluate the claims made in this theory in the light of the discussion in the first section. Chapter 7 focuses on the status of functional categories in **linguistic reconstruction**. After a survey of functional categories in Indo-European, specific issues are discussed, such as the stability/instability of pronouns versus conjunctions. Then, a wider perspective is taken, with evidence from Proto-Uralic, Afro-Asiatic, and Amerind.

The third section of the book is concerned with ***Psycholinguistics***. The special status of functional categories in speech **production and perception** will be discussed in chapter 8. I will begin by considering various models for language production and perception, and then turn to the role of frequency effects. Evidence from both speech error studies and brain imaging studies will be considered. **First and second language acquisition** are the subject of chapter 9. In subsequent sections I discuss the growth in the range of functional categories, first in first language development and then in second language development, before turning to a comparison of the two. Chapter 10 analyses the role of functional categories in **agrammatic aphasia and Specific Language Impairment (SLI)**. I begin by presenting issues of demarcation and definition in the fields of aphasia and SLI studies, and then turn to an overview of the empirical evidence, cross-linguistically. Finally, I discuss various explanatory models that account for the special behaviour of functional categories. In chapter 11 the process of **language attrition** and its effect on functional categories is highlighted. Are there patterns to their decay when a language is no longer used by a speaker or group of speakers? Is the process gradual or abrupt?

The next section is devoted to the topic of *language contact and bilingual speech*. Chapter 12 deals with functional categories in **sign languages**. To be sure, sign languages as such are not contact languages, but their status as relatively 'new' languages makes them similar to creoles; this is why they are included in this section. A second theme, the topic of chapter 13, concerns the exceptional status of functional categories in **code-switching and code-mixing**. After presenting some of the relevant basic facts, I turn to the 4-M model developed by Myers-Scotton and Jake and to the position of functional elements in feature checking theory. After a more theoretical discussion of the role of equivalence, I evaluate the evidence in this domain. On a related topic, chapter 14 surveys the evidence for lexical/functional asymmetries in **lexical borrowing**. I begin with an overview of the evidence for borrowability hierarchies, and then turn to ways to model these hierarchies, including probabilistic approaches. Chapter 15 is dedicated to functional categories in **pidgin and creole genesis**. I will begin by describing the loss of functional categories in pidgins, and then the processes of reconstitution, restructuring, and grammaticalisation in creoles. Three case studies will be presented: the long cycle of pidgin and creole genesis in Tok Pisin, and the processes of formation of functional categories in Saramaccan and Negerhollands. Chapter 16 will deal with the special status of functional categories in **mixed languages**. After discussing issues of definition and delimitation, I will discuss a number of cases, including Media Lengua, Michif, Gurundji Kriol, and Copper Island Aleut. I end with a theoretical analysis based on a comparative overview. The final chapter in this section, chapter 17, focuses on the treatment of functional categories in **Foreigner Talk**, the way non-fluent non-native speakers are addressed by mother-tongue speakers. I begin with an analysis of the different types of Foreigner Talk, and then present an overview of the evidence from a number of languages. I conclude with some possible explanatory models.

Finally, I will present some *conclusions* in chapter 18, presenting a modular and multi-dimensional perspective on functional categories. I summarise the main findings from grammar, historical linguistics, psycholinguistics, and language contact studies, and try to integrate the different dimensions in a model. Finally, I turn to evolutionary considerations. In an **evolutionary perspective**, we might postulate an earlier stage in the development of human language without functional categories, following Bickerton and Jackendoff. Then the question arises why functional categories emerged at all.

Grammar

2 Functional categories and language typology

In the European grammatical tradition a tripartite division has been commonly assumed of major parts of speech, minor parts of speech, and secondary grammatical categories (Lyons 1968: 332):

(1)

(a) **Major parts of speech**	(b) **Minor parts of speech**	(c) **Secondary categories**
Nouns	Articles	Case
Verbs	Pronouns	Tense
Adjectives	Auxiliaries	Aspect
Adverbs	Conjunctions	Mood
	Prepositions	Person
	Interjections	Number
		Gender

However, as more non-European languages were studied, it became increasingly clear that this division was not sufficient. Not only were new categories and values for categories encountered, but also the traditional labels, such as 'auxiliary' and 'article', turned out to be too specific. In addition, the distinction between 'minor parts of speech' and 'secondary categories' turned out to be much less sharp than the listing in (1) leads one to believe.

While traditional grammars were concerned with these parts of speech and the development of theories about the meaning of categories in the western European languages, the introduction of structuralism increased both the range of descriptive categories and offered more systematic analyses of these categories. The full range of functional categories in the languages of the world is currently being systematically inventoried, and comparative analyses are being carried out of 'new' categories such as evidentials and classifiers. Typologists are systematically charting the range of the categories observed, as evidenced e.g. in the Rara & Rarissima conference held in Leipzig in March/April 2006. This chapter tries to outline the consequences of this for our view of functional categories.

I will begin by briefly sketching some of the contributions to this domain by the great structuralists Sapir and Jakobson. Then I will turn to some examples of the expansion in the range of functional categories, and I finish by exploring typologically adequate classifications of functional categories.

Structuralism: Sapir and Jakobson

Edward Sapir (1884–1939) and Roman Jakobson (1896–1982) are perhaps the most prominent structuralist linguists who have contributed to our understanding of functional categories. Their work has been very influential, and merits separate discussion. A central notion of the structuralist tradition is that the primary functional categories are the obligatory ones in a sentence, those distinctions that **need** to be expressed. 'The obligatory aspects are marked by means of grammatical devices', Boas (1938: 132) writes, and this insight has been further elaborated by both Sapir and Jakobson.

Sapir's introductory book *Language. An introduction to the study of speech* (1921) is a testimony to the rapidly growing insight into the diversity of linguistic elements, patterns, and structures, as fieldwork in the early decades of the twentieth century progressed. 'Scarcely less impressive than the universality of speech is its almost incredible diversity', Sapir (1921: 22–23) writes. Using simple examples, Sapir points to fundamental notions that need to be expressed in the simple English sentence *The farmer killed the duckling*, in addition to the concrete concepts that are being referred to: Reference (e.g. definiteness), Modality (e.g. declarative), Personal relations (grammatical roles), Number, and Time (1921: 88–89). What is important is that the conceptual analysis is lifted to a level beyond the particular features of English grammar, beyond 'our own well-worn grooves of expression'. This 'destructive analysis of the familiar' allows an insight into other possibilities and concepts. In German, Gender and Case turn out to be important. In Yana, Gender and other notions mentioned play no role at all, but Information Source needs to be expressed (1921: 91). In Chinese, finally, a number of concepts need no expression at all. In Kwakiutl, Spatial Orientation and Visibility would need to be expressed. An important task for linguists then is to discover which concepts are essential and universally present, and which concepts are accidental. Thus Sapir's work contains an outline and research programme for the subsequent work in linguistic typology and universals, returning to the distinction in the classical grammatical tradition between 'accidence' and 'substantives'. Cann (2000: 37) defines Accidence as 'the grammatical (morphological) categories exhibited by a language (such as case, tense, etc.) that are the parochial characteristics of word formation of a particular language' and Substantives as 'the linguistically universal classes and properties'.

Jakobson's work is at the same time less ambitious in not providing an overall research programme, as Sapir does, and yet it is more detailed, in that specific themes are further explored, while the internal structure of the conceptual space for individual domains expressed by morpho-syntactic categories is charted. Thus in papers written from the early 1930s onward the Russian (often more generally Slavic) verbal aspect, the clitic system, the case system, number, and gender are systematically explored (cf. the essays reprinted and collected in Jakobson 1971b), and placed in a more universal perspective. However, at each point, the particularities of the language data analysed rather than a pre-established categorical system is centred upon. In his work, Jakobson tries to set up a binary feature system for each morpho-syntactic domain studied.

The notional classification of functional categories

For a typological approach to functional categories taken in this chapter it is most useful to start out with a notional or semantic definition, following Award's (2001: 726) definition of part-of-speech systems as 'mappings of semantically defined classes of lexical items onto classes delineated by phonological, morphological, and syntactic properties'. Thus the primary intuition of what constitutes a functional category in a given language is notional. Award (2001: 727 *et seq.*), building on work by Anna Wierbizcka and Ray Jackendoff, tentatively defines eight domains about which natural languages provide information:

- person/thing
- event
- situation
- place
- time
- relation
- property
- quantity.

A preliminary classification of different functional categories could thus be made in terms of these eight notions. However, not all of these notions are expressed through functional categories to the same degree. I will begin,

Table 2.1. *A crude sub-classification of three types of functional categories*

	Shifters	Linkers	Projectors
Determiners	+		
Person agreement	+		+
Tense markers	+		+
Modals		+	
Pronouns	+		
Demonstratives	+		
Question words	+		
Quantifiers	+		
Prepositions		+	
Conjunctions		+	
Complementisers		+	+
Connectives and particles		+	

therefore, with a different approach. Functional categories can be viewed as having three main functions:

- Locating the utterance in the context of utterance (indexicals or shifters)
- Connecting and organising parts of the information (connectives or linkers)
- Structuring the clause (structurers or projectors).

Different functional categories are more or less specialised in one of these three functions, as shown in Table 2.1.

I will use this tripartite division to analyse the position of lexical and grammatical categories in a number of domains of linguistic behaviour.

Expanding the range of functional categories in language description

I will give a few examples of how ongoing descriptive work is changing our perception of the range of functional categories. Examples include noun classification, clause markers, and nominal tense.

A first example is the study of noun classification. This phenomenon is well known, but can take a number of forms. Basing his work on Grinevald (2000), Seifart (2005: 8) puts the elements involved in noun classification on the following scale:

(2) lexical   lexico-grammatical grammatical
← --- →
measure terms *numeral classifiers* *noun classes*
class terms *noun classifiers*   *gender*
      verbal classifiers
      . . .

In the Bantu languages, to start at the grammatical end, we have noun class prefixes, which are involved in subject–verb and modifier–noun agreement. A Zulu example is given in (3)(cited from Zeller 2005):

(3) **u**-Mary   **u**-thanda   **la**   **ma**-kati
  CL1a-Mary 1a.sub-like-FV DEM CL6 CL6-cat
  'Mary likes (these) cats.'

The subject 'Mary' and the verb receive a class 1a prefix, and the demonstrative and the object noun are both marked as class 6.

A highly grammaticalised system such as the Zulu one, with extensive agreement, contrasts with a system such as the likewise well-known Mandarin Chinese system, on the middle of the scale in (2). Here a numeral classifier *ge* is exemplified in (4) (cited from Seifart 2005: 11):

(4) sān ge rén
  three CL person
  'three people'

At the other end of the scale we find measure terms, as in German (5):

(5) Ich habe [eine Kiste   Kubanische Zigarren] bestellt
  I   have a.AC case.AC Cuban.AC   cigars.AC ordered
  'I have ordered a case of Cuban cigars.'

In this example, cited from Corver and Van Riemsdijk (2001a: 8), the construction is fully lexical, at first sight. However, these authors argue that there is subtle evidence, including the case agreement in (5) between all four members of the complex noun phrase, that *Kiste* 'case' is on its way to becoming grammaticalised.

In his fieldwork on Miraña in the north-west Amazon, Seifart (2005) has discovered that the classifiers in this language do not fit very easily in the classification implied in (2), where often noun classes (with agreement) are distinguished from classifiers (without agreement). Miraña has a classifier system with extensive agreement as an extra feature. An example is given in (6) (Seifart 2005: 288):

(6)   a:- *nɛ*   tsájhtɛ-*bɛ́*=*nɛ́kU*   tɛ:-*nɛ*   gwatáhko-*hɪ*
       CON-GM.in take-GM.m.s=REC PN-GM.in cover.NOM-SM.2D.round
       'He brought it, the hat.'

       á-*hɪ*-má=nɛ́kU   pɛ-:bɛ
       CON-SM.2D.round-SOC=REC go-GM.m.s
       'And with it (round and flat, i.e. the hat), he left.'

Based on the primary semantic domains of natural gender (within animates) and shape (within inanimates) there are a number of more general and more specific classifiers that can have various referential and anaphoric functions. In (6) these include -*nɛ* 'general class marker inanimate', -*bɛ́* 'general class marker masculine singular', and -*hɪ* 'specific class marker two-dimensional round'. Notice that the class of two-dimensional round objects is a sub-class of the inanimate class. Depending on specific discourse needs, more specific or more general classifiers can be used for the purpose of reference tracking. The Miraña facts go against earlier typological classifications that had been set up in this domain, and expand our perspective on classifiers, bringing them further into the range of functional categories.

Seifart (2005) proposes to separate the derivational from the agreement uses of nominal classifiers; what is special, semantically, about Miraña is that the semantic domain of shape is so crucial to classifying and sub-classifying inanimate objects, even in an agreement system. Seifart's work is typical in showing that further detailed descriptions of unknown languages can substantially increase our knowledge of the way language and cognition interact. Even in a domain where much descriptive and typological work had been done, such as noun classification, more can still be accomplished.

A second area concerns various types of clause markers. Consider the sentences in (7), from Cuzco Quechua (cf. e.g. Faller 2003; sentences adapted from Cusihuamán 1976: 243):

(7)   (a) Sumaq-ta-**má**   papa-qa   t'ika-yu-sha-sqa.
           pretty-AC-IMP   potato-TO flower-AU-PR-SD
           'Look how pretty the potato plants are flowering!'

       (b) Sumaq-ta-**n**   papa-qa   t'ika-yu-sha-sqa.
           pretty-AC-AF   potato-TO flower-AU-PR-SD
           'The potato plants are flowering pretty (I notice).'

       (c) Sumaq-ta-**chá**   papa-qa   t'ika-yu-sha-sqa.
           pretty-AC-DUB   potato-TO flower-AU-PR-SD
           'The potato plants are perhaps flowering pretty.'

     (d) Sumaq-ta-**si**   papa-qa   t'ika-yu-sha-sqa.
           pretty-AC-REP potato-TO flower-AU-PR-SD
           'The potato plants are flowering pretty, they say.'

There is a grammaticalised set of particles in Quechua which mark focus (through the place where they are attached) and in addition function as evidentials, exclamatives, and validational markers. Thus -*má* indicates that the speaker is impressed, -*n* denotes that the speaker is sure about the knowledge source, -*chá* expresses doubt, and -*si* marks hearsay.

    Similar phenomena have been discovered in many other parts of the world. While in Quechua the clausal particles are clausal enclitics, in other languages we find separate particles, a part of speech to which I will return in the next chapter.

    A third example of the expansion of our view of functional categories resulting from a wider range in descriptive studies is nominal tense. Nominal tense can refer to the temporal reference of the noun phrase itself, as in (8a) and (8b) (from Nordlinger and Sadler 2004: 781) from Guaraní:

(8)   (a) O-va-ta   che-róga-kue-pe.
             3-move-FU   1s-house-PST-in
             'He will move into my former house.'

      (b) A-va-va'ekue hóga-rã-pe
             1s-move-PST 3.house-FU-in
             'I have moved into his future house.'

Here the house can be referred to as 'past' (8a) or 'future' (8b) independently of the tense of the clause.

    In other cases, the tense reference is clausal, even though the tense is morphologically expressed on the noun phrase. A typical example is provided by the Australian language Kayardild, as described by Evans (1995) (examples cited from Nordlinger and Sadler 2004: 792). In this language the case markers, glossed as M.PROP and M.LOC, are marked for tense distinctions:

(9)   (a) Ngada   kurri-nangku mala-wu   (balmbi-wu).
             1.s(NOM) see-NEG.POT sea-M.PROP morrow-M.PROP
             'I won't be able to see the sea (tomorrow).'

      (b) Ngada   kurri-nangku mala-y   (barruntha-y).
             1.s(NOM) see-NEG.POT sea-M.LOC yesterday-M.LOC
             'I could not see the sea (yesterday).'

Temporal reference is not marked on the verb here.

In Movima, the tense reference marked on the article can be either to the noun phrase (10a) (Haude 2006: 162) or to the clause (10b) (Haude 2006: 165):

(10) (a) Aj<a>lo:maj loy os   no:no di'   pa:ko.
          narrate<DR> ITN ART.n.PST pet   REL dog
          'I'll you you about my (former, deceased) dog.'

      (b) jayna n-os   imay-ni   jayna tivij-ni   os
          DSC obl-ART.n.PST night-PRC DSC pain-PRC ART.n.PST
          chodo :wi
          stomach
          'Then at night, my stomach hurt.'

The neuter past article thus has a different scope, depending on the type of referent and the discourse context. Thus Movima provides a mixed system with properties of both Guaraní and Kayardild. This type of system was assumed not to exist by Nordlinger and Sadler (2004), but Haude's new fieldwork has shown it to be possible.

These three areas, classifiers, clausal particles, and nominal tense markers, are typical examples of the expanding range of facts about functional categories at our disposal due to more and more detailed language descriptions.

Towards a new classification

The broader view of the expressive semantic possibilities of human language resulting from the extensive efforts at language description of the past decades has enriched our view of functional categories in a number of respects:

- their morphological status
- the categories distinguished and the semantic sub-classification of the values encountered
- the weakening of the noun/verb distinction
- the linkage or alignment of feature realisations of functional categories with respect to one another
- the link to non-notional categories
- dynamicity and paths of change in meaning and use.

I will discuss these one by one.

Status. Within several linguistic traditions, formal and functional alike, the common assumption now is that lexically independent and dependent functional elements may have the same status. Thus, there is no separate grammatical status for clitics, and the inflection/derivation distinction is incorporated into a general distinction of lexical and functional processes.

Inventories. There has been a general extension of feature inventories, both in terms of the categories distinguished (e.g. evidentials), but also in the actual distinctions made. Thus there is considerable literature on fine-grained tense systems (including systems with absolute reference, e.g. the time of tomorrow), gender and classifier systems, and personal reference systems with many types of arrangements well beyond the traditional first/second/third person system. Aspectual systems have become very refined as well.

It should be kept in mind that we also find cases where negative results are obtained. One of the findings of recent descriptive and comparative studies is that certain functional categories that were supposed to have been universal are actually absent from some languages. Thus pronouns as a distinct grammatical category have been claimed to be lacking in Japanese and Burmese (Mühlhäusler 2001b: 741). Similarly, the language Morwap distinguishes 1 from not-1, but does not distinguish second from third person. Finally, languages like Awyi have the 1/2/3 distinction in their pronouns, but no singular/plural distinction.

Nouns versus verbs. In traditional accounts, but also in some typologically informed accounts such as Croft (1991: 70), it is assumed that different functional categories are directly linked to different lexical categories. However, current research shows that the idea of non-overlapping sets of categories in all domains is mistaken. There are numerous crossings between these domains. I will give a few examples regarding the noun/verb distinction:

- Many languages show the phenomenon of verbal number (as distinct from affixal agreement), even though number is often assumed to be a typically nominal category.
- I have discussed earlier the phenomenon of nominal tense systems.
- Classifiers were assumed to be part of the nominal domain, but occur verbally as well.
- Particularly since the work of Baker (1988) it is clear that there is a link between case markers or adpositions and verbal applicatives, even if researchers disagree about the exact nature of that link.
- Similarly, there can be links between deictics (nominal domain) and evidentials (verbal domain) in different languages.
- Kirtchuk (2000) stresses the relation between deixis and noun classification in the Guaycuruan language Pilagá.
- Within verb morphology new categories have been discovered, such as verbal stem markers, different types of incorporated elements, bound numerals, demonstratives, etc.

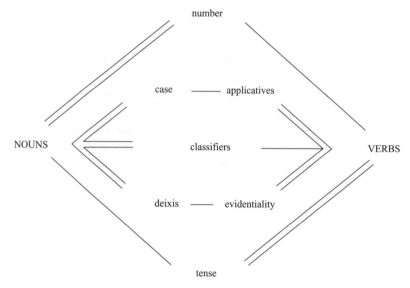

Figure 2.1 *Primary (═) and secondary (—) links between the two main lexical and a number of functional categories*

This leads to a more complex view of functional and lexical categories in the verb and noun domain. A first sketch of this is given in Figure 2.1. Certain functional notions, such as Aktionsart (lexical verbal aspect) and (In)alienable possession are directly linked to major lexical categories (verbs and nouns, respectively), while others, such as Person, are related to several different major categories. Here languages differ considerably. Some functional categories are obviously preferentially linked to one category, while only in specific languages, or specific parts of the world, are they linked to others.

Linkage between functional categories. There are different alignments of feature realisations with respect to one another. To give a few examples from the previously mentioned Rara & Rarissima conference, Pilot-Raichoor (2006) shows that negation in Dravidian languages is a special verbal tense. Peter Schmidt (2006) shows that in a number of linguistic areas (Australian Aboriginal languages, north-east Caucasian languages, and modern Indo-Aryan languages) adverbials can agree in case and person with arguments in the sentence. De Vogelaer and Van der Auwera (2006), to give yet another example, show that person agreement and person clitics can target 'yes' and 'no' in certain Dutch dialects:

(11)   (a) Gaa-n   ze   morgen   naar Gent?
            go-AGR PN.3p tomorrow to Ghent
            'Shall they go to Ghent tomorrow?'

        (b) Jaa-n-s
            Yes-AGR-CLI.3p
            'Yes, they shall.'

What is so special about these three cases – negation as a tense form, agreeing adverbials, and inflected 'yes' – is not so much the categories themselves, which are fairly standard, but rather the combination or linkage between different minor categories.

New notional categories. A number of researchers have shown that the semantic realisation of a given notional category can be quite diverse, and sometimes lead to notional realisations which we would not commonly associate with functional categories, since they involve fairly concrete notions, drawn from the real world. The category of pronoun can be combined with a host of other categories (Mühlhäusler 2001b: 742):

- kinship
- interrogativity
- tense
- gender
- number
- topic/focus
- animacy
- social status and distance.

Some of these combinations are familiar to speakers of European languages, while others are clearly novel.

Binnick (2001: 558–560) argues that there are three types of tense systems:

- *deictic* (oriented with respect to the moment of speech)
- *relative* (oriented with respect to some other temporal reference point)
- *metrical* (oriented with respect to the moment of speech but with absolute time intervals).

An example of this last category would be [±hodiernal] '±more than one day away'.

Mühlhäusler (2001a: 568) notes that recent research has shown that there are three perspectives on space:

- *intrinsic* to the type of object, e.g. *in front of the car*
- *deictic*, i.e. oriented with respect to the position of the speaker/hearer, e.g. *to the left of the car*
- *absolute*, in terms of geographical coordinates, e.g. *to the north of the car.*

Corbett (2001: 818–819) concludes that the category 'number' can have at least the following manifestations:

- singular
- dual
- plural
- trial
- paucal.

One language, Sursurunga, is reliably reported to have a quadral category as well, according to Corbett, citing Hutchisson (1985).

Dynamicity and polysemy. A final finding from the descriptive and typological tradition concerns the dynamicity in the meaning of many functional categories. English *have* can have locational, possessive, and aspectual meanings, in the progression from content word to function word. The same holds, of course, for many other function words in English. Extensive language description has revealed that this is a common feature of morphemes in many languages.

An example is the Cuzco Quechua verbal suffix *-pu*, which can have the following meanings (Cusihuamán 1976, 215–216):

(12)   With movement verbs: 'return to the place of departure'
Kuti-pu-rqa-n.
return-BEN-PST-3
'S/he returned (to his/her place).'

(13)   With different verb classes: 'the action realised results in a fixed state'
Valicha-qa   Lima-ta-s   ri-pu-n.
Valicha-TO   Lima-AC-REP   go-BEN-3
'They say that Valicha went to Lima (to stay).'

(14)   With any verb: 'the action realised is for the benefit of someone'
Alli-chu   unu-man   ri-rqa-pu-wa-y!
good-Q   water-to   go-EXH-BEN-1ob-IM
'Please go and get me some water!'

The unitary gloss for *-pu*, BEN 'benefactive', certainly does not cover all meanings of this form, which may be related, but are nonetheless distinct.

Conclusions

In this chapter I have shown that under the influence of the structural description of hitherto undocumented languages, the notional classification of functional categories has been refined and the range of categories extended, now including various types of classifiers and deictics, nominal tense markers, etc. The links between the notions embodied in different functional categories have become more diverse, and the absolute separation between the nominal and the verbal domain has weakened. The existence of widespread polysemy of functional items, often on a concrete/abstract scale, has triggered the study of grammaticalisation processes that I will discuss in chapter 7.

3 Lexical, morphological, and phonological dimensions of functional categories

In chapter 2, I showed how the description of non-European languages has enriched our view of functional categories. The question raised in this chapter is whether functional categories have a special lexical or morphological status in the languages of the world. Can they be distinguished on the basis of their lexical realisation or morphological properties alone? My answer will be 'no', although it will also become clear that in many languages they have some special properties.

Lexical realisation

The first observation to be made is that functional categories are lexically a quite heterogeneous group. Functional categorical distinctions or 'morphological categories' can be realised in a great many different ways, including:

Lexical elements. Obviously, some functional categories are separate words, the class referred to as function words:

(1)   Dutch *nergens* '(lit.) nowhere' (van Riemsdijk 1978)
Dat   gaat   nergens   over!
that go.3s.PRE   NEG.IND.QA.LOC   about
'That is not about anything!'

Clitics. In many languages, functional categories are expressed with different kinds of clitics, both specal clitics and phonological clitics. A typical example is Romance languages such as Spanish, where third person reflexive *se* marks argument realisation or voice:

(2)   Vende.   'S/he sells.'
Se vende. 'It is sold.'

Clitics will be further discussed in chapter 6 on the syntax/phonology interface.

Affixes. Another possibility is the use of affixes, as in Yurakaré (van Gijn 2006: 52):

(3)   ana-kka-0=ti   ka-l-i-sibë-0
              DEM-MEA-3=DS 3s-AFO-VBL-house-3
              'When he was this big, she made him a house.'

There are two stems, *ana* 'this' and *sibë* 'house', to which various affixes and prefixes are attached, as well as enclitic elements. The switch reference marker =*ti* is analysed as an enclitic by van Gijn (2006). Object person marking takes the form of a prefix, while subject person marking is suffixal. There is good reason here to assume that third person subject is actually a null suffix rather than simply absent.

Suppletive processes. Suppletion of one stem by another frequently marks a functional categorical distinction, as in the paradigm for the verb 'be' in many European languages. Take the example of French:

(4)   suis   '1s.PR'
           es   '2s.PR'
           sommes '1p.PR'
           était   '3s.IMPP'

Consonant and vowel alternations. As is well known, in Classical Arabic the simple root form for 'write' can have the following manifestations, depending on voice and aspect:

(5)   katab   perfective active
           kutib   perfective passive
           aktub   imperfective active
           uktab   imperfective passive

Here the distinctions are indicated by vowels, and particular vowel combinations are associated with a mood and a voice distinction. Thus the component morphemes of these forms can (at least) be split into (6a) and (6b):

(6)   (a) k t b   'write'
           (b) a a   perfective active
               u i   perfective passive
               a u   imperfective active
               u a   imperfective passive

Through association rules (McCarthy 1982), the vowels and consonants are mapped onto consonant/vowel skeletons, so that the right word forms are created.

Reduplication. Reduplication can have a number of meanings in the languages of the world. One of them is stative predicate formation, as in Eastern

Table 3.1. *Classification by Alpatov (1979) of functional categories into three morpho-lexical groups or expression types*

	Flexions	Formants	Function words
Non-phonological changes on morphemic boundaries	+	−	−
Insertion as lexical units	−	−	+

Maroon Creole, a generic name for a creole language known also as Ndyuka in Suriname (Migge 2003b: 61):

(7)   A   atuku   ya   lepi-lepi.
        DET soursop here ripe-ripe
        'This soursop is not quite ripe yet.'

The element *lepi* 'ripe' by itself has an active or processual reading.

Null elements. Of course, it is always hazardous to postulate null elements. The reason van Gijn (2006: 144) adduces to assume a null third person subject marker in Yurakaré is that the 3p marker $-0 = w$ can then plausibly be seen as the combination of a null element and the plural enclitic $= w$.

Compounding. Compounds by definition cannot be used to create inflections, since they always result in new lexemes. However, compounding is productive in the formation of English quantifiers such as *anybody*, *anything*, etc.

On the basis of this brief survey the conclusion must be that:

(8)   Functional categories do not receive a uniform lexical expression in the
        languages of the world.

This also holds within a particular category or a particular language. In English, for instance, tense is marked either with a suffix (*-ed*), with a vowel change (*give/gave*), a suppletive form (*go/went*), or a separate auxiliary (*will*).

With regard to their realisation, Alpatov (1979), cited in Testelets (2001), splits functional categories into three morpho-lexical groups or expression types, on the basis of two criteria. His classification is given in Table 3.1.

Subsequently, different languages are classified typologically as to the degree to which they rely on these expression types:

(9)   Turkish   formants
        Japanese   flexions and formants
        French, Hungarian flexions, formants, and function words

I think this classification is a bit of an idealisation, but clearly languages differ in their expression of functional categories. Theoretically, there could also be languages where functional categories are not expressed at all, the so-called 'amorphous' languages, like the putative example of Old Chinese as preserved in poetry. In Old Chinese, the amount of other morphology presumably was also null.

These differences, linked to overall differences between these languages, would suggest that there is no relation whatsoever between lexical realisation on the one hand and notional and grammatical status on the other. Gil (2001: 1282) writes about quantifiers, to give just one example: 'There is probably no language within which there is a formal category consisting exactly of all quantifiers but no other expressions.' There may sometimes be a relation between lexical form and grammatical function, however, and certainly in a statistical sense.

A case study: Quechua

To take a typical example, consider Quechua. I will use examples from Cuzco Quechua, citing from Cusihuamán (1976). In Quechua there are at least two major word classes, nouns and verbs, while adjectives, adverbs, and postpositions share many features with nouns, at least morphologically. Examples are given in (10):

(10)   muna-   'want'
        puri-   'walk'
        warmi   'woman'
        rumi   'stone'
        sumaq   'beautiful'
        hanqa   'immediately'

Most of these elements are bi-syllabic; in addition there are some words with more syllables. There are a few mono-syllabic elements in the language. The entire set of mono-syllabic verbs is given in (11a), and of non-verbs in (11b) (excluding pronouns, etc. for the moment):

(11)   (a)   ri-   'go'
              ni-   'say'
              qu-   'give'
              ka-   'be'
        (b)   hoq   'one'
              ñan   'path, road'
              ña   'already'
              as   'a little'

It is clear the number of these is very limited, and largely includes high-frequency elements. The verb *ka-* 'be' and the numeral *hoq* 'one' can be considered functional elements as well, but it is not possible to simply state that all mono-syllabic elements are functional.

There is a pronominal sub-class of the nominal elements, which is mixed from the perspective of syllabicity. I present them with their traditional labels, with the bi-syllabic roots in bold:

(12)　　(a) *Personal pronouns*
　　　　noqa　1s **noqa**-yku　1p.exc
　　　　　　　　　noqa-nchis　1p.inc
　　　　qan　2s (qan-kuna　2p)
　　　　pay　3s (pay-kuna　3p)

　　　　(b) *Demonstrative pronouns*
　　　　(an)kay　　'this'
　　　　(an)chay　　'that'
　　　　(an)**chahay**　'yonder'

　　　　(c) *Interrogative pronouns*
　　　　pi　　　　'who'　　may-na　　'how'
　　　　ima　　　'what'　　**ima**-yna　'how'
　　　　may　　　'where'　　**hayk'a**　'how much'
　　　　may-qen　'which'　**hayk'aq**　'when'

　　　　(d) *Quantitative pronouns*
　　　　kiki-　　'self'　　**sapa**　　'alone, each'
　　　　waki-n　'some'　　**llapa/llipi**　'all'

It is clear that in this group of words the proportion of mono-syllabic roots is higher, yet we cannot conclude that the group as a whole is mono-syllabic. There may be an overall correlation within the group between semantic complexity and bi-syllabicity. It should be kept in mind that the elements in (12) morphologically and syntactically behave like ordinary nouns in most respects; it is only their meaning which makes them classifiable as functional categories.

Most of the functional categories in Quechua are not roots, however, but affixes and clitics. Again we can observe a correlation with the different categories between formal and semantic complexity. I first turn to case marking, as representative of nominal morphology:

(13)　　*Case marking*
　　　　-ta　　accusative　　-paq　　benefactive
　　　　-man　dative　　　　-manta　ablative
　　　　-pi　　locative　　　-rayku　reason
　　　　-wan　instrumental　-kama　until
　　　　-q/-pa　genitive

Notice that the more peripheral oblique cases in the second column have the more complex forms. For verbal morphology I will take the domain of verbal 'derivation' markers as illustrative:

(14)   (a) *Verbalisers*
       -cha   'factive'   -ya   'transformative'
       -na   'placement'   -lli   'auto-transformative'

       (b) *Lexical suffixes*
       -naya   'desiderative'   -raya   'persistive'
       -ykacha   'simulative'   -paya   'frequentative'
       -y/rpari 'intentional'   -nya   'continuative'
       -pata   'imitative'   -ymana   'memorative'
       -pasa   'despair'   -tiya   'exaggerative'

       (c) *Syntactic suffixes*
       -pa   'repetitive'   -na   'reciprocal'
       -yu/yku   'augmentative'   -ru/rqo 'exhortative'
       -ri   'inchoative'   -ysi   'assistive'
       -chi   'causative'   -ku   'reflexive'

       (d) *Directionals*
       -mu   'translocative'   -pu   'regressive'

These suffixes are roughly located from the verbal root outwards, preceding the verbal inflection. The elements in (14c) have syntactic properties in that they tend to be somewhat flexible in their position (cf. Muysken 1988a). The elements in (14b) function as a type of secondary root, and have the morphological complexity of roots, while the other elements tend to be mono-syllabic. Notice that their meanings tend to be much more general than those of the lexical roots.

The enclitics finally, which function as clausal particles, are generally mono-syllabic. What the Quechua data show is that differences in formal complexity exist both within the domain of roots and of that of affixes, and tend to correspond to differences in semantic complexity. An absolute lexical/functional distinction cannot be drawn, however, in either domain. Leaving aside the issue of whether there is a sharp break, these data certainly support the observation in (15):

(15)   More functional categories are segmentally and morphologically simple in Quechua than lexical categories, but there is no absolute dividing line.

This accords with Lehmann's notion of attrition (1982: 164) as a feature of grammaticalisation processes.

Other criteria

I now turn to a number of morphological and lexical criteria that could be used to distinguish the class of functional elements: open and closed class, independent coining, paradigmatic organisation, suppletion, syncretism, no selection in collocations, absence of derivational morphology, special morphological status of derivational processes, and compounding in category innovation.

Open and closed classes. An often invoked criterion is open versus closed class. Following this criterion, grammatical elements involve an obligatory choice (from the members of a small set, often a paradigm) in speech production, and lexical elements involve a free choice. Nouns and verbs typically belong to open classes, pronouns typically to closed ones. However, the open/closed class distinction is not clear-cut. Adjectives and adverbs in many languages form an open class, but in some languages a small closed class, as argued by Schachter (1985) e.g. for Yoruba. The same point has been made by Foley (1986) for verbs in some Papuan languages. There are often only a limited number of coordinating conjunctions and adpositions in a language, but equally often elements could still be added to these categories. In Dutch, for instance, the prepositional *be-* prefix (found in *binnen* 'inside' from *in*) can be added to the cardinal points 'north' and 'south' to yield the prepositions *benoorden* 'to the north of' and *bezuiden* 'to the south of'. Many more peripheral conjunctions and prepositions can be easily replaced, and may be replaced more rapidly (in terms of types) than content words, in terms of their percentage of the total set of conjunctions or adpositions. Thus the criterium of closedness is not easy to apply in many cases.

Independent coining. Over and above the open/closed class distinction Emonds (1985: 159) has suggested that the 'conscious coining of new lexical entries by speakers is allowed only in open categories'. Leaving aside the question of how conscious a given process must be, this criterion disregards the issue of compound formation in functional categories (see below). While forms like *somebody* show this for older stages, an area of innovation that is still ongoing concerns the various forms for the second person plural in English, of which the following is just a small selection:

(16)   y'all
        youse
        youse guys
        you-uns
        you guys
        yous
        yis

Table 3.2. *Part of the Dutch non-personal pronoun paradigm (based on van Riemsdijk 1978)*

Definite	Universal quantifier	Negation	Wh	Distant	Human	R	Word
−	−	−	+	−	+	−	wie
−	−	−	+	−	−	−	wat
−	−	−	+	−	−	+	waar
+	−	−	−	+	±	−	deze [+PROX] die [−PROX
+	−	−	−	+	−	−	dit [+PROX] dat [−PROX]
+	−	−	−	+	−	+	daar
+	−	−	−	−	+	−	hij/zij
+	−	−	−	−	−	−	het
+	−	−	−	−	−	+	er
−	−	−	−	−	+	−	iemand
−	−	−	−	−	−	−	iets
−	−	−	−	−	−	+	ergens
−	−	+	−	−	+	−	niemand
−	−	+	−	−	−	−	niets
−	−	+	−	−	−	+	nergens
+	+	−	−	−	+	−	iedereen
+	+	−	−	−	−	−	alles
+	+	−	−	−	−	+	overal

Paradigmatic organisation. An often invoked criterion would be whether a given closed class is paradigmatically organised, i.e. whether the elements in it are defined in opposition to each other (present versus past, singular versus plural, definite versus indefinite, etc.). Thus, paradigmatic coherence refers to the tightness of organisation of a given sub-category. The pronoun system is tightly organised, and it is difficult to imagine English borrowing a new pronoun to create a first person dual in addition to first person singular and plural. Pronoun and tense systems particularly tend to show a high degree of symmetry, and the formations in (16) may be due to paradigm pressure.

A number of functional category systems are paradigmatically organised. An example is the cluster of paradigms described by van Riemsdijk (1978) for Dutch in Table 3.2. In Dutch, there is an abstract grammatical feature [±R], which can have a locative interpretation (and thus might be seen as a case feature), but also characterises those elements or constituents extracted out of a prepositional phrase. Other features in this cluster are [± Human], [± Wh], [± Neg(ation)], [± Definite].

Features of the system in Table 3.2 are:

- partial morphological similarities (the elements marked '+' in the column [R] indeed all contain an *r*-sound; the [+Neg] elements all start with an *n*)
- many irregularities and cases of suppletion (e.g. *hier* instead of *dier* for [+R, +Deictic, −Distant])
- gaps (e.g. no [+Human, +Wh, +R] form, although in informal language the [−Human] *waar* form may be used here in relative clauses)
- cases of syncretism (e.g. *die* for [+Plural] as well as [−Neuter] distant deictics)

Another example is the much more complicated paradigm for Movima third person referential elements (Haude 2006: 143), presented in Table 3.3.

The paradigm in Table 3.3 shares some of the features with the earlier Dutch case, although there are no gaps and no syncretism. In the paradigm we find the combination of vowel alternations, affixes, and clitics provides a rich array of morpho-syntactic distinctions.

However, can we conclude that paradigmatic organisation is limited to functional categories? It is true that it is mostly characteristic of case, tense, agreement, and pronominal systems. However, we may find tight paradigmatic organisation outside the realm of function words, e.g. in kinship terminology. An example is the Latin system for male kin:

(17)　(a) pater 'father'   frater 'brother'   filius 'son'
　　　(b) patruus 'father's brother'   avunculus 'mother's brother'
　　　(c) patruelis 'father's brother's son'   amitinus 'father's sister's son'
　　　(d) consobrinus 'mother's brother's son'   matruelis 'mother's sister's son
　　　(e) fratuelis 'brother's son'   sobrinus 'sister's son'

Notice that most of these forms are not lexically related; in fact internal relatedness increases if the female terms are also included.

However, paradigmatic organisation is rare outside of the domain of functional categories; it may not be a defining lexical feature of functional categories, but is prominently associated with them.

Suppletion. Emonds (1973) has suggested that a suppletive relationship is something that characterises function words in particular, but not content words. Compare the opposition *walks/walked* to that between *is* and *was*. This was illustrated in example (4) with the verb 'be' in French. Similarly, the relation between elements such as *this* and *that* and between *I* and *we* is suppletive,

Table 3.3. *The morphological structure of the third person referential elements in Movima. Bracketed elements refer to segments that only occur in certain phonological environments or that are clearly additional markers. Root elements are underlined*

Marker	Morphemes	Masculine	Feminine	Neuter	Plural
DM.spk	R(+ʔ)	u:(-ru)	i:ni	ay(ru)	i:(-ri)
BP	R+prs	u-ʔ	(i)<ʔ>ne	a-ʔ	i-ʔ
BP.a	R+abs	u-s	(i)<s>ne	a-s	i-s
ART	R+DET	u=s	i<ʔ>ne=s	A=s	i=s
ART.p	R+pst+DET	u-so=s	i<s>n-o=s	O=s	i-so=s
DM.p	R+pst+DM	u-so-ʔ	i<s>n-o-ʔ	o-so-ʔ	i-so-ʔ
PRO	R+prs+PRO marker	u-ʔ-ko	i<ʔ>ne	a-ko	i-ʔ-ko
PRO.a	R+abs+PRO marker	u-s-ko	i<s>ne	a-s-ko	i-s-ko
ART.a	abs2+R+DET	k-u=s	k-in-o=s	k-o=s	k-i=s
DM.addr	abs2+R+dst(+ʔ)	k-u-l(-ru)	k-i<l>ni	k-a-l(-ru)	k-i-l(-ri)
DM.a	abs2+R+ʔ+DM	k-u-ro-ʔ	k-in-o-ʔ	k-o-ro-ʔ	k-i-ro-ʔ
DM.po	abs2+R(+dst)+ TRC.hand	k-u(-l)-pa	k-i(<l>)ni-pa	k-o(-l)-pa	k-i(-l)-pa
DM.std	abs2+R(+dist)+std	k-u(-l)-reʔ	k-i(<l>)n-eʔ	k-o(-l)-reʔ	k-i(-l)-reʔ
DM.nst	abs2+R(+dst)+'lie'	k-u(-l)-de:	k-i(<l>)ne-de:	k-o(-l)-de:	k-i(-l)-de:
DM.el	abs2+R(+dst)-elʔ	k-u(-l)-wa	k-i(<l>)ni-wa	k-o(-l)-wa	k-i(-l)-wa
DM.appr	abs2+R+dst+NEG.Nʔ+ʔ	k-u-l-aʔ-wa	k-i<l-aʔ>ni-wa	k-o-l-aʔ-wa	k-i-l-aʔ-wa
DM.rtr	abs2+R+dst+ʔ+DM	k-u-l-ro-ʔ	k-i<l>n-o-ʔ	k-o-l-ro-ʔ	k-i-l-ro-ʔ

Note: Special abbreviations in this table: R = root; BP = bound pronoun; abs = absential; pst = past; dst = distal; DM = demonstrative; PRO = free pronoun; spk = proximate to speaker; addr = proximate to addressee; std = standing; nst = non-standing; el = elevated; appr = approaching; rtr = retreating; '_' = affix boundary; '=' = clitic boundary.

along the same lines. However, the case of *go/went* in English suggests that this is a mistaken idea: *go* may be a function word some of the time, but its past is always *went*. Similarly, the relationships in *bad/worse* and *good/better* are suppletive. What can be said for most cases is that the categories expressed by suppletion (single/plural, present/past, basic/comparative) are paradigmatic. We can only recognise a suppletive category if there is a paradigm. What gives the impression of limitation to functional categories is that in a language like English suppletion is limited to highly frequent elements. Likewise, in kinship paradigms there are many cases of suppletion, as in the Dutch terms for in-laws, where *zwager* is a suppletive form:

(18)   schoondochter   'daughter-in-law'
         schoonzoon   'son-in-law'
         schoonmoeder   'mother-in-law'
         schoonvader   'father-in-law'
         schoonzuster   'sister-in-law'
         zwager   'brother-in-law'

Syncretism. Just like suppletion, syncretism is a property of paradigms (Baerman, Brown, and Corbett 2005): a single form is used to express various morpho-syntactic categories. A typical example is Latin *-ibus* as the third, fourth, and fifth declension plural dative **and** ablative form. Again, syncretism is typical of functional category paradigms, and might thus be seen as a defining characteristic of functional categories. However, we also find it in kinship systems. Thus English *uncle* refers to both of the Latin categories *patruus* 'father's brother' and *avunculus* 'mother's brother'. Indeed, anthropologists distinguish between different types of kinship systems (e.g. the 'Omaha' type or the 'Crow' type) precisely in terms of the syncretisms that characterise them.

No selection in collocations. It has been suggested that functional categories have less of a chance of being an inherent part of a collocation. This is partly correct; many collocations do contain functional categories. However, the functional categories are the selected element, not the selective element. In the expression *addled brains* the adjective *addled* selects *brains*, not vice versa. In the expressions *high/low esteem* and *high/low tide*, *esteem* and *tide* select *high/low*, not vice versa. Thus, in collocations adjectives can select nouns, or nouns adjectives. However, in the expression (*that is*) *the pits* (*a pits), the noun *pits* selects *the*, just as in *the bottom of the barrel* (**a bottom of the barrel*), *bottom of the barrel* selects *the*. However, there are no cases of a functional category selecting a certain noun or adjective in a collocation. A possible exception might be a particular category that only occurs in a few frozen expressions, such as the Dutch genitive pro-clitic in *'s nachts* 'at night', *'s avonds* 'in the evening', and *'s morgens* 'in the morning'. However, I will assume that this is a phenomenon of a different nature, and in any case, the nouns in these expressions have a particular shape as well, and could be said to select the genitive pro-clitic *'s*.

Absence of derivational morphology. A further criterion would be whether a certain class of elements can undergo morphological derivations, like noun, verb, or adjective, or not, like demonstrative and auxiliary (Abney 1987). On the whole, English functional categories cannot undergo derivational processes, with the possible exception of prepositions, depending on how complex prepositions are analysed. Neither would one expect derivational morphology in this domain, since it does not require new forms. If we had more affective derivational morphology, a different picture might emerge. An interesting test case in this respect is the Spanish diminutive (*-it(o/a)/-ecit(o/a)*), which is quite productive. In various varieties of South American Spanish (notably in Mexico and the Andes) it can occur on nouns (19a), adjectives and adverbs (19b), but also on deictic locative adverbs (19c), time adverbs (19d), quantifiers and numerals (19e), demonstratives (19f), prepositions (19g), and even gerunds (19h):

(19) (a) mujer-cita   woman-DIM
           perri-ito   dog-DIM
    (b) barat-ito   cheap(ly)-DIM
           rapid-ito   rapid(ly)-DIM
    (c) aqui-cito   here-DIM
           alli-cito   there-DIM
           ahi-cito   yonder-DIM
    (d) ahor-ita   now-DIM
           despues-ito   after-DIM
           antes-ito(s) que before-DIM that
    (e) tod-it-ito-s   all-DIM-DIM-p
           dos-ito-s   two-DIM-p
           un-ita   one-DIM
           cualquier-ita   any-DIM
    (f) est-ito   this-DIM
           es-ito   that-DIM
    (g) contr-ita   against-DIM
    (h) corriend-ito   running-DIM
           calland-ito   being silent-DIM

I have not encountered instances of diminutives with personal pronouns (**ell-itos* 'they-DIM'), and undoubtedly there are other restrictions as well, but it is not clear that these restrictions would be due to the functional category status of these items.

Special morphological status of derivational processes. Inflection is the grammaticalised part of word formation, and inflectional affixes should be considered functional categories in their own right, and derivational affixes could be considered their lexical counterpart. Therefore, if functional elements have a special morphological status, we would expect special morphology for inflection. However, languages use the same morphological processes, overall, for inflection and derivation. Thus in Arabic, complex consonant/vowel alternations are used both for derivation and for inflection. In English and Dutch, the various morphological techniques available (prefixing, suffixing, vowel change, etc.) play a role in both inflection and derivation. In Yurakaré, prefixes and suffixes can be both inflectional and derivational. This was noted by Sapir (1921) in his famous dictum: 'Pattern is one thing, the utilization of pattern quite another.'

Compounding in category innovation. Abney (1987: 266–267 fn.) writes that 'adpositions can freely appear in compounds; other functional elements are uniformly excluded from compounds'. However, the formation of complex functional categories often takes place via compounding. An example is the formation of quantifying elements in English:

(20)

	body	*one*	*thing*	*where*
every	everybody	everyone	everything	everywhere
any	anybody	anyone	anything	anywhere
some	somebody	someone	something	somewhere
no	nobody	no one	nothing	nowhere

Abney (1987: 287 fn.) notes the contrast between [*New York*] *lover* and *[*The Bronx*] *lover*, and claims this is due to the inability of functional categories to occur in morphologically complex words. Whatever the merit of the observation, it does not hold for compound nominal expressions.

We can conclude from this survey of morpho-lexical features that there are gradual differences lexically and morphologically between lexical and functional categories, but not absolute differences justifying a principled distinction.

Language processing is more or less automaticised and rule governed. Lexical processing is not automatic but occurs on an item by item basis, while grammatical processing involves more automatic processes. As lexical elements are used more frequently, and their processing becomes more automatic, they turn into grammatical elements. Functional categories are in this sense the debris of automaticised processing; they constitute lexical material dragged along in the process of automaticisation.

Primitives at the interface

In this section I will discuss a few phonological properties of functional categories from the perspective of the syntax/phonology interface. I will start with a brief discussion of the phonological weight of functional categories. Then I will turn to clitics, their properties, and special behaviour.

A notable feature of functional categories is their limited phonological weight. From the perspective of phonology it has been claimed that functional categories have limited phonological weight, e.g. in containing at most one foot, and that they are integrated into a neighbouring phonological word. The precise formulation and empirical basis for these claims will be examined in detail. The main question to be raised is: do phonological rules crucially make reference to the notion of functional category as such?

Cutler and Norris (1988) argue that non-affixal functional categories lack metrical stress, while Cutler and Carter (1987) have shown that initial strong syllables are uncommon for functional categories, although frequent with lexical categories. In their discussion of phonological reduction as a concomitant of 'morphologisation', Hopper and Traugott (2003: 155) distinguish two dimensions:

- on the syntagmatic dimension, there is a quantitative reduction in terms of the number of segments constituting a morpheme;
- on the paradigmatic dimension, there is a qualitative reduction in the nature of the segments allowed.

Inkelas and Zec (1995: 543–544) write: 'Only a subset of morphological entities known as words – commonly those that belong to open classes such as nouns, verbs, or adjectives – acquire the status of phonological words (see, e.g. Nespor and Vogel 1986).' They go on to state (1995: 544): 'In English, for example, it is well-known that function words such as pronouns and prepositions do not, except in positions of contrastive emphasis, receive the same degree of word stress that content words exhibit.' Cross-linguistically, as well, functional categories are exempt from word-level rules and violate morpheme-structure constraints, including minimal prosodic word size.

With respect to tonal patterns, function words appear to show special behaviour as well. Newman (1995: 776) writes that in Hausa: 'Whereas content words (especially nouns and verbs) have the body to carry distinctive tone, with short unstressed grammatical morphemes, a very specific tone, whether it be high or low, has very little saliency. What works well for short words, clitics, and affixes is for the morpheme to join up with a substantive word to become part of a tonal melody whose preferred tune will in many cases be H-L or L-H.'

Similarly, Selkirk and Shen (1990) argue for Shanghai Chinese that: 'The function word necessarily loses its tone (Obligatory Tone Deletion) and receives tone either from the preceding lexical item (Left Right Association) or via Default Tone Insertion.' Relevant functional categories involved include aspectual particles, personal pronouns, and interrogative particles. They start by proposing the Shanghai Chinese Prosodic Word Rule:

(21)   Prosodic Word: {Left, Lex^0}
         where Lex^0 stands for word belonging to the lexical categories N, V, A.

Because of several problems, in part involving strongly versus weakly embedded post-verbal prepositions, the rule was modified to the Shanghai Chinese Major Phrase Rule:

(22)   Major Phrase: {Left, $Left^{max}$}

Selkirk (2004: 464) lists English determiners, prepositions, auxiliaries, modifiers, complementisers, conjunctions, and particles as functional categories. Functional categories can be PWds (prosodic words) or prosodic clitics. In the latter case they can be free clitics, internal clitics, or affixal clitics (2004: 465). She goes to write (p. 466) 'whether a function word in a particular syntactic configuration in a particular language is a prosodic word or not, and if not, what type of prosodic clitic it is, depends crucially on the interaction of various well-attested types of constraints on prosodic structure'. However, this does not mean that it is necessary to formulate a phonological definition of function word. Indeed, 'the set of constraints governing the interface between morphosyntactic and prosodic structure makes no reference to functional categories at all' (Selkirk 2004: 468). Thus in phonology, the notion of function word is an entirely negative one: all elements count as such that are not content words.

Clitics

Others have tried to relate clitic status to belonging to the class of functional categories. Whatever categories one has in mind, the claim is clearly too strong: by no means all functional categories are clitics, but the reverse claim, that all clitics are functional elements, is much more justified.

On the basis of surveys of the domain of clitics such as Klavans (1985) and Halpern (1998), we can conclude that at least the following categories can be realised as clitics:

(23)   auxiliary   personal pronoun
       reflexive/reciprocal   negation
       case   conjunction
       voice   mood
       discourse connective   evidential
       adverbial   determiner
       adposition   complementiser

Thus we can safely conclude that all clitics are functional categories, in the rough sense of including some adpositions and adverbials. Spencer (1991: 350) writes: 'Typically, clitics are function words, such as modal participles [sic, intended is particles] (e.g. interrogative participles), conjunctions, pronominals, or auxiliary verbs.' The converse is not the case of course: not all functional categories are clitics.

In the literature, three types of clitics are often distinguished, following Zwicky (1977; cf. also 1990):

- simple clitics, which can be derived from full forms through simple rules of phrase phonology
- special clitics, which are allomorphs of full forms
- bound forms, which lack a corresponding full form allomorph.

Ignoring many complicated issues in the study of clitics, many of which are alluded to in Spencer (1991), an issue relevant here is to what extent the special position of clitics is syntactically or phonologically determined. Klavans (1985) argues that both factors play a role.

Conclusions

We can conclude from the above survey that indeed there is an overall correspondence between the functional status of an element and its form, but that this correspondence cannot be captured by structural principles. Rather, it should be captured by optimalisation procedures at the syntax/lexicon interface. While the study of the phonology/syntax interface has shown that functional categories often show special phonological behaviour, we cannot conclude that the notion of functional category as such needs to be invoked in the study of this interface.

4 Semantics and pragmatics

Frequently it is claimed that functional categories are different from lexical categories in having an abstract meaning. This holds both for functional categories in the way I have been discussing them in the previous chapters and for a special class of elements often analysed as functional, namely discourse markers. First, I will try to make the claim about the special semantic status of functional categories more precise and see whether it can be made testable, in the light of recent models of the syntax/semantics interface and interpretability. In the second part of the chapter, I will turn to discourse markers. If these should be treated as functional elements at all, they have a status and behaviour rather different from other categories. The discussion in the first section owes much to Cann (2000), the most lucid exposition of the semantic issues surrounding functional categories that I have encountered, even if I do not follow his distinction here between I- and E-language categories (cf. Chomsky 1986a).

Elements can be interpreted in various ways:

- through reference to a notion in the cognitive system
- through deixis
- through knowledge of the constructions they are part of
- through paradigms
- through discourse patterns.

In this chapter, I will deal with the last four possibilities for interpreting an element.

Semantic features of functional categories

There have been frequent comments about the special semantic status of functional categories. I will discuss a number of criteria: abstract meaning, no modification, theta-assignment, relation to ontology, sense relations, meaning coercion, meaning flexibility, semantic projection, and selectional restrictions.

Special abstract meaning. Sometimes, a semantic distinction is made between auto-semantic elements (content words, with a concrete meaning) that have a meaning by themselves, and syn-semantic elements (function words), that have an abstract meaning that depends on the context. Sapir (1921: 93) speaks of 'radical concepts' (expressed by content words) versus 'relational concepts' (expressed by functional categories). However, there may be functional elements that have no evident semantic interpretation at all, not even in conjunction with a content word, for example *of* and *that*. In fact, there is quite a bit of discussion on this issue. On the one side of the spectrum, there is the view that some functional categories are purely manifestations of structural relationships. On the other side, we find the idea that functional categories (almost) always have an independent meaning. Langacker (1991: 111) writes that 'most if not all grammatical morphemes are meaningful, and make active semantic contributions to the expressions in which they appear'. In his view, the idea that there is a large difference in the contribution to meaning of lexical and functional elements is mistaken: 'In reality, however, both lexical and grammatical morphemes vary along a continuum in regard to such parameters as the complexity and abstractness of their semantic representations' (pp. 110–111). One of the examples he cites involves two overlapping continua:

(1)   (a) *lexical*:   ostrich bird   animal thing
       (b) *functional*:   above may have of

While *ostrich* surely has a much more concrete meaning than *of* (which according to many researchers often has no meaning at all), the meaning of *above* is no less concrete than that of *thing*. Langacker refers to the special features of the meaning of functional categories in terms of schematicity (1991: 292): 'So-called "grammatical morphemes" are symbolically minimal, and while often phonologically specific, semantically they are quite schematic.' This notion of schematic meaning is highly theory-specific, however. There is no escape from the fact that the 'meaning' of certain specific functional categories, like determiners, complementisers, and modality markers, if we can speak of meaning at all, is very different from that of lexical items. However, abstractness of meaning is not something limited to functional categories.

No modification. Since they have no independent meaning, functional elements cannot be modified as such (Fukui and Speas 1986). We cannot say (2a), where *very much* modifies the auxiliary, but we can say (2b), where *really* modifies the entire verb phrase:

(2)   (a) *He very much must go.
       (b) He really must go.

Similarly, there is the contrast between (3a) and (3b):

(3)   (a) She smiled wickedly.
       (b) *She has wickedly.

Functional categories like auxiliaries and determiners can indeed not be **modified**, while negation possibly can:

(4)   (a) He didn't at all like the present I gave him.
       (b) He is not at all the person I thought.
       (c) not bad at all

Theta-assignment. Yet another approach would be to distinguish theta-assigning from non-theta-assigning categories (Grimshaw 1990). Functional categories are assumed 'not to enter into theta-marking', either as receivers or as assigners of a particular thematic role, as stressed by Myers-Scotton (1993). In itself this is correct, but lexical categories differ among themselves in the degree to which they assign thematic roles. Verbs are very active, most nouns and adjectives are not, while prepositions do assign thematic roles.

Relation to ontology. For lexical categories there is a clear relation to ontological properties which they denote, while for functional categories there is no such relation. Consider the contrast between *chair* and *of*. Rather, these categories 'constrain relations between denotational classes' (Cann 2000: 45). However, Cann notes that a number of non-functional elements, like *seem*, *appear*, *four*, and *a big chunk of* also constrain relations between denotational classes.

Talmy (2001a) suggests three specific features as characteristic of closed class items, which in his view include everything but nouns, verbs, adjectives, and ideophones. Referents of closed class forms are 'bulk neutral' (they cannot represent specific sizes or distances), they are 'token neutral' (they cannot refer to a specific instance of e.g. a spatial relation), and they are 'substance neutral' (they cannot refer to any specific substance). Bulk neutrality and token neutrality are highly plausible, but it remains to be seen whether come classifiers do not refer to substances, such as water.

Sense relations. Lexical elements 'are linked in complex arrays of sense relations' (Cann 2000: 45) like synonymy and hyponymy, functional elements are not. Thus *cat*, *dog*, amd *hamster* are all *pets*, but there is no lexical item covering *can*, *will*, and *must*. *Auxiliary* or *modal* is a meta-term. We cannot say *I modal go*. Semantic relations between functional elements are defined in terms of features characteristic of the class as such: definiteness, etc.

Meaning coercion. Lexical elements, when combined, have meaning that corresponds to the whole, and their individual meaning is to some extent coerced by the overall construction, leading to metaphors, non-compositional meanings, etc., as in *The book was killed*. This does not hold for functional elements. Cann (2000: 47) cites the example of *all some books*, which becomes incomprehensible rather than that the meaning of either *all* or *some* is extended. This criterion is not watertight. Thus *must* can have a deontic and an epistemic reading, as in:

(5) (a) You must go. (deontic)
     (b) You must be Oscar. (epistemic)

The difference is related to the stativity of the predicate involved. Active predicates induce or coerce a deontic meaning, as in (5a) (compare epistemic *You must be going*), while stative predicates coerce a deontic meaning.

Flexibility in meaning. This difference is probably related to the fact that the meaning of lexical items is generally extendable and adaptable, while that of functional items is not. This quality of lexical items of being extendable in meaning should be distinguished from broadness. Cruse (2000: 90) does not stress the meaninglessness of functional categories but rather the limitations on their meaning: functional categories 'must have a meaning which is flexible, or broad enough, or sufficiently "attenuated" not to generate clashes too easily, and it must signal contrasts which recur frequently'. However, this notion of flexibility is hard to pin down, and is in apparent contrast with what was just stated about meaning coercion.

Semantic projection. Abney (1987: 56) defines functional elements 'as those elements which possess the feature [+F]'. [+F] means that an element f-selects its complement, which 'corresponds semantically to the "passing on" of the descriptive content of the complement'. Abney (1987: 57) distinguishes c-projection (category projection) from s-projection (semantic projection). The following example illustrates what is meant by s-projection. In (6) the relations between *fell* and *tree* and between *woodsman* and '[fell tree]' remain stable independently of the number of functional categories surrounding these elements:

(6) (a) The **woodsman fell**-ed the **tree**.
     (b) [[The **woodsman**] [must [have [**fell**-ed [all [the **tree**-s]]]]]].

The semantic information in these elements is passed on, projected, even though these elements are embedded in complex functional projections.

Selectional restrictions. While functional categories are strongly sub-categorised for a particular type of category as its complement (*the* always takes a noun complement), they are not subject to selection restrictions, like lexical items may be: *to fell* (*a tree*) can only be said of tree-like objects. Thus, as noted in chapter 3, they are not the selective element in collocations.

The syntax/semantics interface and interpretability of features

Anderson (1982), in his well-known paper 'Where's morphology?' argues that inflectional elements in the word are those elements which participate in grammatical processes. In the same vein, we can argue that those features involved in agreement or concord phenomena, features which are doubly expressed in the sentence but receive a single interpretation, must be functional in nature. A selective list of such features is given in (7), with relevant examples:

(7)   (a) *Gender*
             la   casa   blanca
             DET.f   house.f   white.f
             'the white house' (Spanish)

        (b) *Number*
             Les   soldats   marchent.
             DET.p soldier.p   walk.3p
             'The soldiers walk.' (French)

        (c) *Person*
             she eats

        (d) *Case*
             de   Bello   Gallico
             about war.n.OB Gallic.n.OB
             'about the Gallic war' (Latin)

        (e) *Negation*
             Je   ne   regrette   rien.
             I   NEG   regret.1s   nothing
             'I do not regret anything.' (French)

        (f) *Tense*
             He said the car was rusting because of the humidity.

        (g) *Modality*
             This substance may possibly be hazardous to your health.

        (h) *Wh*
             [CP **Was**ᵢ glaubte Miró [CP **welches Bild**ᵢ Picasso tᵢ gemalt hatte]?
             what believed Miró which image Picasso painted had
             'Which image did Miró believe that Picasso had painted?' (German)

(i) *Definiteness*
Het   bruin-e paard/een   bruin paard
DET.DEF.n brown-AGR horse/DET.IND brown horse
'the brown horse/a brown horse' (Dutch)

(j) *Location*
In dem   Garten/ in den   Garten
in.LOC DET.m.DA garden/ in.DIR DET.m.AC garden
'in the garden/into the garden' (German)

(k) *Transitivity/voice*
ruwa-pu-wa-y-ta   muna-pu-wa-n
make-BEN-1ob-INF-AC want-BEN-1ob-3
'He wants to make it (for me).' (Cuzco Quechua)

A possible counter-example to the restriction of concord or agreement to functional categories may be verbal reduplication in predicate cleft constructions, as in Papiamentu and other Caribbean creoles, or the related West African languages:

(8) ta traha e ta traha
    FOC work 3s ASP work
    'He is really working.' (Muysken 1978)

It is interesting that prepositions do not seem to participate in concord in the sense that we find the same preposition repeated.

Deletability and expression as a null form

One feature of functional categories is that they are often deletable. Examples include complementisers in various languages, such as Dutch and English:

(9) (a) The girl that I saw yesterday.
    (b) The girl I saw yesterday.

(10) (a) Ik heb   geprobeerd om je te bellen.
      I have.1s tried   for 2s to call
   (b) Ik heb   geprobeerd [0] je te bellen.
      I have.1s tried   2s to call
      'I have tried to call you.'

Similarly, in a creole language like Saramaccan, tense markers generally only occur if the tense reference is understood from the discourse context:

(11) a (bi) nángó alá
    3s PST go(DUR) there
    'He went there.' (de Groot 1981: 17)

Thus tense markers and complementisers are sometimes deletable. The same holds for some negation markers in negative concord contexts, as in (12):

(12)   Je (ne)   mange pas.
       I   (NEG)   eat   NEG
       'I do not eat.' (French)

Notice that this does not hold for lexical nouns and verbs, except in gapping contexts of course. The question remains as to what status to assign to this feature. In a number of languages, adpositions can be absent in relative clauses with an invariant conjunction. An example from Quebec French is provided by Auger (1994), who recorded and analysed the following three utterances:

(13)   les   anciennes places **que** je restais
       DET.p old.p.f place.p   that I   stay.
       'the old places that I lived' (p. 75) (locative absent)

(14)   la   manière **qu**'on est élevé là
       DET.f manner   that-one is   raised there
       'the manner that we were raised' (p. 76) (*de* 'of' absent)

(15)   j'ai   des   voisins   [0] je parle temps en temps
       I-have of.DET.p neighbour. p   I talk time to time
       'I have neighbours [that] I talk (to) once in a while' (p. 76) (*à* 'to' absent)

Generally, these elements can be omitted on the basis of recoverability.

The special status of discourse markers

The special status of discourse markers within the family of functional categories first became clear to me in the study of the role of these markers in code-mixing. The following example illustrates the relevant pattern, which contrasts with that of other functional categories in code-mixing (cf. chapter 13). It is a Dutch utterance from a Moroccan Arabic speaker with a single Arabic word.

(16)   Ik ben een dokter *wella* ik ben een ingenieur.
       I am a doctor or I am an engineer
       'I will become a doctor or an engineer.' (Nortier 1990: 142)

Normally the community language forms the grammatical base (providing the syntax and function words), with the dominant language providing isolated lexical items or syntactic islands (Myers-Scotton 1993). Here the pattern is reversed. In fact, the only case of 'reverse' mixing is that of discourse markers, interjections, and clausal conjunctions (reinterpreted then as discourse markers). Reverse mixing is highly uncharacteristic for lexical elements and clause-internal function words. The Arabic conjunctions in (17) illustrate the type of elements that participate in the reverse pattern:

(17)   walakin   'but'
         9la-heqq-aš   'because'
         wella   'or'
         be-l-heqq   'but'

The pattern has been found in many other settings as well. Some examples are Swahili/French switching (de Rooij 1996), and the Spanish of Quechua–Spanish bilinguals in Bolivia (Albó 1988). De Rooij notes in his very detailed study that French discourse markers such as *bon* 'well', *non* 'no', *mais* 'but', *puisque* 'because', *lorsque* 'since', *donc* 'thus', *alors* 'then', *et puis* 'and then', as well as the complementiser *que* 'that', play a central role in bilingual Shaba Swahili/French discourse. It is precisely their status as non-Swahili items that allows them to play this role (cf. Gumperz 1982). Thus there is good reason to further explore the status of discourse markers.

Blakemore (2004: 221–222) list two features as central to the definition of discourse markers: (a) their meaning is not described in terms of truth-conditional semantics; (b) they play a role in establishing connectivity in discourse. Sometimes they are said to have **procedural** rather than **propositional** meaning. There is no definitive list of discourse markers in any language, and neither can there be, since new discourse markers may emerge all the time. Three types of elements should be distinguished which cannot be interpreted in terms of truth-conditional semantics:

(18)   (a) discourse markers, such as *well*, *but*, *so*, *indeed*, *in other words*
         (b) discourse adverbials, such as *frankly*, *reportedly*
         (c) expletives, like *damn*, *good grief*

It is clear that some of the notions expressed by these elements in (18b) have been studied from the perspective of functional categories in the typological and descriptive literature, e.g. under the heading of evidentials. Others, the category (18c), will be discussed below under the heading of interjections. There are various positions in semantics and pragmatics with respect to the interpretation, definition, and classification of discourse markers. Here I will take the fairly concrete proposals made by Schiffrin (1987) as my starting point.

Schiffrin (1987: 31) operationally defines discourse markers as 'sequentially dependent elements which bracket units of talk', and more theoretically as 'devices which provide contextual coordinates for ongoing talk'

Table 4.1. *Primary (marked !) and secondary (marked *) functions of discourse markers on the different levels of discourse structure (based on Schiffrin 1987: 316, Figure 10.2)*

	Information state	Participation framework	Ideational structure	Action structure	Exchange structure
interjections:					
oh	!	*		*	
well	*	!	*	*	*
phrases:					
y'know	!	*	*		*
I mean	*	!	*		
conjunctions:					
and			!	*	*
but			!	*	*
or			!		*
so			!	*	*
because			!	*	
adverbs:					
now		*	!		
then			!	*	

(p. 41, p. 326). In discourse, several levels or planes are operant simultaneously (p. 25): **information state** (the organisation and management of knowledge and meta-knowledge), **participation framework** (the roles of the participants), **ideational structure** (the proposition), **action structure** (the (speech) act), and **exchange structure** (the turn). Discourse markers help link these different levels and situate the ongoing talk with respect to these levels. In her book, based on a large corpus of sociolinguistic interviews, Schiffrin analyses a number of different markers: *oh, well, and, but, or, so, because, now, then, y'know,* and *I mean.* Notice that grammatically these elements have widely different functions: interjections (*oh, well*), conjunctions (*and, but, or, so, because*), adverbs (*now, then*), and small phrases (*y'know,* and *I mean*). Functionally, they differ as well. Each of these markers primarily relates to one level or plane in the discourse, as shown in Table 4.1.

The conjunctions and adverbs all have their primary function in ideational structure, but secondary functions on a variety of other levels. The interjections have their primary function at the levels of information state and participation framework. Notice that *well* functions on all levels. The phrases *y'know* and *I mean* likewise are primarily focused on at the levels of information state and participation framework, but have a variety of functions as well.

The multi-functionality of discourse markers can be illustrated with the use of *now* in the following bits of monologue:

(19)   (a) They have an open classroom at Lansdon.
        (b) **Now** there's lots of the mothers in that room are very upset about it.
        (c) I'm not. (p. 234)

(20)   (a) They're using socialism to fight capitalism.
        (b) **Now** can you understand that? (p. 240)

In (19b) the function of *now* is to create an implicit comparison between various opinions (ideational structure), while in (20b) *now* is added to mark a shift from the speaker's opinion to an appeal to the hearer's understanding (participation framework).

It is clear that discourse markers are recruited into their current role via various processes of language change. These are the main topic of Traugott's work (e.g. 1982) in this area.

Interjections

Leaving aside the category in (18b) of discourse adverbials, I now briefly turn to interjections. Ameka (1992) distinguishes four kinds of interjections:

- Expressive   (ouch, wow)
- Directive   (hush, hey)
- Phatic   (mhm, yes)
- Descriptive   (wham, bang)

The last category is also referred to as ideophones, elements which play a grammatical role in many languages (cf. Voeltz and Kilian-Hatz 2001).

The expressive type of interjection is almost the reverse of a functional category in some sense. Cusihuáman (1976: 287–288) provides a list of the rich variety of expressive forms for Cuzco Quechua:

(21)   Achacháw!   'Damn!'
        Alaláw!   'Cold!'
        Akhakáw!   'Hot!'
        Añañáw!   'Tastes good!', 'Looks good!'
        Añakáw!   'Tastes good!'
        Atatáw!   'How ugly!', 'How nasty!'
        Atatachaláw!   'How cute!'

Haw!	'Spicy!'
Achakáw!	'Ouch!'
Achaláw!	'Bold of you!', 'Like this?'
Hananáw!	'Tired!'
Akakalláw!	'Too bad!'
Haliyáw!	'A hail storm!'
Ahaháw!	'Funny!'

Most of these forms have a fixed skeleton of the form /(h)aC$_i$aC$_i$áw/, with a few variations in length, consonants, and initial sound. They are not onomatopoeic, but highly expressive, and their form conforms to general Quechua phonotactic restrictions. At the same time, it is different from that of ordinary Quechua words, which tend to be bi-syllabic and generally end in a vowel. Klamer (2002) has documented the special lexical forms of Dutch and Kambera for highly expressive elements.

Conclusions

In this chapter a number of semantic and pragmatic aspects of functional categories were surveyed. I conclude that very few semantic features, if any, unambiguously characterise a class of elements that may be reasonably termed functional categories. In the domain of semantics, the absence of sense relations among functional categories and the fact that functional category features sometimes remain uninterpretable at the syntax/semantics interface (since they participate in agreement) are among the clearest properties that are not found in the domain of lexical categories. As to discourse markers and interjections, these generally are found at the lexical/functional divide.

5 Theoretical syntax: the generative tradition

While typologists stress the gradual transition between lexical and functional categories, generative syntacticians have tended to make a sharp distinction, which plays a central role in some of the theories of syntax proposed. In this chapter I will evaluate this claim.

First I will review the history of functional categories in the generative tradition, starting with the work of Chomsky in *Barriers* (1986b) and of Abney (1987), work which has established the importance of these categories in syntactic theory. In these works it was postulated that functional categories were syntactic heads in their own right. Earlier generative grammar had recognised functional categories, but a first theoretical treatment of these came in the work of Abney, who extended the discussion about functional categories to the noun phrase. Guéron, Hoekstra, van Riemsdijk, and Grimshaw developed a notion of 'extended projection', in which the projections of lexical categories are wedded to the projections of related functional categories.

Then I will turn to extensions of the inventory of functional categories, such as Cinque's and Rizzi's work, which charted the course for cross-linguistic comparative work in this area and postulated universal complex functional projections in the Inflection Phrase (IP) domain involving a series of semantic categories.

The reason for selecting the generative tradition over other grammatical traditions is that within this tradition functional categories have probably been treated mostly as autonomous entities (as opposed to say, features on a lexical head). Furthermore, it is the tradition I am most familiar with and can describe with least fear of serious misrepresentation.

In the second part of the chapter I deal with various theoretical aspects of functional categories, some of them the object of considerable debate. A series of researchers, starting with Fukui and including Kayne, has closely linked cross-linguistic variation to functional categories and parameters. Baker has attempted to counter claims by typologists about the universality of lexical categories by shifting the burden of variablity to inventories of functional categories. The third part evaluates the various special properties that have been proposed for functional categories in the generative literature. In the fourth part, I look at the treatment of one special category, P, which has been particularly intractable in this research tradition, and discuss this category in three languages: Quechua, Saramaccan, and Dutch.

Historical overview

I will begin then, with a brief historical overview of the treatment of functional categories in the generative tradition.

Functional categories as heads. Earlier generative approaches (e.g. Chomsky 1965) mostly dealt with functional categories at the level of features further specifying major categories. It was in the mid-1980s that the idea that functional categories might be heads in the sense of X-bar theory first became prominent. An important step in generative syntax had been made with the adoption by Chomsky (1970) of the general X-bar schema for the projection of lexical categories, and this same schema was adopted for functional categories in Chomsky (1986b) and Abney (1987). Chomsky (1986b) in *Barriers* proposed that INFL be the head of IP, which formerly was the category S, and that COMP be the head of CP, which had been known as S-bar. The resulting structure is as in (1):

(1)

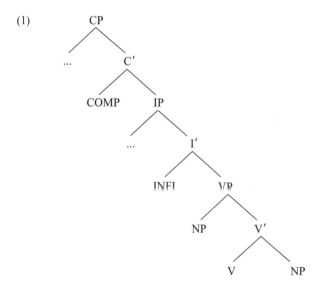

Abney (1987) extended the notion that INFL and COMP are heads in their own right to the noun phrase and the adjective phrase, and proposed structures such as the following (from Abney 1987: 25, 319):

(2) (a)

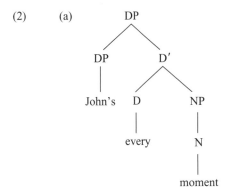

(b)

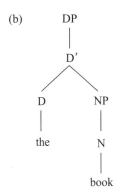

(3) (a)

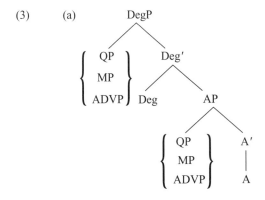

(b) If it's already needlessly long, it won't hurt to make it [six inches]
[more] [needlessly] long.

(Here QP = quantitative degree phrase, MP = measure degree phrase, and
ADVP = adverbial degree phrase.)

Categorical identity. Given the proposals by Abney (1987) and the ensuing
work, the next step was to establish a taxonomy of functional categories, based
on the idea that groups of functional categories might share a crucial feature
with a particular lexical head. Guéron and Hoekstra (1988) developed the notion
of T-chains, where the verb was assumed to be the anchor for a projection chain
including Agreement, Tense, and Comp. Van Riemsdijk (1990) and Grimshaw
(1991) limited the wild growth of categorial projections somewhat by elaborating on the idea that each functional projection has the same categorical features
as one of the lexical projections, a principle van Riemsdijk refers to as the Categorical Identity Thesis. In the spirit of these proposals, Radford (1993) argues
that Det, N, Q, and A are all nominal in nature, specific instantiations of the
category [+N].

Van Riemsdijk (1990: 231), for example, assumes that every lexical category
has its functional counterpart, roughly as in (4):

(4) | | *lexical [−F]* | *functional [+F]* |
|---|---|---|
| (a) [+N,−V] | N = noun | n = determiner |
| (b) [−N,+V] | V = verb | v = inflection |
| (c) [−N,−V] | P = preposition | p = directional particle |

Directional particles include elements such as *zu* in the German example (5):

(5) auf mich zu
on 1s.AC to
'towards me'

Notice that van Riemsdijk's model only allows one kind of functional category
per lexical category. Such a restriction is absent in other proposals.

Encyclopedic inventories. Based on an extensive survey of adverbs, modals,
and auxiliary expressions in different languages, Cinque (1999) developed a
complex, supposedly universal, hierarchy of the functional projections that
hold at the level of the IP or the clause, in his view. The list given in (6)
goes from the topmost position in the clause to the lowest position above the
verb:

(6) *Functional projections in the IP*

Mood	Speech act	T	Anterior
Mood	Evaluative	Aspect	Terminative
Mood	Evidential	Aspect	Continuative
Mood	Epistemic	Aspect	Perfect
T	Past	Aspect	Retrospective
T	Future	Aspect	Proximative
Mood	Irrealis	Aspect	Durative
Modality	Necessity	Aspect	Generic/progressive
Modality	Possibility	Aspect	Prospective
Modality	Volitional	Aspect	Singular Completive I
Modality	Obligation	Aspect	Plural Completive
Modality	Ability/Permission	Voice	
Aspect	Habitual	Aspect	Celerative II
Aspect	Repetitive I	Aspect	Singular Completive II
Aspect	Frequentative I	Aspect	Repetititve II
Aspect	Celerative I	Aspect	Frequentative II

This proposal is part of a series of attempts to account for the range of notions expressed and distribution of lexical elements encountered in many languages through a brute force stipulation of a functional category hierarchy (cf. the survey in Newmeyer 2005: 82). Empirical support for such a hierarchy comes from the fact, already noted by Bybee (1985), that there are many cross-linguistic similarities in the distribution of various modifiers with respect to the verb. Rizzi is one of the architects of this research programme, which he labels the Cartography of Linguistic Structure. In this programme, the assumption is made that 'it is reasonable to expect that clauses should be formed by a constant system of functional heads in all languages, each projecting a sub-tree occurring in a fixed syntactic hierarchy, irrespective of the actual morphological manifestation of the head (as an affix, as an autonomous function word, or as nothing at all)' (Rizzi 2004b: 4). Obviously, as can be gleaned from (6), the cartographic approach has led to a wild proliferation of syntactic positions. Rizzi (2004b: 6) tries to contain the damage by suggesting the possibility that 'each core category may, in fact, be shorthand for referring to a more articulated structural zone'. An illustration of this is (7), where in Rizzi (1997) the following general assumption is made for the structure of the left periphery of the sentence:

(7) *The structure of the left periphery*

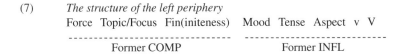

Force Topic/Focus Fin(iteness)   Mood Tense Aspect v V
------------------------------   ----------------------------
            Former COMP   Former INFL

Similar efforts to the one involving adverbs in the Cartography programme include Cinque (1994), who distinguishes for the category AP (where
one wonders, incidentally, about the cognitive foundations for heads like
'Nationality'):

(8)   Quality
         Size
         Shape
         Colour
         Nationality

Beghelli and Stowel (1997) propose to split up the Quantifier Phrase into a
number of separate projections as well:

(9)   Wh
         Negation
         Distributive
         Referential
         Share

The theoretical justification for these elaborate sets of projections comes from
(a) semantics: the need to link a range of semantic and pragmatic distinctions to specific functional heads in the syntactic tree corresponding to diverse
constituents; and (b) word order: the need for landing sites for a variety of
constituents that can be moved to the left periphery of the clause. Empirically,
the support comes from cross-linguistic studies such as Julien (2002), who
documents common patterns of modification for different categories.

Theoretical considerations

With this historical overview in the background, I will now turn to various theoretical considerations that have been brought forward with respect to functional
categories: their universality, whether they project uniformly or not, obligatoriness, relation to parameters, and relation to interpretability.

Universality. Steele is one of the first to explore the cross-linguistic value
of a functional category, conjointly with a group of colleagues (Steele *et al.*
1981). Auxiliaries are typically a 'cluster' category, in her view. The definition
she gives is 'those constituents which may contain only a specified (i.e. fixed
and small) set of elements, crucially containing elements marking tense and/or
modality, will be identified as non-distinct' (1981: 21).

There is much debate on the question as to whether all functional distinctions
are universal, even if not universally lexically realised. While Cinque and Rizzi

make universalist assumptions, others have proposed alternatives. Thráinsson (1996) contrasts different versions of the Structural Uniformity Hypothesis with the Limited Diversity Hypothesis. The Structural Uniformity Hypothesis has a strong version and a weak version (1996: 255):

(10)   (a) *Strong*
          UG determines for each language a universal set of functional categories and their hierarchical arrangement;

      (b) *Weak*
          UG provides a universal set of functional categories and their hierarchical arrangement, and from this set each language selects a sub-set.

Ouhalla (1994) questions the uniform hierarchical arrangement and suggests that the order of Tense and Agreement may differ from language to language. Thráinsson (1996: 257), however, does not suggest order differences, but a parametrised merger of specific categories in different languages, and proposes the Split IP Parameter: in some languages Tense and Agreement are merged, and in others they may be split. The Limited Diversity Hypothesis holds that: (a) there is a universal set of features specified by UG; and (b) per language there are differences in the realisation of functional categories in different clause types, and per language the order may vary in the functional categories.

From the perspective of language description and typology taken in chapter 2, the Structural Uniformity Hypothesis by no means embodies a necessary claim, and is in fact, rather nonsensical. Languages not only differ in whether certain categories are overtly realised or not, but also in the way these categories are organised altogether. The extension of the range of functional projections may in fact be arbitrary from this perspective. It is ironical, in this context, that Croft (1991: 144) uses non-universality as an argument for assigning adpositions to the set of non-lexical categories.

Uniform projection. The assumption that lexical and functional categories project in the same way is generally adopted, one of the exceptions being Fukui and Speas (1986). They assume that functional categories have a fixed two-level structure, as in (11a), while lexical categories have a flexible recursive X' projection, as in (11b):

(11)   (a) $[X''$ Spec $[X'$ X Comp$]]$
      (b) $[X'$ Mod $[X'$ ... $[X'$ X Comp$]]]$

Functional heads can only have one Specifier in Fukui and Speas' proposal (1986: 133), moved there from a position in the complement, while lexical heads can have multiple modifiers, pending semantic interpretability. Additionally, in their proposal, a language like Japanese lacks COMP, INFL, and DET (and thus supposedly all functional heads in the sense of Abney (1987)), and hence it has no true specifier positions. The limited projection of functional categories in the Fukui and Speas proposal is linked to the semantic restrictions on them, e.g. not being able to be modified.

Obligatory in every constituent or not. A further theoretical issue is whether within a given language a constituent always has the same internal structure. Boas (1938: 132) has pointed to a crucial feature of functional categories: they lead to obligatory choices in a particular language. Thus, if a language has a [+ definite] determiner, this feature needs to be marked with every noun. Along these same lines, Sapir and Swadesh (1964) [1946] speak of 'obligatory categories in grammar', and thus suggest these categories must always be present. This obligatory status of functional distinctions, once grammaticalised, does not mean that these distinctions are universal; rather the contrary. Each language makes its own distinctions in Boas' view.

Costa and Gonçalves (1999), however, stress the fact that within a language, clauses may differ in terms of complexity. One of their examples involves Portuguese clause-union-like causative constructions, as in (12) (p. 63):

(12)   Os   pais   mandaram   sair   os   meninos.
         The parentsmade   go.out.INF the children
         'The parents made the children go out.'

Following a respectable earlier tradition, Costa and Gonçalves (1999: 65) argue that these types of complements of a causative verb are defective clauses, lacking functional categories such as C, AgrS, T, and Neg.

A similar point can be made with respect to the contrast between (13a) and (13b) (p. 66):

(13)   (a) O Paulo cuidadosamente tinha simpaticamente lido bem o livro à avó.
              The Paul carefully had kindly read well the book to the grandfather.
              'Paul carefully had kindly read well the book to the grandfather.'

         (b) * O Paulo leu cuidadosamente simpaticamente bem o livro à avó.
              'The Paul read carefully kindly well the book to the grandfather.'

Here Costa and Gonçalves (1999: 66) argue that the (13b) example is ruled out because each adverb needs a position licensed by a separate lexical head, and in (13b) there is only the past tense verb *leu* 'read', no auxiliary *tinha* 'had', as in (13a).

The idea that there may be internal variation in the structure of a constituent probably gains plausibility once we turn from clauses to other constituents.

The degree to which we find functional skeletons realised differs considerably between different categories. In the clausal domain we very often find tense and agreement features, while in the nominal domain agreement is rare. The adjectival domain likewise is not very rich in agreement or other functional categories. Rijkhoff (2002: 195) shows that in his balanced typological sample of 52 languages, 10 languages always cross-reference possessors, and 8 do so in restricted contexts. In the other languages there is no possessor agreement. Musgrave (in prep.) argues that there are good reasons not to assume that the categories Tense and Determiner are present in the grammar of Standard Malay. Thus the apparent obligatoriness of certain functional categories in the clause may be due to the Extended Projection Principle (Chomsky 1981) or a similar principle (which ensures subjects); this principle does not hold in noun phrases.

Functional categories and parameters. Fukui (1988) was one of the first to explicitly formulate the idea, which since then has become current in the generative tradition, that parameters are linked to functional categories. His Functional Parametrisation Hypothesis holds that only functional categories are subject to parametric variation. In the more recent literature, Kayne (2005) is a typical advocate of this position as well, assuming that there is a universal underlying VO word order, coupled with object movement rules triggered by feature strength settings of case parameters. Baker (2003) has stressed the relation between lexical and functional categories. Assuming that parameters linked to functional categories are what makes languages different, the inventory of lexical categories can remain uniform.

Feature strength and interpretability. In the Minimalist Program functional categories were parametrised, initially, in terms of feature strength: strong features could be interpreted as such, weak features had to be moved so as to become interpreted. More recently, this has been rephrased in terms of interpretability of features at the interface with Semantic Interpretation or Logical Form (LF). As noted in Chomsky (1995: 232): 'If F is strong, then F is a feature of a non-substantive category and F is checked by a categorial feature.' Of this basic idea a host of alternative new formulations are around. I will refrain from presenting these here since new versions are appearing continuously.

Diagnostic criteria

Given the theoretical importance of the distinction, various grammatical criteria have been proposed in the generative tradition to distinguish content words from function words. It should be kept in mind that the categorical definition of functional category can only be a negative one:

(14)   Syntactic heads which are not defined in terms of [±N, ±V].

It is worthwhile quoting the main source for the lexical/functional distinction in detail directly (Abney (1987: 64–65) terms it 'thematic/functional' distinction): 'The properties which characterize functional elements, then, are:

(1)   Functional elements constitute closed lexical classes.
(2)   Functional elements are generally phonologically and morphologically dependent. They are generally stressless, often clitics or affixes, and sometimes even phonologically null.
(3)   Functional elements permit only one complement, which is in general not an argument. The arguments are CP, PP, and (I claim) DP. Functional elements select IP, VP, NP.
(4)   Functional elements are usually inseparable from their complement.
(5)   Functional elements lack what I will call "descriptive content". Their semantic contribution is second-order, regulating or contributing to the interpretation of their complement. They mark grammatical or relational features, rather than picking out a class of objects.'

Abney further notes that characteristic (5), previously discussed in chapter 4, is the crucial one, and gives a definition of 'descriptive content' 'a phrase's link to the world' (1987: 65). Characteristics (1) and (2) were dealt with in chapter 3. Only two characteristics are strictly syntactic, (3) and (4)

Criterion (3) actually contains several components: (a) there is an obligatory complement; (b) this is always categorically specific; (c) it is a non-argument. Criterion (4) makes a single claim. I will begin by discussing these four claims, and then turn to other proposed criteria or diagnostic features.

Obligatorily transitive. An important diagnostic characteristic according to Abney (1987) is whether elements are transitive, i.e. obligatorily have a complement. Auxiliaries and determiners belong to the class of functional elements because they have an obligatory complement, while nouns and verbs do not because they need not have a complement: **I saw the. *Do you know if?* Abney (1987: 285 fn.) notes that pronouns, if analysed as instantiations of the category D, are in fact counter-examples to the claim that functional categories are obligatorily transitive. Depending on the analysis of intransitive prepositions and independently used quantifiers, these would also count as counter-examples.

Single category. Abney (1987: 55) states that 'C and I do not take multiple arguments, but only one IP, or one VP, respectively'. Typically, complementisers, auxiliaries, and determiners combine with only one syntactic category, i.e. they take a category specific complement. In the simple inventory of categories presented by Abney, this is indeed unproblematic. Recall, however, the large inventories provided by Cinque and Rizzi. The only way to maintain there that a functional category takes a single type of complement is to make all these categories obligatory, even when they do not appear to be filled in. This will be at least problematic for projections like Negation, which may or may not be present (unless they are subsumed under Polarity or Force). Prepositions, which can often take either DP and CP as their complement, would not be functional in this respect.

Non-argument. The final component of Abney's characteristic (3) concerns the non-argument status of complements of functional categories. If we take DP, CP, and PP as the only argument categories, this will work on the whole, since auxiliaries would take some type of VP as their complement, and determiners NP. However, notice again that prepositions would qualify as functional for this diagnostic characteristic, since they take a DP or CP, as noted above, hence an argument. Also, it could be that in more complex trees, such as the ones envisaged by Cinque or Rizzi, CP could be the argument of some higher functional projection.

Not separable from their complement. The last diagnostic characteristic mentioned by Abney is that functional categories cannot be separated from their complement. Indeed, we do not find stranding of determiners: *House, he saw the*. However, Cann (2000: 43) mentions the case of auxiliaries:

(15)   Lou said he must go to town, and so go to town he must ——.
        Eaten shrimp I certainly have ——!

The same holds for prepositions:

(16)   (a) Who did you give the book to ——?
        (b) Who did you go out with ——?

Thus this diagnostic characteristic is not really watertight with respect to the categories we would want to consider.

Other criteria have been mentioned in the literature as well: being a landing site for movement, and being structurally rigid.

Landing site. In a theory which assumes that all leftward syntactic movement is to specific specifier positions, having a wide range of functional heads in the left periphery provides a number of landing sites for movement. This criterion would support the cartography approach of Cinque and Rizzi. However, it is strongly theory-dependent, and hence relevant to the approach taken in this book.

Categorial specificity. To some extent, lexical elements may occur in different environments, and remain interpretable. Cann (2000: 43) provides the following pair:

(17)   (a) Kim hit a slow ball. (N)
        (b) Kim slow balled it into the back of the net. (V)

It is the presence of *a* and *-ed* which determine the nominal and verbal interpretation of *slow ball*. Of course, *slow* and *ball* are also categorially specific, but they are more flexible and allow coercion in a different syntactic context by a functional element.

The functional skeleton and rigidity. To my mind the most substantial finding of the generative tradition, starting with Chomsky (1957), is the existence of fairly rigid, morpho-syntactically conditioned, structures, particularly for clauses in many languages. Successful work in this area concerns *do*-support and the auxiliary system of English, the interaction of clitics, tense, and negation in French, verb second phenomena in German and Dutch, the interaction of clitics and verb clusters in Italian, etc. This research has resulted in the postulation of functional skeletons in these languages: skeletons involving the agreement, tense, negation, and complementiser systems. The rigidity criterion corresponds to what Lehmann (1982) calls the resulting syntagmatic invariability of the process of fixation in the grammaticalisation process.

Notice that this functional skeleton is only indirectly related to lexical elements. Positions in the skeleton may be realised by words, clitics, affixes, or null elements. In Warlpiri, the constituents of the clauses can move fairly freely, as has often been noted. However, the auxiliary system is solidly in place in the clause in second position (Hale 1983). Similarly, in the Panoan language Capanahua (Peru), there is a rigid second position for the affirmative marker (which may be either a modal or an evidential) (Loos 1969: 91):

(18)   (a) mani ta howi-ti-?-ki
             banana AF ripe-TF-PRE-AF
             'The bananas are ripening.'
        (b) mani ta ? in his-i
             banana AF 1.s see-PRE
             'I see bananas.'

We also find evidence that in some languages discourse structures are defined by skeletons (Kiss 1995).

Insertion. From the discussion in the papers in Corver and van Riemsdijk (2001b) it is clear that the grey area between functional and lexical categories emerges because either (a) lexical categories end up in functional positions, or (b) lexical categories lose semantic content, and hence become more limited in their combinatory possibilities. This makes it necessary to make a distinction between words and affixes and the positions that these elements may occupy. Thus we may think of the skeleton purely in syntactic terms, not in terms of the elements inserted into syntactic positions. However, that cannot be right either, since insertion is constrained. In the ideal case, there is a one-to-one mapping between lexical items and positions in the syntactic tree. This one-to-one mapping certainly holds for lexical items, in all versions of grammatical theory. However, for functional categories there could be a mapping asymmetry, in that a lexical + a functional element could together be inserted into a single syntactic position, in lexicalist models.

The category P

Baker (2003) has argued that prepositions are universally a functional rather than a lexical category. His arguments are:

(a) Others have made a similar claim (p. 304)
(b) P is a closed class (p. 304)
(c) 'Adpositions do not take part in derivational morphology, either as inputs or as outputs to word formation rules' (p. 305). This mirrors Aronoff's (1976) Major Category Restriction.
(d) Prepositions cannot be incorporated.

Disregarding (a), I will discuss the other arguments one by one. Arguments (b) and (c) have been dealt with in chapter 3 on the lexicon and morphology: these are at most tendencies that hold for these categories, and they are not essential to them. The fourth argument is curious to me, given the extensive work on particles and incorporation in the generative tradition, culminating in den Dikken's book, where it is claimed (1995: 12) that 'the particle is optionally incorporated into the verb in the course of the derivation'. Thus these four arguments are not really convincing. Notice that the category P does not fit into the functional skeleton discussed above very easily.

In the generative literature there has been extensive discussion and going back-and-forth on the issue of whether adpositions are functional categories or not. I will present three case studies showing different degrees of richness in the domain of adpositions. I will start with Quechua, as a system with the syntactic category P but no lexical instantiations of this category. Then I turn to the Maroon Creole language Saramaccan, for which claims had earlier been made about the overall absence of adpositions, but with a limited, well-defined set. Finally, I turn to Dutch, with a rich and complex set of adpositions.

In **Ecuadorean Quechua**, we have the following types of PPs (Muysken 2005):

(19)   [Pedro-ta yalli]   yacha-n-mi.
        Peter-AC exceed know-3-AF
        'She knows more than Peter.'

(20)   [Misa khipa-ta]   shamu-nga-mi.
        Mass back-AC come-3FU-AF
        'S/he will come after Mass.'

(21)   [Kan-rayku]   shamu-n-mi.
        you-because come-3-AF
        'S/he comes because of you.'

In Muysken (2005) I argue that in (19) the element *yalli* 'exceed' is an uninflected serial verb, while in (20) the element *khipa-ta* 'back' is actually a noun. For (21) I assume an empty P position, licensed or 'morphologically controlled' by the case marker *-rayku* 'because'. For all three bracketed constituents in (19–21) it makes sense to treat them as PPs as regards their external distribution. However, there are no lexical elements in the language that can be considered Ps.

Saramaccan has three core prepositions, *ku* 'instrumental, comitative, NP-coordination', *a* 'locative, directional', and *u* 'possessive, benefactive' (Muysken 1987). All three have a wide semantic range:

(22)   Mi   sinkíi **ku** di   bóto, y-a   ó   paká u   de.
        1.PO body WI DET boat 2s-NEG FU pay   for them
        'My services and the boat, you don't need to pay for them.'

(23)   A bi   kó   **a**   u   akí
        3s PST come LOC 1p here
        'He came to us (here).'

(24)   di   wósu **u**   dáta
        DET house BE doctor
        'the doctor's house'

In addition to these three basic prepositions, there are a number of more specific ones:

(25)	téé	'until'	(< Port até 'until')
	sóndo	'without'	(< Du zonder 'without')
	bóíti	'except'	(< Du buiten 'outside')
	kuma	'like, as'	(< Port como 'like')
	ufó/bifó	'before'	(< E before)

To form more complex locative expressions, [locative P + NP +locative noun] combinations are formed, involving the following postpositions/nouns:

(26)	báka	'behind'
	bándja	'next to'
	básu	'under'
	déndu	'inside'
	édi	'cause'
	fési	'in front of, before'
	líba	'above'
	míndi	'middle of'

It should be noted that Saramaccan also has a rich class of serial verbs, including dative *dá* 'give'. Contrary to Sranan, however (Jansen, Koopman, and Muysken 1978), these verbs never acquired prepositional characteristics.

Turning now to **Dutch**, we note that it has a rich and complex system of adpositions (cf. e.g. Zwarts 1995, 1997). There are various ways of classifying them. To give just one example: basing himself particularly on the criteria listed in Abney (1987), Zwarts (1995, 1997) has tried to classify the Dutch prepositions, which show a quite complex interaction with the oblique pronoun *er* 'there'. The problem is that each criterion yields different results; no unified classification emerges. Fundamental from the grammatical point of view is the distinction between those prepositions that allow a [+R] pronoun, and hence can be stranded, and those that do not. Examples include:

(27)	(a) er-aan	'there to'
	(b) *er-met	'there-with'
	*er-aangaande	'there-concerning'
	*er-via	'there-via'

Roughly 25 prepositions allow [+R], and 57 do not (Zwarts 1997: 1093–1095) (criterion [1] in Table 5.1). The class that does not is larger, includes new formations and borrowings [2], and generally contains longer forms [3]. Thus it is tempting to define that latter class (class (b)) as lexical, and the former class (class (a)) possibly as functional. However, criteria [4] and [5] point in the other direction: contrary to what would be expected of lexical categories, the (b) class is obligatorily transitive [4], as noted by Zwarts (1997: 1100), and cannot be the input to word formation rules [5]. In addition, many elements in the (a) class can be modified, while elements in the (b) class cannot [6]. If we consider which prepositions have a grammatical role (if any, criterion [7]), the following would be the most likely candidates in Dutch:

(28)   grammatical: aan 'to'   dative
                        van 'of'   genitive
                        door 'by'   expression of underlying subject in
                                         passives
                        te 'to'   infinitive complements
                        om 'for ... to ...'   'purposive complements'

These five prepositions do not share many other features, however, in Table 5.1.

Another feature of Dutch prepositions is that some of them have a now opaque morphological relation to each other (see also chapter 3):

(29)   uit 'out'   buiten 'outside'
        in 'in'   binnen 'inside'
        over 'over'   boven 'above, over'

The morphological process involved, describable as transitiviser *be-* prefixation and nominaliser (?)'-en* suffixation, is also involved in the derivation of other prepositions (cf. chapter 3):

(30)   [noord] 'north'   benoorden 'north of'
        [zuid] 'south'   bezuiden 'south of'
        [neer] 'down'   beneden 'below, beneath'
        [zijde] 'side'   bezijden 'beside'

However, not all complex prepositions derived in this way have the same characteristics. Those in (29) allow [+R] pronouns, while those in (30) do not.

Another relevant feature of Dutch adpositions is that sometimes there is a (semi)suppletive relationship between a form that occurs with and without [+R] elements (criterion [8]) (Zwarts 1997: 1095):

(31)   *er-met   er-mee   'there-with'
        *er-tot   er-toe   'there-to' (purposive)
        *er-naar   er-heen/er-naar-toe 'there to' (directional)
        *er-van   er-van-daan   'there from'

The pattern is far from regular and there are meaning changes between the [−R] and the [+R] forms.

A final observation is that sometimes the same form can be non-directional as a preposition and directional as a postposition:

Table 5.1. *A sample of the Dutch prepositions classified for eight diagnostic features*

	[1] Allow [+R]	[2] Open	[3] Long	[4] Not obligatorily transitive	[5] Input morph	[6] Allow modification	[7] No grammatical role	[8] Postposition
te	−	−	−	−	−	−	−	−
van	+	−	−	−	−	−	−	−
aan	+	−	−	−	+	−	−	−
door2	+	−	−	−	+	−	−	+
om	+	−	−	+	+	+	−	−
naast	+	−	−	−	+	+	−	+
toe	+	−	−	−	+	−	+	+
heen								
mee								
over	+	−	−	+	+	+	+	+
uit								
door1								
in	+	−	−	+	+	+	+	+
bovenop	+	−	+	−	−	+	+	−
onderin	+	−	−	−	−	−	−	−
naast								
behalve	−	+	+	+	−	−	+	−
via								
middels								

(32)   (a) in de tuin   de tuin in
                  'in the garden'   'into the garden'
        (b) op de tafel   de tafel op
                  'on the table'   'onto the table'

In Table 5.1 these properties are systematically listed for a number of prepositions, arranged roughly and very intuitively from functional to lexical. However,
no clear pattern emerges so far with respect to these specifications. Clearly, the
traditional features that could be used do not yield a clear lexical/functional distinction among the different prepositions, which corresponds with other aspects
of their form or behaviour, nor an argument for labelling them as functional
categories as a group.

Many more details can be noted about Dutch adpositions. However, it is fairly
clear that:

- They constitute a fairly large lexical class
- There are complex morphological relationships between them
- Their distribution and use are quite complex and often lexically deter-
  mined.

Conclusions

To start with the adpositions, there are clear differences between the way adpositions are realised as a lexical class in different languages. In Ecuadorean
Quechua, there are postpositions syntactically, but there is no independent lexical class. Saramaccan has a modest number of prepositions, with their own
grammatical properties (e.g. they do not allow preposition stranding, contrary
to verbs). Dutch has a complex, rich and still-growing system, with its own morphological complexities. Nonetheless, nothing is accomplished by claiming that
this class of elements is functional in nature.

Claiming that adpositions are functional does not tally with the basic insight
of the generative tradition with respect to this book, that is that functional categories provide the structural skeleton for the main constituents of the sentence,
namely the clause and in some languages also the noun phrase and possibly
other types of phrases. Skeletal elements are complementisers, agreement and
tense markers, and in some languages also case markers and determiners.

Other elements may share some semantic, morphological, and phonological properties with these skeletal elements, and hence resemble syntactically
functional categories, but they do not have the central properties of unique
categorical selection and non-modifiability of functional categories from the
perspective of syntactic processing.

Historical linguistics

6 *Grammaticalisation*

In the previous four chapters I have tried to evaluate the status of functional categories from a number of perspectives: typology and language description, morpho-phonology and the lexicon, semantics and pragmatics, and generative syntax. I now turn to functional categories in historical linguistics.

An important area within historical linguistics is the study of grammaticalisation processes. Grammaticalisation is the recruitment, across time, of lexical elements for grammatical purposes. Meillet (1912) was one of the first to draw attention to the phenomenon of grammaticalisation, which he defines as 'l'attribution d'un caractère grammatical à un mot jadis autonome' [attributing a grammatical status to a word that was autonomous before]. This definition still stands, although it is now extended to include grammaticalisation of dependent morphemes rather than words.

An example of the type of phenomena involved in grammaticalisation is the Tense Modality Aspect (TMA) system of Pichi, the English lexicon pidgin/creole of Malabo studied by Yakpo (in prep.). Pichi distinguishes a core from a non-core TMA-system, represented schematically in Tables 6.1 and 6.2. The core system in Table 6.1 is more of an integral part, in other words more grammaticalised, than the non-core system in Table 6.2.

In both tables, the Pichi particles or auxiliaries are derived from (mostly English) words with a different status and syntactic function. Pichi can be said to have recruited its TMA-system from other elements:

- sometimes reducing their phonetic shapes (making it shorter): *dè* < *there*, *jis/jOs* < *just*;
- generally modifying their meaning somewhat (making it more abstract): Future < *go*, Subjunctive < *make*, Proximative < *want*;
- and changing its grammatical status (making it more specific and less flexible) to that of a pre-verbal marker with a fixed position, while originally it may have had a more varied distribution.

Table 6.1. *Core Pichi TMA-system*

Category	Marker	Focal function	Default tense deixis	Source word
Tense	bin	past	past	been
	kan	consecutive	past	come
	gó	future	future	go
Modality	mek	subjunctive	future	make
	fO	conditional	past	for
		obligation	present	
Aspect	0	perfective	past/present	
	dè	imperfective	present	there
	kin	habitual	present	can
	dOn	perfect	past	done
	nOba/nEva	negative perfect	past	never
	verb~verb	iterative		

Notice that in one way the Pichi data do not fit into Meillet's definition: the grammaticalised words become part of a new system, but they do not necessarily lose their autonomy in a lexical sense, i.e. they do not turn into prefixes of the verb. In some creoles, like Saramaccan (see chapter 15), there is evidence that the pre-verbal TMA-particles become a phonological cluster with the negator and possibly also with the unstressed clitic pronouns, but not with the verb that follows them. There are also cases which do not fit Meillet's definition in another way: derivational affixes may become grammaticalised, as well as lexical words. Thus in Cuzco Quechua, the suffix *-pu-*, described in chapter 2, has acquired a range of more abstract meanings but is now also in a fixed morphological position in the word, at the end of the string of derivational affixes but preceding the inflectional affixes (Cusihuamán 1976, 216):

(1)   Alli-chu unu-man ri-rqa-pu-wa-y!
       good-Q   water-to   go-EXH-BEN-1ob-IM
       'Please go and get me some water!'

Hopper and Traugott (2003: xv) also include constructions in the range of elements that can be grammaticalised and define the process as 'the change whereby lexical items and constructions come in certain linguistic contexts to serve grammatical functions and, once grammaticalised, continue to develop new grammatical functions'.

Table 6.2. *Non-core Pichi TMA-system*

Category	Auxiliary	Focal function	Source word
Aspect	bigin (dè)	ingressive	begin
	(jis/jOs) kOmOt	egressive	just / come out
	finis	completive	finish
	stil	continuative	still
	want	proximative	want
Modality	gEt fO	obligation	get for
	nid fO	necessity	need for
	sabi	mental ability	<Port saber 'know'
	fit	physical ability	fit
	want	desire	want

There is little disagreement about the facts of grammaticalisation: everyone will acknowledge that it occurs with some frequency in the history of natural languages. Where authors disagree is on the nature and status of the phenomenon. Newmeyer (1998: 239) writes that grammaticalisation 'is nothing more than a label for the conjunction of certain types of independently occurring linguistic changes'. In contrast, Hopper and Traugott (2003: xvi) refer to it as 'not only changes observable across time, but also to an approach to language study, one that highlights the interaction of use with structure, and the non-discreteness of many properties of language'. Thus grammaticalisation has to some extent become a pawn or a knight in the formalist–functionalist debate.

An important insight is provided by Meillet when he writes of the trigger for the process of grammaticalisation ([1912] 1921: 139): 'Mais ce qui en provoque le début, c'est le besoin de parler avec force, le désir d'être expressif.' [But what triggers its beginning is the need to talk with force, the desire to be expressive.] This insight has been elaborated upon and refined in Hopper and Traugott (2003: 92), who speak of 'subjectification' as an important semantic/pragmatic dimension of the early parts of a grammaticalisation process. Subjectification is the 'relatively abstract and subjective construal of the world in terms of language'. Other researchers have focused upon the later stages in the process, where morphological and phonological reduction and bleaching become more important.

Thus, it is important to emphasise the diachronic dimension of the grammaticalisation process; in its different stages, different aspects are relevant. Croft (1991: 142–146) introduces the notion of 'transitory category' for those elements which are permanently on their way to being grammaticalised and will necessarily end up as affixes. Examples include auxiliaries and adpositions, in his view. Their frequent, if not universal, appearance would not result from their 'basic pragmatic propositional function' (Croft 1991: 144), as with adjectives, nouns, and verbs, but from a 'diachronically unstable universal process', and 'displays a cline of behavior rather than a prototypical core'. However, we saw in chapter 5 that in Dutch adpositions are a stable lexical class.

In this chapter the status of the grammaticalisation process as such will not be the central focus. After these introductory remarks, three issues will be discussed:

- To what extent do the different dimensions of the grammaticalisation process: morpho-lexical, semantic, phonological, syntactic, co-occur in actual changes?
- Which functional categories frequently tend to emerge out of processes of grammaticalisation, and which ones rarely, if ever, do?
- How successful are recent proposals by, e.g. Vincent, van Gelderen, and Roberts to link grammaticalisation theory to generative models of functional categories? Do they provide additional insight into the process?

These three questions will be taken up in subsequent sections, before a more general perspective is sketched. A further question is: are some functional categories not involved in grammaticalisation processes, but rather remain stable? This question will come up in the next chapter on linguistic reconstruction.

Different dimensions of the grammaticalisation process

Do the different dimensions of the grammaticalisation process: morpho-lexical, semantic, phonological, and syntactic, co-occur? In the previous chapters a picture of functional categories was sketched suggesting the relative independence of the various dimensions involved in their definition. This raises the empirical question as to what extent the different dimensions of grammaticalisation co-occur in the processes of change. Hopper and Traugott (2003: 103) are wary of attributing a central role to semantic bleaching, and write: 'The important claim should not be that bleaching follows from generalization, but rather that meaning changes leading to narrowing of meaning will typically not occur in grammatizalization.' Likewise, the phonological effects of grammaticalisation may correspond to a late stage in the process. I will use their textbook on the phenomenon as the basis for Tables 6.3 to 6.6, where I try to establish, for all the changes discussed by these authors in sufficient detail, whether it involves the four dimensions I am focusing on.

I have divided the changes they discuss across four language groups (leaving out the changes which are only postulated as probable occurrences, possible very recent changes in English, and grammaticalisation processes linked to language contact): English, Romance, other Indo-European, and non-Indo-European. The results in the resulting tables are interesting in that they show that two factors play an important role in characterising the changes studied:

- whether or not we have detailed knowledge of the history of the language involved;
- the time depth of the changes mentioned.

For English, with detailed knowledge and relatively limited time depth, the changes involving grammaticalisation are often defined syntactically and semantically. They do not always have a morpho-lexical and phonological dimension, as with OE 'demonstrative' *þæt* > Present-day English *that* (complementiser, demonstrative), but may well, like OE *hwile þe* 'that time that' > Present-day English *while*.

For Romance, often the whole development from Latin to the modern Romance languages is taken into account, and very frequently involves all four dimensions. Examples would be Latin *ille* 'demonstrative' ultimately ending up as French *il* 'pronominal subject clitic', or the Latin demonstrative *hoc* being transformed into French *ça*.

For changes in the other Indo-European languages, the picture is a bit more mixed, but often all different dimensions are involved as well, as with IE **kanta bʰumos* 'sing we.are' > Latin *cantabimus* 'we will sing'.

For the other language families referred to by Hopper and Traugott sometimes most or all of the four dimensions are involved, but in those cases where we lack historical sources or time depth is limited, the phonological and morpho-lexical dimensions are not involved. This is mostly because the connection between different forms has been postulated on the basis of formal resemblance rather than of detailed knowledge of the path of change involved.

Frequently emerging functional categories

Which functional categories frequently tend to emerge out of processes of grammaticalisation? By now a large literature about the semantic and syntactic aspects of grammaticalisation processes has become available, much of it summarised in the very interesting book by Heine and Kuteva (2002), essentially a compendium of all types of putative grammaticalisation. An example would be

Table 6.3. *An overview of the changes in English treated in Hopper and Traugott (2003) under the label 'grammaticalisation' with respect to the four dimensions involved: morpho-lexical, phonological, semantic, and syntactic*

English	Morpho-lexical	Phonological	Semantic	Syntactic	Pages in Hopper & Traugott
ME be going to > gonna	+	+	+	±	1–3, 68–69
OE þa while þe 'that time that' > PDE while	+	+	+	+	4
ME let's > PDE lets	+	–	+	+	9–13
OE had 'person, condition, rank' > -hood 'property'	+	±	+	+	39–40
OE verbs > EME modals	+	±	±	+	55–58
OE siþþan 'from the time that' > because	–	±	+	–	81–84
OE hwile þe 'temporal' > PDE while 'contrast'	±	–	+	+	90–91, 107
OE do 'active' > dummy	–	±	+	+	95
E considering verb > conjunction	–	–	+	+	108
OE an 'one' > PDE a/an	–	+	+	+	119
OE to 'directional' > PDE 'infinitive'	–	–	+	+	190
OE 'demonstrative' þæt > PDE 'that' (complementiser)	–	–	+	+	190–194
English relative clauses	±	±	±	+	196–203

Note: OE = Old English, ME = Middle English, EME = Early Middle English, PDE = Present-day English.

Table 6.4. *An overview of the changes in the Romance languages treated in Hopper and Traugott (2003) under the label 'grammaticalisation' with respect to the four dimensions involved: morpho-lexical, phonological, semantic, and syntactic*

Romance	Morpho-lexical	Phonological	Semantic	Syntactic	Pages in Hopper & Traugott
Lat N illorum > Istro-Romanian -lor 'm.GEN.p'	+	+	–	+	8
Lat cantare habemus 'sing we.have' > Fr chanterons 'we will sing'	+	+	+	+	8, 52–55
Lat ille 'demonstrative' > Fr il 'pronominal agreement'	+	+	±	+	15
OFr pas 'step' > pas 'negator' OFr point 'point' > point 'negator (emph.)'	+	–	+	+	32, 117–118
Lat hoc > Fr ça	+	+	+	+	94
Lat -mente > Romance adverbial -ment etc.	+	+	+	+	140–141
Lat ad > Romance a 'infinitive'	–	+	+	+	189

Table 6.5. *An overview of the changes in other Indo-European languages treated in Hopper and Traugott (2003) under the label 'grammaticalisation' with respect to the four dimensions involved: morpho-lexical, phonological, semantic, and syntactic*

Other Indo-European	Morpho-lexical	Phonological	Semantic	Syntactic	Pages in Hopper & Traugott
O Norse úlfr hinn 'wolf that' > úlfr-inn 'wolf-the'	+	+	?	+	8
IE *kanta bʰumos 'sing we.are' > Lat cantabimus	+	+	+	+	9
Older Gr thelô hína 'I wish that' > MGr tha 'future'	+	+	+	+	24, 99–100
Indo-Aryan verbs > vector verbs	–	–	±	+	112–114, 116
O Polish copula > M Polish past tense	+	+	+	+	145–148
O Icelandic sik > sk 'reflexive'	+	+	+	+	159–161
O Persian rādi 'goal' > Modern Persian -râ 'AC'	+	+	+	+	165–168
Germanic and Scandinavian posture auxiliaries	–	–	+	+	206–207

Table 6.6. *An overview of the changes in non-Indo-European languages treated in Hopper and Traugott (2003) under the label 'grammaticalisation' with respect to the four dimensions involved: morpho-lexical, phonological, semantic, and syntactic*

Other	Morpho-lexical	Phonological	Semantic	Syntactic	Pages in Hopper & Traugott
Ewe bé 'say' > bé 'that' (complementiser)	+	–	+	+	13–15
Gã kʼɛ 'take' > accusative	–	–	±	–	96–97
O Finnish genitive >M Finnish subject of perception complement	–	+	±	+	104–106
O Finnish se 'demonstrative' > M Finnish determiner	–	–?	+	–	129–130
17ᵗʰ c Chin ba 'take' > M Chin ba 'object marker'	–	–	+	+	28
O Malay watu 'stone' > M Malay satu 'a/an'	+	+	+	+	119–121
Buryat Mongolian pronouns > verb endings	+	+	–	+	141
O Akkadian quotative 'say' > subordinating conjunction	+	+	+	+	194–196
Lhasa verb chaining > inflection	+	+	±	+	204–206

that the word for 'eye' in certain languages came to mean 'before' (Bambara) or 'in front of' (Baka, Susu, Bambara) (pp. 128–129), or that the word for 'house' came to mean 'at' or 'next to' (Swedish, Akkadian, Kagaba, Haitian) (pp. 176–177). Table 6.7 is based on this book. The table was distilled from the text and should be interpreted with considerable caution, for a number of reasons: (a) Heine and Kuteva give a list of all the changes they are familiar with, but there may be many more; (b) often the list is not historical, in that the directionality is assumed rather than documented, e.g. Quechua instrumental *-wan* is assumed to be derived from comitative *-wan*, but there are no language-internal facts suggesting that the converse could not have been equally true; (c) the table contains my interpretation in syntactic categorical terms of what is analysed and presented in semantic terms; this may have caused misinterpretations; (d) the figures represented the number of processes listed, not the number of languages per process, and there are wide differences between the processes in this respect; (e) for the sake of simplicity, I have sometimes collapsed categories carefully distinguished by Heine and Kuteva.

In spite of all these caveats, a number of conclusions can be drawn from the Table. First the perspective of the source categories:

(a)   There are many processes of reanalysis of verbs as auxiliaries or case markers / adpositions. Likewise verbs can be reanalysed as conjunctions, copulas, adverbs, and voice markers.

(b)   There are a great many types of reanalysis of nouns as case markers and adpositions. There is also a diversity of processes by which nouns are grammaticalised as classifiers, numerals, and pronouns. Perhaps surprisingly, nouns can also be grammaticalised as other categories, such as conjunctions and copulas or possessor verbs.

(c)   There are many paths known by which case markers/adpositions change meaning but remain of the same category. Sometimes case markers or adpositions turn into auxiliaries, conjunctions, or copulas/possessor verbs.

(d)   Deictic elements may be the source for conjunctions and pronouns.

(e)   Adverbs may turn into auxiliaries or change meaning within the adverb class.

(f)   Copulas and possessor verbs may turn into auxiliaries or different kinds of copulas/possessor verbs.

(g)   There are many processes by which conjunctions can change meaning, remaining within the same category.

(h)   In addition to these more frequently listed grammaticalisation paths, there are others which may be less expected.

Table 6.7. *The number of grammaticalisation paths for different categories listed in Heine and Kuteva (2002)*

	Ca	Aux	Co	Cp	Nm	Pro	P	Ad	Voi	De	Dei	Det	Cla	Ne
V	25	71	11	8	2			7	5					3
N	60		5	4	9	14	1	3					7	
Ca	34	7	11	5					1					
Dei			5	1		3	1				2	1		
Ad		3	2			1	1	4						
Cp		8	2	6			1							
Pro			1	1		5		1	4					
Num					9	1		1						
Wh	1		3			1								
Co			9				1							
A		2								2				
P					2		1							
Aux		13												
Voi									1					
Neg							1							
Nm					1									

Note: Ca = case marker and adposition; Aux = auxiliary; Co = conjunction, complementizer, subordinator; Cp = copula and possessive; Nm = nominal modifier (gender, number, diminutive, etc.); Pro = pronoun, agreement, reflexive, reciprocal; P = clausal particle (focus, question); Ad = adverb; Voi = voice (passive, anti-causative, medial); De = degree marking element (e.g. intensifier); Dei = deictic (demonstrative, here, there); Det = determiner; Cla = classifier; Ne = negation.

Taking the target categories as central, it is clear that adpositions and auxiliaries have emerged via the most diverse paths. It should be kept in mind that these are also semantically very complex categories. In Table 6.8 the different meanings given for these categories are listed, illustrated here just for the letters A–C in the lexicon provided by Heine and Kuteva (2002).

Table 6.8 shows the considerable semantic complexity of the elements involved.

Grammaticalisation theory and generative models of functional categories

How successful are recent proposals to link grammaticalisation theory to generative models of functional categories? Starting around 2000, several researchers have tried to link the discussion of grammaticalisation to work in the generative tradition on functional categories, much of this work building on Roberts and

Table 6.8. *Notions involved in case markers/adpositions and auxiliaries in Heine and Kuteva (2002), letters A–C*

Case markers/adpositions	Auxiliaries
ablative	ability
according to	andative
across	aversive
after	causative
agent	change-of-state
allative	completive
around	continuous
before	
behind	
benefactive	
beside	
between	
cause	
comitative	
common comparative	
comparative, equative	
concern	

Roussou (2003) (cf. also the comments in Haspelmath 1994). These researchers account for the emergence of functional categories within the T (tense), C (complentiser), and D (determiner) complexes through the mechanism of grammaticalisation. While Newmeyer was critical of the concept of grammaticalisation, it is clear that it has been embraced enthusiastically by many researchers in the generative tradition, leading to some fruitful new analyses.

Using data mostly from English, van Gelderen (2004) argues that the process of grammaticalisation is driven by Economy principles developed in the Minimalist Program. She argues that two types of languages can be distinguished (often referred to as 'configurational' and 'non-configurational'), in terms of the layer of structure best articulated: 'some languages are more "lexically-oriented", i.e. towards the VP, and others more "grammatically oriented", i.e. towards the IP. The CP in many languages is necessary to accommodate questions, topics, and other discourse information, but is not integrated into the grammatical system' (2004: 252). In van Gelderen's view, Old English is more lexically-oriented, and Modern English more grammatically oriented, and the development of English can be viewed in terms of grammaticalisation, here conceived of as the articulation of IP and CP structure. Two principles drive the process of grammaticalisation:

(2)   *Head Preference*, or *Spec to Head Principle* (2004: 11)
        Be a head, rather than a phrase.

(3)   *Late Merge Principle* (2004: 12)
        Merge as late as possible.

These two principles, which van Gelderen claims are motivated outside language change as well, drive change. An example of Head Preference is that in relative clauses, relative *that*, a demonstrative in the specifier position of the CP in Middle English, becomes a head in C in modern English. A second example would be the change from head *not* to clitic −*n't* and the introduction of a new phrase, such as *no thing*, in specifier position.

An example of Late Merge (which ultimately goes back to Lightfoot's (1979) work on Transparency) would be the development of a separate category of modals out of a sub-class of main verbs. Van Gelderen makes the point that grammaticalisation always involves a move upward in the syntactic projection: it leads to the articulation of higher structure.

In the same vein, Osawa (2003) argues that there is a parallel between the development of English child language (cf. chapter 9) and the history of English in that both early child language and Old English lacked functional projections while Present-day English and adult English obviously have them. Limiting ourselves here to Old English, he argues that the determiner system was absent: demonstratives functioned as deictic elements, but were nouns. Case marking was triggered thematically rather than syntactically. There was no syntactic Tense category, as shown e.g. by the absence of *do*-support. While much can be said against Osawa's analysis (e.g. Old English sentences are very very different from early child language, with extensive inflectional morphology), his ideas point in the same direction as those of van Gelderen.

Tremblay, Dupuis, and Dufresne (2005) provide an interesting account of the development of two types of prepositions in French: obligatory transitive prepositions such as *sur*, in (4a), and intransitive prepositions such as *dessus*, in (4b):

(4)   (a) Je m'assieds   sur   la   table.
            I   1s.ob-sit.1s   on   DET.f table
            'I sit down on the table.'

        (b) Je marche dessus.
            I   walk   on
            'I walk on it.'

In Old French, both prepositions could be either transitive (5a) and (6a), or intransitive (5b) and (6b):

(5) (a) et   fetes   escrivre **sus**   la   tombe ...
         and make-IM   write-INF on   the grave ...
         'and let it be written on the grave ...'

     (b) et   metent **sus** ce qu'il   cuident ...
         and put.3p on   what'they consider.3p ... (2005: 110)
         'and they put on what they consider ...'

(6) (a) **desus** la   tombe qui   estoit   merveilleuse et   riche
         on   DET.f grave REL.su be.PST marvellous.f and rich.f
         'on the grave which was splendid and rich'

     (b) après firent   metre **desus** letres qui   disorient ...
         after make.PST.3p put   on   letters which said ... (2005: 111)
         'afterwards they had letters put on which said ...'

In Old French it was possible as well to have verb + particle combinations such as *cort sus* 'attacks' (lit. runs on) and *mis sus* 'accused' (lit. put on). In Old French, in contrast with Modern French, verbs needed a particle (7a) or a prepositional phrase (7b) to mark direction (2005: 113):

(7) (a) si   **entrerent**   **enz** et   voient le   leu   si bel
         and enter.PST.3p in   and see.3p DET place so beautiful.m
         'and they went in and saw the so beautiful place'

     (b) il   **entrerent**   **dans** la   grant sale
         they enter.PST.3p in   DET.f great.f hall
         'they went into the great hall'

Then, a number of things gradually changed. The verb *entrer* came to be used directionally, as in Modern French, and the productive use of directional verbal particles disappeared. Originally, the particles of the type *de+sus* were morphologically complex, and could not be used in verb + particle combinations, but gradually their morphologically complex status became opaque. By the time of the Renaissance, doublets had come into existence (2005: 116), and the present development towards two classes of prepositions, transitive and intransitive, was the result of a tendency towards the elimination of these doublets.

Conclusions

We can conclude from the above brief survey that the extent to which different dimensions are involved in grammaticalisation differs somewhat from case to case; often semantic changes are involved, but phonological and morpho-lexical changes may lag behind. Many different categories are involved in grammaticalisation processes. In particular, auxiliaries, adpositions, and conjunctions are categories that often result from grammaticalisation processes, as noted previously by Croft (1991). Generative models of syntactic change have successfully incorporated the notion of grammaticalisation, and in some cases given some of its features a stronger theoretical foundation.

7 Linguistic reconstruction

In the previous chapter I dealt with the dynamicity of functional categories. Here the question is raised of their potential stability over time. It has been claimed that at least some sub-systems of functional categories (e.g. pronouns and question words) remain relatively stable in the course of language change, i.e. do not change very rapidly, and hence can often be reconstructed for the proto-language in individual language families, while others are highly changeable (conjunctions and auxiliaries). Mallory and Adams (2006: 415) write: 'Generally, along with numerals and some kinship and body terms, the most persistent elements in any language tend to be basic grammatical forms, such as pronouns and conjunctions.' This claim of stability and persistence will be examined for three well-established families with different time depths, and one putative language family, and the basis for a possible differentiation between functional categories will be explored.

A certain class of grammatical elements, a sub-set of the shifters, has proved to be remarkably stable in the process of regular language change (while undergoing a number of more or less regular sound changes). This can be illustrated with the Indo-European proto-form for 'what' and its descendants (from Beekes 1995: 203–207):

(1)   *'what, which' in Indo-European*

Proto-form	*k^we-/k^wi-, adjectival *k^wo-
Sanskrit	kás, kā's, kát/kím
Old Church Slavonic	kþto, čþto
Hittite	kuis, kuit
Homeric Greek	tís, tí
Latin	quis, quid, quī, quae, quod
Gothic	hwas, hwo, hwa
Avestan	kə, -ciš/-cit
Old Irish	cía

In most branches of the Indo-European language family, the word for 'what' can be directly related to the proto-form. The class of elements which show this stability tend to be the ones that form a tightly organised paradigmatic set, such as the set of first and second person pronouns (Beekes 1995: 208; Mallory and Adams 2006: 415). Grammatical elements that do not belong in this category, particularly linkers and most functional categories proper, tend to be much less stable.

Many scholars have commented on making use of the stability of certain parts of the functional category system in establishing the most conservative parts of a language family. Malcolm Ross (2005) successfully explores the possibility of establishing preliminary family groupings among the Papuan languages on the basis of pronoun systems, and concludes that this is indeed a possibility. When a group of geographically contiguous languages shares a number of pronominal elements, there is great likelihood that they are related (at least in the case of New Guinea). We cannot conclude, however, when they do not share these elements, that they are not related, since pronouns can, and often do, undergo erosion.

Vincent (1993) draws attention to the rapid emergence of new functional categories through the process of grammaticalisation, but acknowledges the fact some some categories are perhaps quite stable across time (Meillet and Vendryes 1927). In a similar vein, Kortlandt (1995) writes: 'When we look at language interference in bilingual communities, it appears that there is a marked difference in the ease of linguistic borrowing between grammar and lexicon, between bound and free morphemes, and between verbs and nouns. As a result, the older strata of a language are better preserved in the grammatical system than in the lexical stock, better in verb stems and pronouns than in nouns and numerals. The wide attestation of Indo-European numerals must be attributed to the developments of trade that accompanied the increased mobility of the Indo-Europeans at the time of their expansions.'

However, when we compare the stability or instability of pronouns versus that of conjunctions, we must conclude that the stability of a given class of functional categories must be measured on several dimensions (Ross 2005):

(a) Are elements in the class easily transferred from one language to the other? Transferability or borrowability has to do with many things, including the degree of paradigmaticisation of a given class and its open/closed status.

(b) Do elements in the class easily undergo phonological erosion? Capacity to undergo erosion has to do with the position of an element in the prosodic word.

Table 7.1. *Rating of a few classes of functional categories in terms of their instability on three dimensions*

Category	Borrowing	Erosion	Grammaticalisation
Discourse particles	High	High	High
Interjections	High	High	Low
Prepositions	High	Low	Low
Open sets of pronouns south-east Asian style	High	Low	High
Deictic elements	Low	High	High
Closed sets of pronouns Indo-European style	Low	High	Low
Modals	Low	Low	High
Question words	Low	Low	Low

(c) Are elements in a class likely to be grammaticalised and acquire new functions? Likelihood of undergoing grammaticalisation has to do with semantic properties and relation to various grammaticalisation paths.

Applying these criteria to a number of functional category types suggests marked differences. Table 7.1 provides a first schematic rating of a few categories on these three dimensions.

High on all three instability dimensions are discourse particles, which are notoriously unstable, and low on these three dimensions are question words. They are not borrowed easily, tend to occur in emphatic positions and are hence little subject to erosion, and do not easily participate in grammaticalisation (except in that they may become relative particles and then perhaps conjunctions more generally). Other items are in between these two extremes.

Functional categories in Indo-European

Of course, an evaluation of the claims about relative stability should start with Indo-European, perhaps the best studied 'deep' language family. In addition to well-known branches such as Indo-Iranian, Balto-Slavic, Greek, Italic (including Latin), Celtic, and Germanic, there are smaller branches (many of which are now extinct) such as Tocharian, Thracian, Anatolian (including Hittite), Armenian, and Albanian. Beekes (1995) provides one of the most up-to-date reconstructions of Indo-European, and on his account Table 7.2 is based. This table simply surveys the different functional categories of the Indo-European

Table 7.2. *The possibility of reconstructing different functional categories for Proto-Indo-European (PIE) according to Beekes (1995)*

Category	Comments	Beekes
articles	no articles in PIE	94
nominal number	singular, dual, and plural in PIE	173
nominal gender	feminine, masculine, neuter in PIE	91, 174
nominal case	eight cases in PIE	173
adjectival infl.	same categories as the noun	197–9
adjectival degree	comparative and superlative in PIE; no suppletion	199–200
demonstratives	deictic and anaphoric in PIE, combinable with adverbs	201–2
question words	basic interrogative in PIE, Wh+-*tero* > 'which of two'	203–6
relative pronouns	possibly a strategy with question words in pre-head restrictive RCs, and anaphoric deictics in post-head non-strictive RCs	207
personal pronouns	a three-person system in PIE with 1st and 2nd sg and pl reconstructible, and 3rd derived from demonstratives	207–9
reflexives	a basic accusative reflexive *se* in PIE, with genitive and dative inflections	209–10
possessives	a 1st and 2nd sg and plural form in PIE, 3rd p = 'own'	210–1
numerals	numerals fully reconstructible in PIE	212–7
prepositions	no prepositions in PIE, later prepositions < adverbs	220–2
negation	negative indicative (*ne*) and prohibitive in PIE	222
voice	no passive in PIE, but a stative middle	225–6
agreement	all person endings reconstructible in PIE	232–44
alignment	ergative in PIE	252–4
mood	indicative, subjunctive, optative, and imperative in PIE	245–9
tense/aspect	aorist and present in PIE	253
coordination	'and' and 'or' in PIE	233
subordination	no subordination markers in PIE	233

languages in terms of the possibility of reconstructing a proto-form for each category.

We can conclude that, on the whole, functional categories in the nominal system have survived intact, but not in the verbal system.

The evidence from Proto-Uralic

The Uralic language family consists of about 30 languages with approximately 20 million speakers. The name of the language family refers to the Ural

mountain range, since the area of central and northern Russia west of the Urals
is the most likely homeland of the family. Countries with a significant number
of speakers of Uralic languages include Estonia, Finland, Hungary, Norway,
Romania, Russia, the province of Vojvodina (in Serbia), and Sweden. Well-
known languages in the family include Estonian, Finnish, and Hungarian. Dat-
ing from around the third millennium BC, the Uralic family is relatively young,
when compared to Indo-European and Afro-Asiatic (cf. also Austerlitz 1987;
Comrie 1988).

The Proto-Uralic case system can largely be reconstructed, although there
is some disagreement between the authors about the specific details. Collinder
(1960: 282) provides the following forms:

(2)   *-0   nominative
        *-n   genitive
        *-m   accusative
        *-na~ *-nä   locative
        *-ta ~ *-tä separative

Raun (1988: 558) largely confirmed Collinder's account and claimed that there
was a six person case system:

(3)   *-0   nominative
        *-m   accusative
        *-n   genitive
        *-na   locative
        *-t   allative
        *-ta   ablative

Décsy (1990), finally, argues that there was no genitive and accusative in Proto-
Uralic, and that there was two main locative cases:

(4)   *-na~ *-nä   essive I
        *-ta ~ *-tä   essive II
        *-ka ~ *-kä   lative I
        *-nja ~ *-njä or *-na ~ *-nä   lative II
        *-la ~ *-lä   lative III

In Collinder's view, the Proto-Uralic nominal plural was *t (1960: 297), but
Raun (1988: 556) claims that number cannot be reconstructed. Collinder also
reconstructs *ka ~ *kä + *-n ~ *-ń for dual (1960: 303).

The verbal system cannot be reconstructed, according to Collinder (1960:
308), but Raun (1988: 562) reconstructs *k for imperative mood and *ne for
subjunctive mood, but is not able to reconstruct a tense system for Proto-Uralic.

Sinor (1988: 462) claims that there was a finite verb agreement system, and negation marked on the agreement. The agreement forms are closely related to the pronouns (see below; cf. Raun 1988: 561).

The form *-m* is the first person marker, as well as the pronoun, according to Collinder (1960: 308), while Raun (1988: 561–562) and Décsy (1990: 57) provide much more complete paradigms for the personal pronouns, although some reconstructions are tentative:

(5)   *Raun*   *Décsy*
   1s   *mi ~ *me-nä   me
   2s   *ti ~ *te-nä   te
   3s   s tä

   1p   *m8"   *me(kä)
   2p   *ti ~ *te   *te(kä)
   3p   *tä(kä)

A number of other pronouns have been reconstructed as well, but there is less agreement with respect to the demonstratives.

(6)   *Raun*   *Décsy*
   *ći~ će   'this'
   *e   'this'
   *ta   *tä   'this'
                   *te   'there (near you)'
   *to   *tjo   'that'
   *o   'that'
   *ki/*ke   'that (over there)'
                   *na/*nä   'this, (that)'
                   *no   'those that'
                   *me   'here'

According to Décsy there is a close link between some of the demonstratives and the personal pronouns. Finally, Décsy (1990: 57) reconstructs a few of the interrogative pronouns: *ko ~ *ke* 'who' and *mi* 'what'.

Altogether, a good deal of the Proto-Uralic functional categories seem to be reconstructible.

The evidence from Afro-Asiatic

The Afro-Asiatic languages constitute a language family with over 350 languages, spread throughout North Africa, East Africa, the Sahel, and Southwest Asia (including some 200 million speakers of Arabic, of course). This highly diverse language family is also closely linked to the development of writing;

some of the oldest writing systems involved Afro-Asiatic languages. Afro-Asiatic is a family with very great time depth; it may have split up at least 15,000 years ago. The family includes the following language sub-families:

- Berber languages
- Chadic languages
- Egyptian languages
- Semitic languages
- Cushitic languages
- Beja
- Omotic languages

Typical features of the Afro-Asiatic languages include two genders in the singular, with the feminine marked by the /t/ sound; VSO typology, often developing towards SVO; in phonology, a set of emphatic consonants, variously realised as glottalised, pharyngealised, or implosive; a template morphology, in which words are affected by internal changes, but also carry prefixes and suffixes.

Hetzron (1990) argues for internal dialect variation in the earliest stages of Proto-Afro-Asiatic, based on the pronoun system. He adduces evidence from first person singular independent pronouns (p. 580), prefix-conjugations (p. 584), first and second person singular oblique pronouns (p. 586), and addressing particles (p. 589), to argue for the internal diversity of the proto-language. Bender (1990) surveyed the functional categories of Omotic in the light of the overall Afro-Asiatic family. It is clear from the work of both authors that functional categories play an important role in the reconstruction of the original family.

Hetzron (1987: 649–651) reconstructs a number of the general features of Proto-Afro-Asiatic. These include:

(7)   *t   feminine
         *k   second person
         *mut 'die'
          an   'I'
          k   'thou'

The general association of *u* with masculine forms and *i* with feminine forms shows up in different branches as well in the words for *he/she*:

(8)   šu:/ši Akkadian
         uu/ay Somali
         -o/e-   Kafa

In the demonstrative system there is possible opposition as well between m.s/f.s./p. in different branches of Afro-Asiatic:

(9)   w /   θ /   -
         n /   t /   n
         ku /   ti /   hu
         p /   t /   n

Possibly masculine singular *w* and *p* are linked to *ku*. The feminine singular forms are quite similar, in any case.

Hetzron argues that Proto-Afro-Asiatic shows prefixal conjugation:

(10)   1s   *? or *a
         2s/3fs   *t
         3 other   *y

Vocalic changes are another feature reconstructable for the whole family, as is a *ma-* nominaliser.

The evidence from Amerind

Citing earlier less systematic work by Edward Sapir and Morris Swadesh, and extending their account with his own interpretations of the data of a vast number of languages, Greenberg (1987: 44–57) cites the pronominal markers of the North and South American languages as evidence for his postulated language family Amerind. His proposal is that the basic pronominal forms, with a basic focus on first person *-n* and second person *-m*, were:

(11)   1 -iy, **-n**
         2 (-a), **-m**, -p, -b
         3 -i?, -t, -0
         4 -ḳ

Greenberg (1987: 48ff.) discounts the possibility of borrowing ('There are few if any authenticated instances of the borrowing of a first- or second-person pronoun.'), and, in contrast with other researchers such as Campbell (1997), also of chance ('such an accident could hardly have occurred spontaneously anything like a hundred or more times'). It is clear that Greenberg relies on the fundamental stability of pronouns here. Allowing for the fact that some putative Amerind language does not show relics of the forms in (11), he writes (1987: 55) 'no aspect of language – not even pronouns – is completely immutable'. In his chapter 5 Greenberg returns to the issue of common grammatical evidence for Amerind. In addition to the forms discussed, Greenberg tentatively postulates *m* and *t* as distal demonstratives and *k* as a near demonstrative (1987: 255). For the categories number, noun class, and gender, Greenberg considers Amerind proto-forms unlikely, and neither is case system reconstructable, although there is indirect evidence for ergative alignment and allative -*k* appears quite generally. In the verbal domain hortative -*pV* is quite general, while no other form occurs in most of the stocks postulated by Greenberg. Very generally occurring interrogatives begin with a *k*- or *m*- (Greenberg 1987: 316).

There is no need here to summarise the large number of highly critical reviews that have appeared after the publication of Greenberg's work (in particular, pointing out many inaccuracies and misinterpretations), and there can be no doubt that many of his conclusions are premature. Since the early 1980s a large number of detailed studies have appeared, particularly of South American languages, yielding far more adequate and precise data. At the same time, probably teamwork will be indispensable for comparing the vast amounts of data available. Nonetheless, the comparative work carried out by Greenberg (1987) on the lexical and functional categories of the languages of North and South America is very inspiring, for all its failings.

For Greenberg, functional categories do not have a special status, although they play an important role in the argumentation for genetic relationship. Thus, he writes (1987: 19) about the inclusion of Hittite into Indo-European: 'Thus the existence of even a few of such forms as Hittite *eszi* "he is" and *asanzi* 'they are' (cf. Latin *est/sunt*, Sanskrit *asti/santi*) is quite sufficient to exclude accident.'

Conclusions

From this survey of Indo-European, Proto-Uralic, Afro-Asiatic, and Amerind it is clear that among the possibly reconstructable items we find many functional categories, which can be expected given the stability of some of these. However, this stability only holds for some categories in the functional domain, notably for pronominal and gender systems. Several possible dimensions may be distinguished that contribute to the stability of a particular functional category.

Psycholinguistics

8   *Speech production*

There is considerable evidence that functional categories have a special status from the perspective of language production, and language processing in
general; this evidence comes primarily from speech error and brain imaging
studies.

First, speech error studies show interesting differences between lexical and
functional categories. Function words themselves are only infrequently moved
around in those speech errors that are classified as word exchanges (Levelt
1989: 339). Consider a case such as (1), taken from the Fromkin speech error
corpus:

(1)   a language NEED-ER LEARN-S ... < a language LEARNER NEEDS ...

The lexical elements *need* and *learn* are shifted around, but the affixes *-er* and
-s remain where they are.

Second, there is evidence from brain imaging studies that some functional
elements are processed differently from lexical elements. In a number of studies,
including Neville *et al.* (1992), Brown *et al.* (1999), and Osterhout *et al.* (2002)
different Event Related Potential (ERP) effects were observed for the processing
of open and closed class items.

In addition, a number of other types of studies have reported on differences between these two classes of elements: lexical and functional. While
the research on speech production working within the speech error paradigm
has tended to stress the differences between lexical and functional categories,
the overview in Levelt *et al.* (1999), which mostly relies on evidence from
reaction time studies and modelling techniques, downplays the contrast. In this
chapter, I will focus on some of the early speech error studies and on the ERP
studies, and try to answer two questions with respect to these areas of research:

(a)   Which functional categories are considered in these studies; in other
       words, where is the line separating lexical from functional drawn? Are

just words taken into account or also affixes? No systematic account of the types of categories that play a special role is available yet.

(b) How do we explain the differences between lexical and functional categories in these domains? There are strong frequency effects to take into account: functional categories tend to be much more frequent in ordinary speech than lexical categories. Second, in different processing models (e.g. Garrett 1975; Levelt 1989; cf. also Bock and Levelt 1994) the special behaviour of functional categories is linked to the organisation of the production system. Third, some researchers have assumed word length to be the crucial factor (cf. Zipf 1949).

Production models: evidence from speech error studies

As I have briefly mentioned above, elements such as inflectional affixes and determiners have a strong tendency to be stranded in word exchanges (Levelt 1989: 249). One explanation, explored below, is that closed-class items are not accessed independently of syntactic information (cf. e.g. Shillcock and Bard 1993).

To study the actual distribution of different categories in grammatical speech errors in more detail, I analysed the non-phonological errors in the English speech error corpus collected by Victoria Fromkin and hosted electronically by the Max Planck Institute in Nijmegen, and the German speech error corpus collected by Richard Wiese and available through his website. The most typical example involves noun exchanges, as in (2):

(2)   I would rather gamble $125 than have a HOLE full of FLOORS < I would rather gamble $125 than have a floor full of holes

Here the nouns are exchanged, and the functional category stranded is nominal plural. The stranded elements that we find in the Fromkin corpus are all 'bound', i.e. morphologically dependent, forms. They are listed in (3), with a distinction made between the inflectional elements in (3a), and the derivational ones in (3b):

(3)   (a) *inflectional*
        Case endings on pronouns
        3s -*s*
        Comparative -*er*
        Past participle -*ed*
        Past tense -*ed*
        Gerund -*ing*
        Past participle -*en*

Table 8.1. *Exchanges and stranded functional elements in the English part of the Fromkin speech error corpus*

	0	Ca	3sg	pl	Co-*er*	pp-*ed*	pst	-*ing*	-*en*	Ag-*er*	-*ly*	*re*-	V	N	Der
N~N	1			11						1					
A~A	1														
A~N	1			1											
V~Adv				1	1										
N~Adv											1				
V~V		1				1	1	1							
N~V						4	2	1		1					
V~N				1		1		1	1	1					
Pro~N		1													
Pro~Pro		1													
Part~Part	1														
Word-internal compN		1	4							1		2	2	2	3 1
PartAdv	1														

Note: Ca = case marking; Ag = agentive; Co = comparative; pp = past participle; pst = past tense; Der = derivational; Part = particle; compN = compound noun

(b) *derivational*
　　Agentive -*er*
　　Adverbial marker -*ly*
　　Verbal prefix -*re*
　　Derivational suffixes -*hood*, and -*ically* and -*icant*
　　Nominal and verbal heads of compounds and phrases

In Table 8.1 they are listed cross-tabulated with the categories of the elements that are exchanged.

From Table 8.1 it can be inferred that of the stranded elements, 25 are inflectional, and 15 derivational. The large majority of the stranded derivational affixes occur in compound noun exchanges, which may have a special status. Turning now to the elements exchanged, there are 36 lexical category exchanges, including two involving a pronoun, and one involving two particles:

(4) 　*PN~N*: 　PAUL was a student of HIS < He [Allan] was a student of Paul's

(5) 　*PN~PN*: 　I didn't know Ravel had HIM in IT < I didn't know Ravel had it in him

(6) 　*Part~Part*: I will take my MAKE OFF UP < will take my MAKE UP OFF

There are also some word- or phrase-internal exchanges, including:

(7)   I'm sorry I didn't RECALL your TURN sooner < I'm sorry I didn't return your call sooner

In (7) the prefix *re-* is stranded. Notice that the prefix *re-* in English is quite autonomous; it can be repeated, for instance, as in *re-redo* something.

A second type of error I considered involved misplaced word endings. Here the ending is shifted to an earlier or a later word. Examples are given in (8) (shift forward) and (9) (shift backward):

(8)   V>>V if she want_ to comeS here < if she wants to come here

(9)   V<<V as I keepING suggest_ < as I keep suggesting

In (8) it is a 3s -*s* that is shifted into the complement clause, and in (9) the -*ing* form. The shifted elements encountered in the Fromkin corpus are listed in (10). Again, many are inflectional suffixes (10a), and some derivational (10b). There are also a few independent elements shifted in this way (10c):

(10)   (a) *inflectional*
            3s -*s*
            Genitive -*s*
            Gerund -*ing*
            Copula '*s*
            Plural -*s*
         (b) *derivational*
            Superlative -*est*
            Adverbial -*ly*
         (c) *independent*
            Pronoun
            Particle

In Table 8.2 the frequency of the different errors of this type in the Fromkin corpus are presented. Of the shifted affixes, 25 were inflectional, and 3 derivational.

Notice that this error type is quite frequent in verb + particle combinations:

(11)   V>>Part
         (a) I should be SHUT UPPING < I should be SHUTTING UP
         (b) it COME ONS at < it COMES ON at
         (c) add_ upS to < adds up to
         (d) and Rachel come_ inS < and Rachel comes in
         (e) he end_ upS < he ends up
         (f) when someone come_ upS to me < when someone comes up to me

Table 8.2. *Wrongly attached functional elements in the English part of the Fromkin speech error corpus*

	3sg	Gen	-ing	C -s	Pl	pron	-est	Part	-ly	>>	<<
V~V	1		1							1	1
V~Part	5		1							6	
V~A	2									2	
compN				1	4					2	3
Mod~V	1										1
V-ing					1						1
V~Pron	1										1
N~Pron					1						1
Adv~A							1		1	1	1
N~V	2				2					2	2
V~A								1			1
N~N		1			2					1	2

Note: >> means shifted backward, and << shifted forward; Gen = genitive -*s*; C = copula; Mod = modifier

There are two cases where an element is shifted onto or away from a pronoun:

(12)   N>>PRO   some part_ of ITS are < some parts of it are

(13)   V<<PRO   in order to buildS one career < in order to build one's career

There also a few cases of including an extra gerund affix, sometimes in the context of another gerund (14a), sometimes not (14b):

(14)   (a) *gerund contexts*
            no means of letting the family KNOWING
            The taxi's getting ready to PUSHING him out

         (b) *non-gerund contexts*
            All I can DOING is hope and pray
            As Chomsky and Halle POINTING out ... POINT out
            Let me just TRYING to make my point

It is not clear how to interpret the data in (14). Possibly, it is the unmarked nature of the gerund form which leads to its insertion instead of an infinitive or finite form.

The data presented for German in the Wiese data set for word exchanges (shifted functional categories are not in evidence in these data) show a similar picture to the one given in the Fromkin corpus. They are shown in Table 8.3.

Table 8.3. *Word exchanges and stranded functional elements in the German speech error corpus prepared by Richard Wiese*

	0	Case	3sg	pl	Pp *ge-t*	Inf
N~N	4	1		4		
A~A	1					
A~N		1				
Adv~Adv	1					
V~V			1			
N~V						2
V~N					1	
NP~Pro	1					
P~P		2				
Word-internal						
compN	2	1				

The large majority of word exchanges involve lexical categories, and there are a few cases involving a pronoun or a preposition:

(15)   NP~PN
und ICH war noch sehr jung, als MEINE MUTTER geboren wurde <
and I was still very young when my mother born was
und meine Mutter war noch sehr jung, als ich geboren wurde
and my mother was still very young when I born was
'And my mother was still very young when I was born.'

(16)   P~P
IN der Fensterbank AUF dem Badezimmer habe ich den gesehen <
in the window-sill on the bathroom have I it seen
auf der Fensterbank im Badezimmer habe ich den gesehen
on the windowsill in the bathroom have I it seen
'I've seen it in the bathroom on the windowsill.'

IN'N Aldi ZUM Reisholz < zum Aldi in Reisholz
[into the Aldi to the Reisholz] < [to the Aldi (name of a supermarket) at Reisholz (place name)]

The stranded elements in the German corpus are all inflectional:

(17)   Case endings
3s *-t*
Plural marking
Past participle *ge-V-t*
Infinitive *-en*

It is striking that in the German case there is no report of shifting errors (anticipation and perseveration). It is not clear whether this is due to the way the data were collected or to a difference between German and English morphology (the latter being more 'detached').

If we summarise these data from the perspective of the lexical/functional distinction, we can conclude that for the exchanges it is largely true that lexical elements shift around, and functional elements, in particular inflectional affixes, are stranded. The exceptions to a clear-cut distinction are: (a) in both the Fromkin and the Wiese Corpora a few, although not many, pronouns and prepositions or particles shift around; (b) in the Fromkin corpus, sometimes derivational affixes are stranded, but nearly always in very local exchanges.

Garrett's distinction between functional and positional structure

Garrett (1975) has suggested that different types of speech errors, including a wider variety than illustrated above, correspond to different levels of representation in the production model. Garrett (1975, 1980) makes a distinction between differences between word and sound exchange errors, and anticipation and perseveration errors. In word exchanges, correspondence of the grammatical category is an important issue, while sound exchanges are confined to open-class elements. In anticipation and perseveration errors an open + a closed-class category is involved. Crucial in the model proposed by Garrett, schematically presented in Table 8.4, is that grammatical formatives are part of 'positional frames', so that there is a fundamental distinction here between lexical and functional categories.

Garrett notes (1975: 51) that only very few, namely 2 out of 137 sound exchanges involve closed-class items, while at the next level, 20 out of 97 word exchanges involve closed-class items. The categories of these items are listed in (18):

(18)   10 prepositions
           6 pronouns
           2 determiners
           1 element of a complementiser
           1 negative/temporal qualifier

Prepositions have the property that they do, albeit infrequently, occur in exchange errors: *in* and *to* can interchange positions (see also Butterworth 1989: 115), like other lexical items. They do not undergo sound change errors, unlike true content words. Examples of exchanged particles and prepositions include:

Table 8.4. *Schematic presentation of the different levels of representation in the model proposed by Garrett (1975), with the relevant psycholinguistic processes linking them and the speech errors associated with these processes*

Level of representation	Processes	Error type
Message source (M$_1$, M$_2$, M$_3$, ..., M$_n$)		
Functional level of representation	Semantic factors pick lexical formatives and grammatical relations	Word substitutions and fusions. Independent word and phrase exchanges
Positional level of representation	Syntactic factors pick positional frames and their attendant grammatical formatives; phonemically specified lexical formatives are inserted in frames	Combined form exchanges and sound exchanges, word and morpheme shifts
Sound level of representation	Phonetic detail of both lexical and grammatical formatives is specified	Accommodations and simple and complex sound deletions
Instructions to articulators		Tongue twisters
Articulatory system(s)		

(19)   which was parallel TO a certain sense, IN an experience (p. 51)
    Every time I put one of these buttons OFF, another one comes ON (p. 52)

Garrett (1982) explains the special behaviour of prepositions by assuming that prepositions are lexical elements in what he terms functional structure (lexical/conceptual structure) and subsequently undergo cliticisation and appear as grammatical elements in positional structure (syntax). Speech errors occur after positional structure has been constituted. It may be that the difference between the results for sound exchanges and word exchanges had to do with the length of function and content elements.

Frequency effects

It has been known for a long time that functional categories are highly frequent in spoken and written texts. Consider the 20 most frequent bigrams (sequences of two adjacent words) in the *New York Times* corpus, based on the newswire from August to November 1990 and comprising 14 million words (listed in order of frequency) (cited from Manning and Schütze 1999: ch. 5).

(20)	of the	and the	of a	he (said)
	in the	that the	by the	as a
	to the	at the	with the	is a
	on the	to the	from the	has been
	for the	in a	(New York)	for a

Only in places 15 (*New York*) and 16 (*said*) do the first non-function words appear, and immediately beyond the 20 limit many other functional categories appear. Likewise, in the CELEX database (18 million words) the first 70 most frequent words are function words. However, notice that prepositions, which in other domains are considered marginal to the functional domain, are extremely frequent elements; they occupy positions 1–5 and 8–14 on this list. Frequency has an important role in speech production, and hence functional categories may be accessed much more easily than other words in the mental lexicon.

Thus the data presented and analysed by Garrett as supportive of functional differentiation between open- and closed-class categories could alternatively be analysed in terms of frequency. More frequent items, including functional categories, could be resistant to word exchange errors simply because they are so readily accessible to speakers.

Finocchiaro and Caramazza (2006: 144), in a series of experiments with Italian speakers, show that the production of clitic pronouns is sensitive to the frequency of the nouns that they replace. This suggests that the frequency effect is associated with the level of lexical processing at which the grammatical features (gender, number) of a word are represented. Thus the retrieval of grammatical features follows automatically from lexical node selection for those features associated with lexical items (p. 163).

However, no systematic study has been carried out, to my knowledge, of the relation between word frequency and speech errors. Furthermore, the types of elements that are stranded in word exchanges are not lexical items, but inflections; admittedly frequent, but not subjected to the same word frequency studies.

There is some, albeit disputed, evidence from lexical decision tasks that function words are not subject to the same frequency effects as content words for normal speakers, but that they are for aphasic speakers (Bradley et al., 1980) (cf. chapter 10).

Evidence from neurolinguistic studies

Different studies concerning the processing of language in the brain have similarly revealed differences in the way lexical and functional categories are stored and processed. First of all, there are localisation differences. Second, there are differences in the time course of processing different elements.

With regard to localisation, Pulvermüller (1995) has claimed that closed-class items are stored differently in the brain from open class words. Closed-class items were found to be left-lateralised, while open-class items had a wider distribution. Similarly Bradley and Garrett (1983) report different patterns of hemispheric asymmetries. There is also evidence about the general differences between concrete and abstract words. Binder *et al.* (2005) found that bilateral association areas in the brain are more involved during concrete word processing, while processing of abstract concepts occurs almost exclusively in the left hemisphere. While the traditional assumption might be that the category of functional categories as a block is distinct from that of lexical categories, again as a whole, it may well be that neither cluster forms a unified class. Thus Caramazza and his co-workers have discovered (Shapiro and Caramazza 2003; Shapiro *et al.* 2006) that verbs and nouns are processed in different areas in the brain.

In their survey of the neurocognitive aspects of syntactic processing, Hagoort *et al.* (1999: 282) distinguish between closed- and open-class items in the following way:

(21)   closed: articles, conjunctions, prepositions
         open: nouns, verbs, adjectives

The closed items have a negative peak latency of less than 280 ms, and in this they contrast with open-class items, for which we find 350–400 ms. Also, there some differences between them:

(22)   articles   212
         prepositions   115
         conjunctions   71

In an earlier study Osterhout *et al.* (1997) found somewhat higher negative peak latencies:

(23)   articles   280
         prepositions   320
         pronouns   350
         auxiliaries   360
         nouns/verbs   400

Weber-Fox *et al.* (2006) studied the effects of grammatical categories on children's visual language processing, using Event-Related brain Potential (ERP) measurements. They conclude that (older) children show similar responses to the ones reported above.

Similar to the studies mentioned so far, an earlier study by Neville *et al.* (1992) reports an N280 effect (a negative peak latency in an event-related potential experiment approximately 280 ms after the stimulus) for closed-class items in anterior regions of the left hemisphere, while for open-class items there is an N400 effect (a wave effect on the EEG curve in an event-related potential experiment approximately 400 ms after the unexpected stimulus) in posterior regions.

Nonetheless, the categories vary among themselves, the rankings for different categories differ somewhat, and it is not clear exactly how the distinctions are made. It is also not known yet whether it is length, frequency, or word class that causes the difference between lexical and functional categories in this respect.

Osterhout *et al.* (2002) argue that ERP differences between open- and closed-class words correlate closely with quantitative differences in word length (as well as with frequency differences). Thus a functional distinction between the two word classes may not be needed to account for the special status of closed-class items in neuro-imaging studies.

All studies mentioned so far have concentrated on separate lexical items: articles, prepositions, pronouns, and so on. With respect to functional categories represented as inflectional morphology, Longworth *et al.* (2005) suggest that four patients with damage to the peri-sylvian cortex, who need to process spoken sentences with regular past tense morphology, show evidence in the time course of their processing for the dual root account of inflectional morphology (cf. also Marslen-Wilson and Tyler 2003). In this account there is a difference neurolinguistically between associative memory processes for stored arbitrary information and procedures that combine units of stored knowledge. The patients took longer to process the regular than the irregular past tense forms of the verb, suggesting that the regular ones had to be computed separately.

In line with this study, Newman *et al.* (2007) carried out an ERP study of regular and irregular English past tense inflection. They found that violations of regular past tense marking triggered lateralised anterior negativities (LANs), but not violations of irregular past tense marking. The results are consistent with the view that regular past tenses are composed by a frontal/basal-ganglia procedural system, while irregular past tenses are stored in a temporal lobe-based declarative memory system.

Conclusions

It is clear the lexical/functional distinction plays a role in the psycholinguistic and neurolinguistic study of language processing. However, the definition of what counts as lexical and functional needs further elaboration, since the brain-imaging studies do not make the fine distinctions that can be possible in the analysis of the speech error data. Furthermore, it is not clear to which factors the distinct behaviour of the different types of categories must be attributed. However, the idea that there is a clear neural functional distinction between the category types as such needs further confirmation. Differences are gradient between different category types, and the fact that prepositions rank high in these studies on the functional scale but not in other domains of analysis also suggests that a more systematic analysis of the available data is needed. Finally, word length, frequency, and abstract meaning may play a separate independent role.

9 *Language development*

Humans acquire languages and develop their language abilities under diverse conditions. It may be their first or their second language, and development may take place at different ages. These different conditions also have an effect on the development of functional categories, as will be shown in this chapter.

In first language development generally, lexical categories are acquired before functional categories, with some exceptions. In second language development, a much more chaotic picture emerges. Initially some categories are present in rudimentary form, others not at all. In simultaneous bilingual child language development, the two systems with their respective functional categories tend to be kept apart, although there is some convergence as well.

The present chapter will systematically survey some of the more detailed studies in this area, comparing the various conditions of language development.

First language development

In the study of child first language development the lexical/functional distinction has played an important role. It has been frequently noted that children use very few grammatical elements while in the one-word and two-word stages of language acquisition. Brown (1976 [1973]: 99): 'the sentences the child makes are like adult telegrams in that they are largely made up of nouns and verbs (with a few adjectives and adverbs) and in that they generally do not use prepositions, conjunctions, articles, and auxiliary verbs'. This is the basis for what Brown called the 'telegraphic speech' analysis.

An example is given here from a Dutch dialogue reported by Schaerlaekens (1977: 111), the interest of which hinges on the fact that the adult interprets the child word *lees* 'read' as a reduced form of *vlees* 'meat':

(1)   *Dutch mother–child interaction*

Child: Sijs lees	'Sijs meat/read'
Adult: wil Gijs nog vlees?	'does Gijs want more meat?'
Child: sijs lees	'Sijs meat/read'
Adult: wil Gijs nog vlees?	'does Gijs want more meat?'
Child: neeneen	'nono'
sijs lees	'Sijs meat/read'
Adult: wil Gijs nog vlees?	'does Gijs want more meat?'
Child: kran lees	'newspaper read'

A number of issues need to be discussed when we consider the role of functional categories in child language development.

Potential exceptions to the 'telegraphic speech' analysis of early child language production. There are a number of adult language functional elements that children do use, as pointed out by Park (1970) for German, and acknowledged by Brown (1976 [1973]: 104–106). A list of the main forms is given in (2):

(2)   (a) *German*   (b) *English*

da 'there'	there
dass 'that'	that
ein 'one', 'a'	this
hier 'here'	here
mehr 'more'	more
ander 'other'	'nother
ab 'off'	off
an 'at'	on
auf 'on top'	I
mit 'with'	you
um 'round'	my
weg 'away'	me
zu 'to', 'closed'	

The two lists coincide to a considerable extent, with the proviso that in English the pronoun inventory is richer, while in German it is the inventory of (intransitively or adverbially used) prepositions. Brown insightfully discusses the possible reasons for these exceptions. Key is that these elements may not have a 'functional' status in a proper sense in early child language. Pronouns, for instance, can carry all thematic roles (Agent, Beneficiary, etc.), can have all syntactic functions (Subject, Object, etc.), do not express 'modulations of meaning', and can carry full stress (p. 105).

'Grammatical morphemes', according to Brown, are 'defined by the partial convergence of a large number of characteristics or variables' (p. 106). The

Table 9.1. *Features determining the occurrence of functional elements in early child speech (based on discussion in Brown 1973 [1976]: 113)*

	Features	Occurrence	Examples
I	Minimal frequency High perceptual salience Basic semantic role Invariable in form	Integral part of early child speech	*Here* *Off* *My*
II	High frequency High perceptual salience	In early child speech, but only in fixed routines	Fixed plurals Fixed N *of* N
III	Low frequency Low perceptual salience Variable in form Modulates meaning	Absent from early child speech	

exceptions to the general rule that functional categories do not occur in early child speech are 'simply those words that do not have enough of the determinants working against them' (pp. 106–107). Stated in positive terms, relevant features that could favour early acquisition for Brown include:

- a minimal level of frequency
- perceptual salience, measured in terms of phonetic substance (can be a full syllable or not), possibility of heavy stress and high pitch, possibility of occurring in utterance-final position
- independent semantic role rather than merely the modulation of the meaning of another element
- informativeness rather than redundancy
- invariability of form rather than being conditioned by grammatical, lexical, or phonological factors

A form such as third person singular -*s* in English will score negatively on all of these variables, while *off* will be positively specified: it occurs frequently enough in parental speech, is syllabic, can be stressed, often occurs in final position, has a separate meaning which is generally not redundant, and is invariable in form (pp. 107–109).

Altogether, Brown sets up three general classes of 'functors' on the basis of these criteria, as outlined in Table 9.1. These classes are acquired in different stages, as will be outlined below.

The early acquisition of the lexical/functional distinction. How and when do children catch on to the lexical/functional distinction? According to Janet Werker, Rushen Shi, and colleagues (Shi *et al.* 1999, 2003) infants make use of the fact that function words have different acoustic phonological properties from content words. They tend to be shorter and they have more reduced vowels. Infants are sensitive to these acoustic differences. Newly born babies do not know that lexical words carry meaning and function words do not, but they can perceptually differentiate between them. At the age of six months, they show a preference for listening to the content words.

Using comparative data from Danish, Icelandic, and Swedish, Strömqvist *et al.* (2001) studied the interaction of frequency and stress in the input to explain the emergence of function words in early child language. All of the twenty most frequent words in the input and in the child language itself in the Swedish data were function words, and of the fifty most frequent words in the Swedish child data only three were unambiguously content words: *mamma*, *pappa*, and *tikka* 'look'. The authors speculate that the child starts out with stressed highly frequent function words, and then develops unstressed words in the same class later on.

Shi (2006: 91–99) traces the interaction of phonological and grammatical factors in the early language development of syntactic categories. Citing Juszyk and Aslin's (1995) observation that 'infants' early word segmentation only includes content words', Shi explores the acoustical and phonological correlates of grammatical categories, and observes that it is a universal that function words are phonologically reduced, but the manifestation of this reduction may differ from language to language. Turkish functional categories contain underspecified vowels subject to harmony rules, while Chinese functional categories show predictability of their tones from neighbouring tonal concepts. From a survey of the existing literature (2006: 97–99), Shi concludes that infants are able to categorically discriminate content words from function words in any language.

Hohle *et al.* (2004), using a head-turn preference paradigm, show that German children at 14–16 months old can use the cue of a determiner to establish that the following element has the category of noun. They do not show the same ability with subject pronoun–verb combinations. Analysis of child-directed adult speech shows that determiners and nouns are much more likely to occur, in that order, than subject pronouns and verbs.

Order of acquisition. What is the order in which the functional categories appear in child language? There is a tradition of *Morpheme Order Studies*, in which the L1 morpheme acquisition order is established, starting with Brown

(1976 [1973]), as mentioned above. In his longitudinal study of three children, Brown found the following order:

(3)   *-ing*
        -s (plural)
        irregular past tense (*broke, fell*)
        -'s (possessive)
        copula
        the, a
        regular past tense *-ed*
        -s (3s)
        auxiliary *be*

Brown argues that the order of morpheme acquisition was not dependent on frequency of exposure (in caretaker speech). Instead, the morphemes were acquired in order of syntactic and semantic complexity.

Implications for overall grammatical development. What are the implications of the acquisition of the functional categories for overall grammatical development? There has been considerable discussion in the literature as to whether children 'know' the grammatical and semantic distinctions implied by grammatical elements at a time when they are not yet using these elements. Three main hypotheses can be distinguished (cf. e.g. Sánchez 2003: 8–9):

   (i) **Strong continuity**. The full grammatical skeleton and all functional categories are available to the child throughout their language development. Hoekstra and Hyams (1998) and Verrips and Weissenborn (1992) assume complete functional skeletons from the very beginning. Grammatical differences between different developmental stages are due to lexical development, subsequent learning of selectional or pragmatic restrictions, or the fixing of a specific parameter. Demuth (1994) argues that functional categories are underlyingly present in the course of development but are often not pronounced due to phonological restrictions on word length in early child language.

  (ii) **Maturation**. In early stages there are no functional categories available to the child, only lexical categories, and there is no articulated syntactic structure. Radford (1990) assumes that all functional categories are absent in early child language. Gradually the functional system evolves, as the child becomes acquainted with the different categories characterising it.

 (iii) **Weak continuity**. The X-bar system is available to the child from the beginning, but the functional skeleton emerges as the child gains access to different morpho-syntactic distinctions. Clahsen and Pencke

(1992) assume incomplete specification of functional categories, filled in by the acquisition of morphological patterns.

DeVilliers (1992), in a commentary article on the acquisition of functional categories, concludes on the basis of the available evidence that there must be some development in functional categories. However, Radford's claim that there is a functional category-free stage is not supported by the evidence: from very early onwards, children show evidence for the distinction of various basic functional positions in the clausal skeleton, even if the system does not yet have the same amount of articulation as the adult system. In a detailed study of the development of English determiners, Abu-Akel *et al.* (2004: 419) conclude that children already use articles at the onset of the multi-word stage, at 1.6–2.0 years. In the early stages there are high rates of omission and there is high variability between the children (p. 420). There is a significant decrease in omission at the age of 3.0 for many of the children studied.

Child bilingual development

A number of researchers have tried to study the relation between the development of the two languages in bilingual children, yielding a basic picture of mutual independence, but some evidence of mutual influence as well.

Meisel and a group of research associates have studied French/German and Basque/Spanish simultaneous bilingual language development (e.g. Meisel 1994a), and have argued for the Autonomous Development Hypothesis. In both languages children develop the functional projections, and hence the overall clause structure, independently, on the basis of an initial verbal projection. In (1994b) Meisel particularly cites evidence from one French/German bilingual child, Ivar, and documents how in both French and German finiteness, tense, and agreement start playing a role (Ivar's age is given as years, months, days).

(4)   nonours dort   'teddy sleeps'   Iv2;00,02   (p. 94)
        dort bébé   'sleeps baby'

(5)   presentative *das (ist)*   'that (is)'
        das gita   'that [is a] guitar'   Iv2;0,?   (p. 95)
        das kaput   'that [is] broken'
        das ist mann   'that is [a] man'

(6)   Ivar darf nicht tee   'Ivar may not tea'   Iv2;04,23   (p. 108)

With the emergence of agreement, evidence for the functional projections above VP becomes available (1994b: 118). However, these developments are autonomous in the two languages involved, in Meisel's account. For all intents and purposes, the bilingual children develop like double monolinguals.

Hinzelin analyses Portuguese/German bilingual development, and shows (2003: 131–132) that pronouns are used in subject position at 2;08 for Portuguese, and 2;07 and 2;10 respectively for German. These developments are closely linked to the development of finite verbs in both languages at 2;08 for Portuguese and 2;07 and 3;02 respectively for German. Hinzelin's work supports the Autonomous Development Hypothesis because the setting of the null subject parameter (null subjects allowed in Portuguese, disallowed in German) proceeds perfectly for both languages.

The researchers associated with Meisel's DUFDE project tend to stress the mutual autonomy of the functional category systems of the two languages involved in child bilingual development (e.g. Meisel 1989). A similar set of results has come from work by Genesee and his colleagues (e.g. Genesee 1989). However, the complete autonomy of the two systems has been questioned from various angles.

Working with similar bilingual children to those studied in Meisel's project, Müller and Hulk (2001) argue that under certain conditions there may be mutual influence of the two developing languages. The case they study involves object omission. In Dutch and German, objects can be omitted in sentence-initial position if they have been previously mentioned in the discourse, as in German (7a) and Dutch (7b):

(7)   (a) [0]   Hab ich schon gesehen.
                   have I already seen
         (b) [0]   Heb ik al gezien.
                   have I already seen
                   'I have already seen **it/that**.'

Given the fact that in finite declarative main clauses in German and Dutch the verb is in second position, we can indeed assume that the omitted objects occur in initial position. If some other constituent is in first position, the object cannot be omitted. German and Dutch children very frequently omit the object, particularly in the early stages. Monolingual French and Italian children in the same age ranges omit objects much less frequently. Children bilingual in Dutch/French, German/French, or German/Italian, however, show omission rates for objects much higher than their monolingual French and Italian counterparts. Müller and Hulk attribute the difference to the fact that the clausal domain involving the complementiser system, where we also find the clausal semantic information interacting with discourse semantics and pragmatics, is particularly vulnerable to cross-linguistic influence.

Studying a very different group of children, Quechua/Spanish bilinguals in Peru, Sánchez (2003) has also underlined the possibility for the mutual influence of the two languages. She formulates two hypotheses in this respect, the Functional Interference Hypothesis and the Functional Convergence Hypothesis:

(8)   **Functional Interference Hypothesis**. Functional interference in bilinguals, i.e. the activation of functional features in one language triggered by input in the other language, generates syntactic changes in the bilingual grammars. Interference in lexical entries (n-insertion, v-insertion) does not generate such changes. (p. 13)

This hypothesis limits structural interference between the two languages in child development to the functional domain. The second hypothesis concerns the way that this interference may come about:

(9)   **Functional Convergence Hypothesis**. Convergence, the specification of a common set of features shared by the equivalent functional categories in the two languages spoken by a bilingual individual, takes place when a set of features that is not activated in language A is frequently activated by input in language B in the bilingual mind. (p. 15)

Sánchez compares the marking and positioning of objects in Quechua and Spanish, where possible in these languages, of monolingual children from near the capital of Lima, to two bilingual groups of children from communities elsewhere in Peru. Using bilingual child narratives elicited with an adapted version of the Frog Story, she studied the distribution and marking of direct objects. In traditional Quechua, direct objects are pre-verbal, marked with accusative *-ta*, and often not preceded by a determiner. An example from one of Sánchez' researched communities, Ulcumayo, is given in (10) (p. 91):

(10)   Huk wambra # racha-kta chari-ya-n.
        a   boy   toad-AC   grab-DUR-3s
        'A boy is holding a toad.'

Particularly in the other community studied, Lamas, there is evidence for functional convergence towards Spanish in three respects: (a) frequent dropping of the accusative marker; (b) frequent post-verbal object placement; (c) frequent employment of a determiner, most often the indefinite determiner *suk* 'one'.

For the Spanish of the bilingual children the picture is more complex. There was no clear tendency towards pre-verbal objects in the Spanish of the bilingual children, in contrast with the results in the study by Luján *et al.* (1984) of bilingual Cuzco Spanish. The bilingual children tended to overgeneralise the dative clitic *le* (unmarked for gender) to all object contexts (replacing accusative masculine *lo* and feminine *la*). They also showed a tendency to frequently use null objects when there was an antecedent in the discourse, similar to the bilingual children in the Müller and Hulk study. Both developments could be linked to Quechua influence, but only indirectly.

It is tempting to interpret Sánchez' results in terms of shifts in the mapping between abstract morpho-syntactic features and morpho-phonemic shapes, thus as the results from the shift at the interface. In this way, both types of interlingual influence could be viewed as involving shifts in interface mappings: the syntax/semantics and the syntax/morpho-lexicon interface.

Second language development

In the area of second language (L2) acquisition a number of questions come to the fore with respect to the issue of functional categories.

- Is the order in which morphemes are acquired similar to that found in L1 studies?
- Does the functional skeleton of the L1 play an important role?
- Is there a stage in the acquisition of the L2, e.g. the so-called Basic Variety stage, where functional categories are not present?
- Does the functional skeleton of the L2 develop gradually?
- Is the acquisition of syntactic functional categories in L2 directly linked to the appropriate morphological endings?

These issues will be discussed one by one, starting with a discussion of morpheme order studies.

Morpheme order studies. If L2 acquisition shows the same developmental order as L1 acquisition it may be assumed that L1 and L2 learning are characterised by the same cognitive processes. This finding would downplay the importance of transfer, and provide an argument for a mentalist view, against behaviourism, on the basis of the following reasoning. L1 transfer is not important, therefore transfer of habits is not important, therefore habits were not important. The L2 learner is involved in learning, so they gradually construct rules for the speech they hear using innate mechanisms. If transfer is not important, all second language learners regardless of L1 background should show the same order of development.

Dulay and Burt (1974) studied 60 Spanish and 55 Chinese *child* learners of English, and applied the Bilingual Syntax Measure (BSM) to their spoken output, the result of a narrative task describing a series of pictures. In their study, Spanish and Chinese children had similar scores across the morpheme types.

Bailey *et al.* (1974) looked at 33 Spanish and 40 non-Spanish (Greek, Farsi, Italian, Turkish, Japanese, Chinese, Thai, Afghan, Hebrew, Arabic, Vietnamese) *adult* learners of English, again applying the BSM. Pooled results show similarity to Dulay and Burt (1974), in that Spanish and non-Spanish groups had comparable profiles. However, in spite of the claims by Dulay and Burt, L1 effects were still found in some studies; for example, Japanese learners showed lower accuracy on articles than learners of L1s which used articles (Larsen-Freeman 1975).

However, a number of methodological and conceptual problems remain with respect to the morpheme order studies. First, does correct use of a morpheme in the BSM indicate acquisition? The use of a morpheme in the test context does not necessarily entail the correct use of the morpheme elsewhere. Do orders in the development of accurate use (accuracy orders) of particular morphemes in cross-sectional studies reflect developmental sequences?

Possible other causes for such accuracy orders include:

- perceptual saliency of the morphemes
- semantic factors
- syntactic complexity
- input frequency.

Zobl and Liceras (1994) analyse a number of morpheme acquisition order studies for both first and second language development and conclude (p. 159) that the emergence of functional categories in L1 is category-specific, while their development in L2 is cross-category. In L1 learning, nominal categories are acquired earlier than verbal categories, while in L2 learning no such distinction holds. Furthermore, in L1 development, inflectional elements are on a par with lexical ones in the implementation of functional morphemes, while in L2 development inflectional elements follow lexical elements in the instantiation of functional categories. Zobl and Liceras divide the morphemes into three main groups, for both L1 and L2 development, and the order in the two groups is not identical. In L1 development auxiliary BE is not acquired together with -*ing*, and copula BE precedes auxiliary BE. In L2 development, BE and the determiner are acquired early, since the free morpheme/bound morpheme distinction plays an important role here. Lexical elements thus appear before non-lexical elements, on the whole.

There are several problems with the conclusions reached by Zobl and Liceras. Empirically, they have no account for the early appearance of V-*ing* and for irregular pasts. It is much less evident that there is a sharp distinction to be made, in terms of acquisition patterns, between the three classes. Indeed, second-language learners acquire lexical elements first, but start introducing all kinds of grammatical elements irregularly quite early on.

The L1 functional skeleton. The transfer hypothesis, traditional in the L2 research tradition associated with Contrastive Analysis, assumed an important role for the first language in determining the course of L2 development. This hypothesis for a while receded into the background, but has now been given new fire by the L1 conservation or full transfer hypothesis (Schwartz and Sprouse 1996; van de Craats *et al.* 2000, 2002). The L1 conservation/full transfer hypothesis holds that all L1 functional categories are there at the beginning of the L2 interlanguage. The patterns of Moroccan Arabic and Turkish possessive constructions were found to be directly reflected in the L2 Dutch of Moroccan Arabic and Turkish learners (van de Craats *et al.* 2000).

The findings on the L2 development of Dutch possessives presented by van de Craats *et al.* (2000) concern both Turkish and Moroccan Arabic learners. Here only some of the Turkish data are presented. In Turkish, the attributive possessive construction has the structure [possessor + genitive possessum + personal ending]. In the Dutch interlanguage of Turkish learners, presented in (11) below roughly in terms of the progression in complexity of the L2 representations, there is a tendency towards the order [possessor possessum], different from what we find in most Dutch sentences, and the introduction of a number of elements from Dutch that take the place of Turkish functional elements. These are italicized in (11). Notice that in native Dutch we find pre-head possessors mostly with pronouns (*mijn moeder* 'my mother', with names (*Jans moeder* 'John's mother'), and with a few kinship terms (*mijn moeders huis* 'my mother's house'). Some of the extra Dutch elements introduced in the examples in (11) could be characterised as functional elements, but bear no relation to the elements in the target Dutch noun phrase.

(11)   (a) vriend huis
            friend house
            'my friend's house'

        (b) garage *die* naam
            garage DEM name
            'the name of the garage' (*die* = non-neuter deictic)

        (c) de auto *van* de lichten
            the car of the light.p
            'the lights of the car' (*van* = of)

(d) *die van z'n* ding
   DEM of his thing
   'his thing'

(e) van Omer'*s* huis
   of Omer's house
   'Omer's house'

(f) *van* Henry *z'n* foto
   of Henry his photo
   'Henry's photograph'

(g) *van* Zorro *van* Turks film
   of Zorro of Turkish film
   'the Turkish film [of] Zorro'

(h) *z'n* jongen *z'n* tekening
   his boy his drawing
   'the boy's drawing'

(i) de pan *z'n* deksel
   the pan his lid
   'the lid of the pan'

(j) juffrouw Lia *z'n* feest
   miss Lia his party
   'Miss Lia's party'

(k) Mark en Mieke *z'n* moeder
   Mark and Mieke his mother
   'Mark and Mieke's mother'

(l) Mijn oom *'s* zoon
   my uncle's son
   'my uncle's son'

Thus underlying aspects of the Turkish functional skeleton are retained even though all the morphemes involved are from Dutch.

The Basic Variety. The most systematic exploration of early stages of interlanguage is found in the analysis of the Basic Variety (BV), as introduced by Klein and Purdue (1997): a stage in the language development of many second language learners, a stage incidentally where some learners get stuck, in the process of fossilisation. The lexicon in the BV consists basically of a number of noun-like and verb-like words, and adjectives and adverbs. There is a minimal pronoun system for referring to speaker, addressee, and third referent, and anaphoric reference to animates. There are a few quantifiers, a basic negator, a few prepositions with fairly general meanings, but no complementisers and no inflectional morphology. There are at most a few demonstrative-like determiners, and no expletives (pp. 312–313). Instead of derivational morphology we find various kinds of nominal compounds in the lexicon, such as the following words for 'baker':

(12)   (a) un monsieur la boulanger (French)
            a gentleman the.f baker
        (b) brood baas (Dutch)
            bread boss

Syntax is organised with fairly rigid constraints, leading to an SVO word order (with a few exceptions in the early stages) (p. 314), and there are semantic principles of the type Agent First. Pragmatic constraints include Focus Last and a restriction on NPs with referents already previously introduced in the discourse. Zero anaphora tend to be avoided. These have to be introduced first. Similarly, there are basic patterns for reference to spatial and temporal organisation. The following sentences exemplify a number of the properties of this variety:

(13)   (a) Charlie give present for young children   English BV
        (b) il [setruv] avec la fille   French BV
            he finds.himself with the girl
            'He finds himself with the girls.'
        (c) de mädch gucke de mann mit brott und de mädch wolle   German BV
            essen
            the girl look the man with bread and the girl want eat
            'The girl looks at the man with the bread and wants some
            food.'
        (d) altijd ik les om half twee   Dutch BV
            always I lesson at half two
            'I always have my class at half past one.'

From a more formal perspective, Klein and Perdue (pp. 336–337) assume that a number of features of the skeleton are present in the BV: the category D, since often determiners are present, the category T, since the clauses in BV are finite, and the category ASP, since lexical aspect plays an important role. However, there is no evidence of C, nor of agreement or case features. The cross-linguistically stable and invariant word order of the BV is assumed to be the result of the fact that all features are weak in the BV, and hence do not trigger movement (Chomsky 1995).

Gradualness of development. As in the case of L1 development, different perspectives can be taken on the course of L2 development. The Full Continuity Hypothesis holds that all functional categories are in place from the beginning, originally with L1 settings (and hence is the same as the full transfer hypothesis

Table 9.2. *The development of negation in L2 English (based on Ellis 1994)*

Stage	Specification	Examples
Stage 1	External Neg	No you are playing here.
Stage 2	Internal Neg	Mariana not coming today.
Stage 3	Neg attachment to modal verbs	I can't play that one.
Stage 4	Neg attachment to Auxiliary verbs with target language rule	She didn't believe me. He didn't said it.

of Schwartz and Sprouse cited above). The empiricist approaches would predict that L2 categories are all acquired through input, and maturational approaches would hold that the inventory gradually unfolds either through tree expansion or fuller specification of individual categories

Ellis (1994: 96) argues that 'a close look at individual morphemes shows that they are acquired gradually and systematically'. He discusses pronouns (pp. 96–99) and negation (pp. 99–101) in this context. The development of negation proceeds in four stages, in his analysis, as represented in Table 9.2.

The link between morphological endings and syntactic functional positions. A number of researchers have evaluated the relation between morphological and syntactic acquisition, with respect to functional categories.

Lardiere (1998) analysed the recorded conversations of an Indonesian Malay/Chinese learner of English who had lived in the United States for a number of years, for much of it in an English-speaking environment. Consistently this speaker's variety is characterised by an exactly constant 34% production rate of past tense morphology. In addition, this speaker showed 100% correct nominative case morphology for pronominal subjects throughout, as well as productive use of complementisers in subordinate clauses. Lardiere concludes from this that this speaker had full use of both the T and the C functional projections, but suffered from a mismatch between underlying morpho-syntactic representations and morpho-phonological realisations.

While Lardiere studied a learner with a Chinese language background, Prévost and White (2000) concentrated on two learners of German (one with a Spanish, one with a Portuguese background) and two learners of French, both with Moroccan Arabic backgrounds. All four speakers had been recorded in the ESF project (Klein and Purdue 1997). For all speakers, the percentage of overtly finite verbs after a preposition, an auxiliary, or another verb, was quite low (ranging from 1.3% to 7.2%). This would suggest a correlation between non-finite morphology and non-finite syntax (in all these positions an infinitive is required). Similarly, a large majority of finite verbs preceded the negator (*pas* in French, *nicht* in German). Again, this result conforms to the idea that syntax and morphology go hand in hand. However, non-finite verbs tended to follow the negator, but a substantial number also precede it. Thus there is some overuse of non-finite forms in finite verb contexts. This result is confirmed for other finite contexts, reported on elsewhere in the paper. Furthermore, 95% of agreement marking, when it occurs, is correct for learners of French. For learners of German, the percentage was lower, around 88%. However, most of the 'errors' involved the *-e* form, which can also be interpreted as non-finite. With subject clitics in French, there were also quite a few 'errors', due to overuse of masculine *il* '3.s'. Altogether, the results support the Missing Surface Inflection Hypothesis: when there is inflection, it is used correctly, but sometimes uninflected forms occur in contexts where inflection would have been required. We do not find inflected forms in non-finite contexts, however, something that would be expected if there were no link between syntactic functional categories and morphological endings.

In a similar vein, finally, Herschensohn (2001: 274) contrasts the 'linked morpho-syntax hypothesis' (which assumes that functional categories emerge in the language development process as speakers start realising distinctions from inflectional morphology) with the 'independent morpho-syntax hypothesis', which assumes that mismatches between morphological realisations and syntactic development (where presumably the syntax is ahead of the morphology) are due to 'deficiencies in morphological mapping'. Considering the overuse of infinitival verbs by intermediate learners of French, Herschensohn concludes (p. 75) that these are not root infinitives as seen in the early stages of L1 development (cf. Wexler 1994), but rather examples of missing surface inflection. Thus the linked morpho-syntax hypothesis works well for L1 learners, but for L2 learners the missing surface inflection hypothesis has much more of a chance of being correct.

Conclusions

In language development studies the lexical/functional distinction plays an important role. In first language development, many researchers distinguish between a first phase, in which only a specific set of functional items is present, and a second phase, in which the other categories are gradually acquired. However, the idea that the functional skeleton is completely absent in the earliest stage finds little support. In bilingual child language development there is still disagreement about the degree to which the different languages influence each other. In those cases where there is interlingual influence claimed, it seems that the interface between the functional categories and either the lexical representations or the semantics/pragmatics is central to the process of mutual adjustment. Functional categories are acquired in L2 development in a much more gradual fashion; the L1 functional skeleton plays a central role here.

10 *Agrammatic aphasia and Specific Language Impairment*

There are two areas in the study of language and communication disorders where the lexical/functional distinction has played an important role: agrammatic aphasia and Specific Language Impairment (SLI).

With respect to agrammatic aphasia, Sloan Berndt (1990: xxv) writes: 'In the context of a fairly well-preserved ability to communicate meanings, the agrammatic patient appears to have lost some very essential part of the language system.' Patients speak very haltingly and with lots of pauses; there is less variation in grammatical forms, and patients tend to omit 'grammatical function words and bound grammatical markers'.

SLI is a developmental disorder, in which proficiency scores for first language development fall outside the normal range, although other cognitive capacities do not. In the case of SLI the development of specific functional categories will lag systematically behind what would be expected in typically developing children, depending on the language involved.

For both types of disorders it is claimed that functional categories are particularly affected. However, in different studies different functional categories are highlighted, and a cross-linguistic evaluation of the evidence is needed. I will first discuss agrammatic aphasia in more general terms, before surveying different studies with respect to evidence about special problems in the production of functional categories (leaving aside the much scarcer but equally important evidence about comprehension). In the second part of the chapter I turn to the phenomenon of SLI and then survey a number of studies in this domain, with a cross-linguistic perspective. I conclude with a comparison of the two types of disorders in this respect, with some preliminary conclusions.

Agrammatism

A classical domain where we find a reported asymmetry in the production of lexical elements is with a specific type of aphasic patients, suffering from Broca's syndrome and showing agrammatism. They can speak only in very short sentences, consisting of lexical elements. They have great difficulty building grammatical structures and using the appropriate grammatical elements, both separate words and inflectional endings. An example of Dutch agrammatic speech is (from a pictured scene description task) (Prins 1987: 14):

(1)   krukje ... eh ... vallen ... moet, nee, eh, meisje en jongen.
       stool ... eh ... fall.INF ... must, no, eh, girl and boy

       en eh pikken, hè ... snoepje ... eh koekje.
       and eh steal.INF, right ... candy ... eh cookie

       en vallen ... krukje.
       and fall.INF ... stool

       enne stromen je water.
       and.eh flow.INF you[r] water

       ja, eh ... kinderen ... stromen water en eh, koekjes.
       yes, eh ... children ... flow.INF water and eh cookies

The speaker can use the right content words for describing the scene: 'girl', 'boy', 'steal', 'cookie', 'stool', 'fall', 'water', 'flow', but lacks the grammatical apparatus to put them in a coherent perspective. There is an overuse of infinitives and of the linker *en* 'and', but there are no determiners, logical connectors, tense markers, etc.

Agrammatism research, as part of general research on aphasia, is a highly complex area, for a number of reasons:

   (a) There are many different types of individual patients, who often cannot be neatly classified as Wernicke or Broca or yet another kind of aphasic.
   (b) Broca aphasics have problems in syntax production, but also some-times with word retrieval (particularly of verbs), while Wernicke apha-sics also have some syntactic production problems.
   (c) The severity and precise nature of the deficits vary considerably from patient to patient.
   (d) Patients vary widely as to their performance on different types of tests. Often their comprehension skills are further developed than their production skills.

For these reasons, Kolk (1998) argues for an approach to aphasia in terms of impaired processing limitations rather than of an impaired linguistic rep-resentation. Such representations have been proposed at various points in the past, in terms of the Trace Deletion Hypothesis, the Case-Deficit Hypothesis, etc.

There is a very large literature on agrammatism, and in this literature a number of criteria are suggested to distinguish grammatical from lexical elements. While much research has been done on the agrammatic speech, the following remark by Caramazza and Sloan Berndt (1985: 34) remains valid:

> [Aside from the work by M.L. Kean] there has not been a formal (explicit) distinction drawn between the class of elements omitted and those retained in the speech of agrammatics. Most researchers have, instead, relied on the classical grammatical distinctions among form classes (i.e. function word, noun, adjective, etc.). Whether or not this classical division among lexical items drawn by linguists corresponds to distinctions in a psycholinguistic model of language processing remains to be determined.

No coherent picture emerges with respect to the grammatical elements that are omitted, and indeed Miceli *et al.* (1989) argue that there is considerable variation between patients in this respect.

I will take Miceli *et al.*'s study on Italian aphasic patients as my point of departure, since it is one of the most detailed studies empirically. The main lexical elements found by Miceli *et al.* in the speech of aphasic patients are nouns, adjectives, and main verbs. Adverbs were excluded from the counts of content words because only a few of the patients retained the ability to produce them (p. 452). Both bound grammatical morphemes such as nominal, adjectival, and verbal inflections, and freestanding grammatical morphemes, such as prepositions, definite and indefinite articles, clitics, and auxiliaries, are absent to various degrees (p. 453). Only some patients retained the ability to produce subordinating conjunctions. The same holds for indefinite pronouns, possessive pronouns, and quantifiers. Prepositions were also considerably impaired. Miceli *et al.* (p. 461) conclude that 'no consistent pattern of impairment in the production of freestanding grammatical morphemes is found in our patient series'. Rather, we need scales of retention.

Caramazza and Sloan Berndt (1985: 34–35) report the following overall hierarchy (with descending frequency of omission):

(2)   hierarchy in omission rates

function words	*inflection types*	*morpheme -s*	
determiners	-ed	verb inflection	possessive 's/3.s -s
auxiliaries	-ing	adj inflection	plural -s
prepositions	-s (plural)	noun inflection	
pronouns			
connectives			

It is clear that elements in the core skeleton: Tense, Agreement, and Case, are most easily omitted.

There is no consensus in the literature on the precise criteria for defining the class of missing elements. One theory, mostly associated with the work of Kean (e.g. 1977), is that the fundamental feature of the missing elements is the possibility for them to be unstressed. Goodglass (1968: 206) reports in an early study 'we find that the omission of function words is primarily correlated with the rhythmic patterning of aphasic speech'. A second theory assumes that it is the grammatical status of the elements that is crucial. Bennis *et al.* (1983) argue that of the different uses of some multi-functional Dutch prepositions, the lexical and sub-categorised uses are much harder to process than the syntactic uses for Broca patients, and the reverse for Wernicke patients.

Froud (2001) had a specific patient perform an English reading task, in which both lexical and functional elements had to be read in isolation. This particular patient had a remarkable deficit: lexical elements were read with relative ease, but functional elements were only read correctly 30% of the time. At the same time this patient showed reasonable comprehension and even production of functional elements in extended discourse. Strikingly, all prepositions were subject to considerable difficulties on this task, classing them with the functional elements. Building on work by Smith and Tsimpli (1995) and Tsimpli (1996), Froud speculates that there may be a UG-centred specific functional lexicon, which was impaired with this patient. Better performance on production and comprehension tasks with current sentences would be due to support from the surrounding lexical elements. However, it is not clear how the category P would be directly UG-centred, given its tremendously variable shapes and also sometimes non-instantiation in the languages of the world.

Menn and Obler (1990a) is a massive and fascinating comparative parallel study of pairs of aphasic patients in fourteen countries with reasonably similar clinical syndromes including parallel interviews, story retelling tasks, etc., and also with control speakers for all of the languages involved. After presenting the material for all of these languages and patients in great detail, Menn and Obler (1990c: 1370–1373) try to summarise the data and conclude that some features of agrammatism are characteristic of all languages studied. These include:

- short phrase length
- slow speech rate
- reduced variety in grammatical patterns
- syntactic simplification.

Similarly, omission of free grammatical morphemes obligatory in normal language use is characteristic of virtually all languages studied. The exception may be the Mandarin Chinese patient studied, who is not capable of producing a coherent narrative; in Chinese there are few purely grammatical morphemes, and such as there are are also often optional in normal speech as well. How do Broca's aphasic patients whose native language is Chinese, a language with very limited functional categories, reduce their syntactic productions? In a more recent study by Packard (2006: 334–337) this issue is addressed in detail. Broca's aphasics drastically underuse the noun modifier particle *de* and sparingly use second-position words. These include adverbs, auxiliaries, location words, instrumental markers, and negation elements. Other function words are used very little as well.

Bound grammatical morphemes are not universally omitted, however, with equal freedom. When the omission of a bound morpheme, e.g. as with third person singular *walk-s* on the verb in English, leads to a semantically less marked but well-formed form in the language (*walk*), it is often omitted (cf. also (2) above); however, when it leads to a non-form (**compr* '(stem of) buy' in Italian) or to a semantically marked form, like the imperative singular (*compra* 'buy!'), it is not omitted (cf. also Badecker and Caramazza 1991, 1998; Bates *et al.* 1987). Menn and Obler (1990c: 1370) conclude that 'an explanation of agrammatism that attempts to directly unify the omission of functors and the relative lack of bound grammatical morphemes cannot work in the general case'. The exceptions are few, and include some omissions of *ge-* past particle prefixes in German and some forms in Hebrew. What is striking is that clitic pronouns are retained more often than strong independent pronouns, contrary to phonological weakening accounts of agrammatism such as Kean (1977).

Other results from the comparison of the different studies include that some patients overuse adverbs, extra-clausal conjunctions, and discourse particles, and that on the whole verbs are more frequently omitted than nouns. As to word order, there is a preference for canonical sentence patterns. Comrie (1990), basing himself on the studies by Ahlsén and Dravins (1990) and Magnúsdóttir and Thráinsson (1990), draws attention to the fact that of two agrammatic speakers of Swedish and two of Icelandic, one of each pair tended to not invert the subject and verb when there was an initial adverb (in the Swedish examples cited the linking element *sen* 'then, later', and in the Icelandic examples *svo* or *þa* 'then'). Non-inverted examples from Swedish include (cited from Comrie 1990: 1361):

(3)   (a) sen **jag pratta** ...
            'then I talked ... '

    (b) sen **ham tar** en famn säd
            'then he takes an armful of corn'

An inverted example from the same speaker (much less frequent but the rule in non-impaired Swedish) would be:

(4)   sen **äter han** mat
       'then eats he food'

Comrie tentatively interprets these findings as evidence for an underlying subject-verb order in Scandinavian. However, the German agrammatism data (Stark and Dressler 1990: 321–322) also show a few cases of deviant order which suggest that other mechanisms are at work:

(5)   Und dan **bei den Kinder[n] bin ich** zu Hause geblieben
       and then with the children am I at home stayed
       'and then with the children I stayed at home'
       (standard: Und dan **bin ich bei den Kindern** zu Hause geblieben.)

Here the verb occurs in third rather than second position, even though there has been inversion of the subject and finite verb (*bin ich* 'am I').

(6)   ...weil **das Mädchen hatte sie** immer [eine] rote Kappe auf [de]m Kopf
       ...because the girl had she always [a] red cap on the head
       '...because the girl always had a red cap on her head.'
       (standard: weil **das Mädchen** immer eine rote Kappe auf dem Kopf **hatte**.)
       (non-standard colloquial: weil **das Mädchen hatte** immer eine rote Kappe
       auf dem Kopf.)

Here the lexical subject precedes the verb (followed then by a resumptive subject pronoun), which should be in final position if *weil* is treated like a subordinating conjunction, and after the subject if *weil* is treated, as many German speakers do, as a coordinating conjunction.

(7)   Der Wolf fragt sie, wo **geht sie** hin.
       the wolf asks her, where goes she to
       'The wolf asked her where she is going.'
       (standard: Der Wolf fragt sie, wo **sie** hin **geht**)

Here the verb is in second position in a subordinate clause, while it should occur clause finally.

What these cases suggest is not so much that a competing grammatical rule is operating, but that the agrammatic patients operate without a clearly articulated clausal structure with a functional skeleton, where the presence or absence of Tense and Complementiser positions would trigger the appropriate verb placement rules. It is not clear what rules to use to account for the word order in these sentences, but certainly canonical SVO strategies may be part of what patients operate with in the Germanic languages. It should be mentioned that in the Dutch agrammatism corpus presented and analysed by Kolk *et al.* (1990) most utterances containing a verb show an infinitive in clause-final position. Work by Kok *et al.* (2006), specifically designed to test the productive capacities of nine agrammatic speakers of Dutch with respect to verb placement in main and subordinate clauses, yielded no specific problems in this area. However, they may not have tested for exactly the same patterns as the ones reported on here.

Case marking and adpositions in agrammatic speech

I will now turn to a cluster of related grammatical phenomena in the various case studies (in the order in which they appear in the Menu and Obler (1990a) book: case marking, adpositions, and pronoun usage). An cross-linguistic overview of the findings of the case studies is given in Table 10.1.

In the *English* case study (Menn 1990: 121), pronominal case is not problematic: the right pronouns are used, although one speaker omitted quite a few of them. Genitive -*s* was impaired, however, to some extent for both speakers. One speaker had considerable difficulty with prepositions, even with lexically determined ones (1990: 126).

The *Dutch* speakers reported on by Kolk *et al.* (1990) had great difficulty with personal pronouns, leading to a high omission rate, and the same holds for prepositions, which are omitted in 46% and 85% of the contexts, regardless of whether it was a lexically determined, a locative, or a grammatical preposition.

The two *German* agrammatic speakers showed some case errors in their use of definite and indefinite articles after prepositions. Gender errors were more frequent than case errors. Many pronouns and most prepositions were correct. Examples of case errors include (Stark and Dressler 1990: 297):

(8) (a) mit **ein-en** Korb
         with a.AC basket (should be *ein-em* [a.DA])
         'with a basket'

    (b) für **ein** Mund
         for a.NOMI mouth (should be *ein-en* [a.AC])
         'for a mouth'

Strikingly, one patient produced nine prepositions where these were not required in the context, almost as fillers. An example would be (9) (Stark and Dressler 1990: 357):

Table 10.1. *Percentage of omissions of obligatory free grammatical and lexical morphemes (cell sizes 8 or more). Table 10.1 is based on Menn and Obler (1990c: 1374–1376, Table 1), with a number of changes. The languages and the categories have been rearranged somewhat and a number of cautionary details have been left out of consideration*

	1	2	3	4	5	6	7	8	9	10	11
German	9	35	16	12	28	—	12	0	6	3	
	10	17	52	50	28	—	7	1	13	3	
Dutch	80	96	100	91	100	80	85	6	19	3	
	28	44	85	56	100	96	46	5	39	2	
Swedish		14	50	0	9	—	14	0	18	X	postp. 10
		16	8	4	4	—	7	2	0	X	0
Icelandic	0	—	X	5	4	—	2	X	2	X	infl. 4
	12	—	X	12	18	—	15	X	11		infl. 22
English	6	0	5	26	—	—	0	3	4	1	
	47	56	82	100	67	—	78	30	12	2	
French	13		50	45	15	53	18	0	5	X	
	3		4	9	1	28	2	0	0	X	
Italian	23	?	57	0	8	?	43	0	20	X	
	11	0	8	25	?	12	0	0	3	X	
Polish	—	—	10	?	40	27	3	0	4	X	
Serbo-Croatian	—	—	?	0	?	80	92	8		10	
	—	—	5	2	4	3	6	0		2	
Hindi	—	—	27	20	13	—	0	0	8	X	
Finnish	—	—	36	50	55	—	?	0	18	20	
	—	—	4	0	5	—	0	0	4		
Hebrew	90	—	60	—	80	—	100	1	22	X	object
	42	—		—	34	—	25	?	17	X	object
Japanese	—	—	X	15	—	—	—		26	X	num/object; topic 61
	—	—	X	2	—	—	100	—	11	X	topic 91

Note: 1 definite article 2 indefinite article
3 have/be main verb 4 auxiliary verb
5 strong personal pronouns 6 weak personal pronouns
7 pre/postpositions 8 coordinating conjunctions
9 lexical main verbs 10 nouns
11 other

(9)   Die Kinder wollen **in** wollen Keks
         the children want in want cookies.
         'The children want cookies.'

Magnúsdóttir and Thráinsson (1990: 450–453) report on *Icelandic* agrammatic speakers, one of whom shows particular difficulty in selecting the appropriate case for the noun and associated article (in over 30% of the contexts). For pronouns, there is no wrong selection of case forms, although often (18%) pronouns are omitted. Only 15% of the prepositions were omitted by this speaker (preserving the appropriate case selected by this preposition). As in German, there are some superfluous prepositions, and a number of wrongly selected prepositions.

The *Swedish* speakers described by Ahlsén and Dravins (1990) omit prepositions and pronouns only sporadically. One speaker uses pronouns instead of nouns relatively often, and shows frequent gender (f > m) replacement and some person (3s > 1s) replacement.

Nespoulous *et al.* (1990) describe two *French* agrammatic speakers. Strong pronouns are produced correctly more often (83% and 96% respectively) than clitic pronouns (33% and 68% respectively). Omissions are more frequent than substitutions. Among the clitics, reflexives are the best preserved category (45% and 89% respectively). The majority of prepositions are produced correctly (75% and 91% respectively), and of the omitted prepositions many are lexically determined. Some examples of omitted clitics include (Nespoulous *et al.* 1990: 642):

(10)   (a) Le chaperon rouge [lui] donne le panier.
              'The little Riding Hood [pro.DA.3s] gives the basket.'

         (b) ... va chercher le maïs pour [le] porter en ville.
              '... goes look for the corn in order to take [PRO.3s.m] to town.'

The two *Italian* speakers (Miceli and Mazzucchi 1990) likewise produced strong pronouns (92% and 100% respectively) more correctly than clitic pronouns (33% and 80% respectively). For prepositions, the correct productions are 54% and 92% respectively, with one patient showing frequent omissions, both of prepositions in isolation and of prepositions combined with determiners.

Jarema and Kądzielawa (1990) have analysed the *Polish* speech of one agrammatic patient. In contrast with the Italian and French data, clitic pronouns were correctly supplied more often than strong pronouns (68% versus 53%). The majority of the clitics were reflexives. Omissions were more common than substitutions. Prepositions were overwhelmingly (92%) produced correctly.

Of the two *(Serbo-)Croatian* speakers studied by Zei and Šikić (1990), one speaker omitted 40% of the pronouns (all types taken together), and 92% of the prepositions. The other speaker had an overall 96% correct score on pronouns, and 90% on prepositions.

Bhatnagar (1990) studied one *Hindi* agrammatic speaker, who retained 83% of the pronouns (13% were omitted), and 95% of the postpositions. The greatest impairment of functional categories with this patient concerned clause-final verb morphology.

The two *Finnish* speakers studied by Niemi *et al.* (1990) omitted 55% (mostly in object position) and 5% respectively of the pronouns required. Case marking was largely intact for their adjectives, nouns, pronouns, numerals, and relative pronouns. There were very few errors in the prepositions and postpositions. Striking is the 20% noun omission rate (around 60% of omitted nouns are subjects) with both speakers.

Baharav (1990) studied two *Hebrew* speakers. Pronouns are produced correctly only in 13% and 19% respectively of the cases; one patient omits 80% of the pronouns, while the other omits 34% and substitutes 47% of the pronouns. One speaker omits all prepositions expected, while the other retains 50% of prepositions (with an equal number of omissions and substitutions). Both patients handle the Hebrew object marker *et* fairly adequately.

The *Mandarin Chinese* speaker studied by Packard (1990) did not show any substitutions, the few required pronouns also were produced correctly, and no prepositions were required. Nonetheless, the speaker was not able to produce a coherent narrative, and had recourse to an underemployment strategy for those categories affected by omission and substitution in other languages.

To conclude this overview, Sasanuma *et al.* (1990a, b) studied two *Japanese* agrammatic speakers and one crossed agrammatic patient (Mrs Hayasi, with dextral crossed aphasia). Overall, the picture for the three patients is a high retention rate for most categories (except copulas, auxiliaries, and to some degree verbs), and variable retention of the numerous particles of Japanese. The case particles in this set are summarised in Table 10.2. In addition to a number of central clausal particles, including nominative *-ga*, topic marker *-wa*, and object *-o*, Sasanuma *et al.* (1990a) also cite the frequent omission of the quotative marker *-to*. In contrast the inflection like prodicative conjunctive particle *-te* is never omitted. The morphological class of pronouns is absent in Japanese.

It is clear that language-specific features greatly influence the form that the family of agrammatic syndromes takes (Miceli and Mazzucchi 1990 in particular strongly argue against the idea of a single syndrome). DeVilliers (1974) similarly stresses the diversity between the categories affected in different languages.

Table 10.2. *Precentage of correctly produced case markers for two Japanese agrammatic speakers (Mr Saitoo and Mrs Tanaka) and one crossed agrammatic speaker (Mrs Hayasi) (absolute figures for expected contexts in parentheses; based on Sasanuma et al. 1990a, b)*

	Mr Saitoo	Mrs Tanaka	Mrs Hayasi
Particles total	64 (87)	44 (119)	86 (180)
Nominative *-ga*	40 (15)	8 (24)	79 (33)
Topic *-wa*	80 (5)	–	89 (9)
Object *-o*	50 (2)	25 (4)	54 (15)
Possessive *-no*	50 (6)	50 (10)	100 (3)
Oblique *-ni*	75 (4)	0 (17)	88 (17)
Ablative *-kara*	–	0 (1)	100 (10)
Instrumental *-de*	–	0 (5)	100 (1)

Friederici (1982) compares the contribution of syntactic and semantic factors to the processing of prepositions in twelve German agrammatic patients and twelve patients classified as Wernicke's aphasics. Of 28 target sentences in the production condition 14 included fully lexical prepositions as targets that had to be supplemented in a written sentence with a gap, as in (11a), and 14 sub-categorised prepositions, as in (11b):

(11)   (a) Peter steht (**auf**) dem Stuhl.
                 'Peter stands on the chair.'
             (b) Peter hofft (**auf**) den Sommer.
                 'Peter hopes for the summer.'

There was also a perception condition, in which judgements had to be given.

The agrammatic aphasics did significantly worse in the production task on the sub-categorised prepositions (11b) than on the purely lexical prepositions (11a). For the Wernicke patients the reverse result held. Also, there were a number of cross-category substitutions for the (b) class of prepositions with the agrammatic patients (but not with the other group), and no substitutions of this type with the lexical prepositions. For both groups of patients, scores in the perception condition were significantly higher.

Thus Friederici (1982) provides support for the lexical/functional asymmetry in aphasic production, but in her account it is not word class as such that makes the difference, but rather functional role. In a parallel study, Friederici *et al.* (1982) report on English-language aphasics processing prepositions; a similar overall result was obtained regarding the special status of prepositions, although no difference was made between lexical and sub-categorised prepositions.

Structural interpretations of agrammatic speech

There is a large literature which attempts to interpret the phenomenon of agrammatism from a formal generative perspective. Surveying some of the studies from the 1980s and 1990s, de Roo (1999) distinguishes three positions in this literature:

No functional structure. Ouhalla (1993) distinguishes between the UG lexicon and the grammatical lexicon, and claims that in several agrammatic patients the grammatical lexicon cannot be accessed. Clearly, this statement is much too strong, and others have provided more gradualist perspectives.

Truncated functional structure. Hagiwara (1995), cited by de Roo (1999: 197) claims that 'functional projections that are higher in the structure are more impaired in agrammatic speech than functional categories that are lower in the structure'. The theoretical motivation for this is that 'the few number of times the operation Merge takes place, the more economical the resulting structures are, and the more accessible they are to an agrammatic aphasic'. Friedmann and Grodzinsky (1997) support the Tree Pruning Hypothesis and claim that C, T, and Agr are underspecified in agrammatical production, while an underspecified node cannot project any further.

The Tree Pruning Hypothesis of Hagiwara (1995) does have the advantage that different levels of proficiency can potentially be accounted for: the functional category tree would be pruned at various levels of syntactic articulation, thus theoretically for some patients, only CP and the complementiser would be affected, in others the complementiser and Tense (TP), and in more severe cases, even agreement (AgrP) would have been pruned. It is not clear however, that such a tree pruning metaphor is an adequate model of the aphasia data.

Full functional structure. Here the assumption is that the full functional projection is available, but that other factors hinder the production and comprehension of the full structure. This would be in line with the position of Kolk and his colleagues sketched above.

In addition to these three positions there are other attempts to give a structural account of the impairments known as agrammatism. Wenzlaff and Clahsen (2004) have as their central claim that T/INFL is tense-defective for agrammatic patients, and the specification is for [+ Realis] rather than [+ Past]. In their study it was shown that in aphasic speech conjunctions are retained (2004: 57). Regular noun plurals were produced better than possessive marking. They note that tense is not produced as well as agreement in Dutch, German, and Spanish. For English, however, similar error rates have been reported for 3s -*s* and past tense -*ed*, and in Czech and Greek also it has not been shown that tense is harder to produce than agreement for Broca aphasics. However, at least the English and the Greek data are hard to interpret because tense and agreement morphology are linked together.

Specific Language Impairment

Children with SLI 'show a significant deficit in language functioning yet exhibit normal hearing, no evidence of frank neurological impairment, and no signs of serious impairment of social interaction typical of disorders such as autism' (Leonard 1995: 1270). In particular their grip on grammatical morphology is weak. Summarising some of the evidence for English, Leonard (1995) concludes that children with SLI, while showing almost normal nominal plural morphology, show delays in acquiring regular past *-ed*, the use of articles, third person singular *-s*, copula and auxiliary *-be*, infinitival *to*, complementiser *that*, and auxiliary *do*. They also sometimes substitute *me* for *I*, etc. However, in a detailed study of the spontaneous productions of ten children with SLI Leonard found that these children do have access to a wide range of functional categories in the three principal functional category systems:

(12) (a) D (Determiner)-System   articles
                                    pronominal demonstratives
                                    pronominal possessors
                                    genitive *-s*
                                    non-thematic *of*

      (b) I (Inflection)-System   third person singular *-s*
                                    regular past *-ed*
                                    copula and auxiliary *be*
                                    infinitival *to*
                                    modals
                                    auxiliary *do*
                                    nominative case

      (c) C (Complementiser)-System complementisers
                                    auxiliary inversion
                                    pre-subject question words
                                    indirect questions

Thus the idea that these SLI children did not have access to functional categories cannot be correct. At the same time, these children realised these features less systematically, in those cases where an obligatory context could be established, than a group of controls. Nonetheless, the control children did not have perfect scores either. Leonard explores several possible explanations for the weaker performance of the SLI children. A purely performance explanation and a prosodic explanation are not plausible. A child bilingualism explanation would hold there are two grammars: one (A) with, and one (B) without functional categories, and the SLI children would shift from A to B at a slower rate than normal children. Specific instances of this account would be the Deficit of Agreement theory of Clahsen (1989) and the Optional Infinitive theory of Wexler (1994, 2003). In both a stage A is postulated without a specific property (agreement for Clahsen, finiteness for Wexler), followed by a stage B with that property, and the assumption that SLI slows down the transition. Yet another explanation would be that elements with a short phonetic duration are particularly vulnerable to omission by SLI children. Although there is supporting evidence for the Agreement deficit account, the Optional Infinitive account, and the phonetic duration account, none of them can be complete in itself. There have been a few accounts which try to generalise the general intuition that for children with SLI somehow the more grammatical representations are impaired. Van der Lely (1994) claims that the SLI data can best be accounted for in terms of a Representational Deficit for Dependent Relationships (agreement, case assignment, etc.). Hamann *et al.* (1998), on the basis of German acquisition data, argue for a Minimal Default Grammar for SLI children. In their view children with SLI cannot project a structure that unifies the CP shell with the propositional core of the clause, leading to a lack of coherence for the overall structure. Finally, de Jong (1999) stresses the importance of the impaired representation of Argument Structure in the linguistic knowledge of children with SLI. Bishop and Adams (1989) relate pragmatic to grammatical disorders, stressing that semantic overextensions occur mostly with function words (connectives, auxiliaries, and prepositions).

These accounts lead to partially overlapping predictions, and are often language-specific in their inspiration. A cross-linguistic comparison may be able to generate more comprehensive accounts, and in his 1998 book Leonard compares the available data for a number of languages. Leonard (1998: 93–98) summarises some of the data for Italian. SLI children used significantly fewer articles and clitics than controls, and had particular difficulty with the article *il*, probably for phonetic reasons. Prepositions were much less of a problem for these children. Neither were there great difficulties with noun plurals, adjective gender agreement, and third person singular inflections. The children had difficulty with third person plural inflections, except for bi-syllabic forms such as *fanno* 'they do/make' and *danno* 'they give'. As seen earlier in the agrammatic aphasia studies, omission of inflection markers never leads to a bare form in

Italian, but always to a substitution, generally by a simpler form (e.g. *vedono* 'they see' is replaced by *vede* 's/he sees'). Replacement of a finite verb form by an infinitive is very rare in Italian SLI children.

While Spanish children with SLI were roughly similar to Italian children (Leonard 1998: 98–99), French children showed some differences. This could not be studied with Italian and Spanish (which are both null-subject languages), but French SLI children sometimes have difficulties with subject pronouns, particularly the form *il*. In contrast, articles tended not to be omitted by these children. There is evidence of omission of auxiliaries and copulas, but no replacement of finite forms by infinitives, and infrequent verb-agreement errors. Jacubowicz *et al.* (1998: 132, 147) have also studied French children with SLI and argue that in their production the following three dissociations hold:

(13)   (a) *le* DET > *le* PN, i.e. determiner *le* is produced more than clitic
            pronoun *le*
        (b) NOM Cl (*il*) > AC Clitic (*le*), i.e. nominative *il* is produced more
            more than accusative *le*
        (c) REF Cl (*se*) > AC Clitic (*le*), i.e. they produce more reflexives than
            other clitics

There is no significant difference with normal children with respect to the *le* determiner, but a significant difference with respect to the *le* clitic pronoun. The difference between the two *le* forms constitutes evidence against a surface form oriented hypothesis.

For Hebrew (Leonard 1998: 102–104), the picture is quite complex. Children with SLI learning Hebrew had fewer difficulties with verb endings, on the whole, than with other aspects of verb morphology. Similarly the children with SLI had more difficulty with the accusative *et* marker and possibly also the definite *ha*-pro-clitic. On the basis of these findings, Leonard formulates the hypothesis that non-word-final morphemic material is particularly vulnerable for SLI children.

Children with SLI learning German clearly have considerable difficulty with agreement, and as a consequence, with word order, although there is some disagreement about the precise relation between these phenomena.

Swedish children with SLI appear to have difficulty with indefinite (though not definite) articles, some difficulty with auxiliaries, and some problems with finite verb forms. There are also some word order problems, which parallel some of the word order problems that we saw above for Swedish agrammatic patients (Leonard 1998: 115). The child produced (14a) instead of the required (14b), which involved verb second:

(14)   (a) Sen **jag fick** en kompis där.
             then I had a friend there

        (b) Sen **fick jag** en kompis där.
             then had I a friend there
             'Then I had a friend there.'

Leonard *et al.* (2004) cite Wexler's (2003) Extended Unique Checking Constraint, which holds that in child grammars the D features of DP can only be
checked against one functional category. This constraint explains why English,
Italian, and Swedish children with a similar degree of SLI and of similar age
show different proficiency in producing the target language verb morphology.
Italian children are much better than English children in producing agreement
but this is explained because they only need to check Agreement features. This
cannot be the explanation for why Swedish children also perform much better.
here the explanation would be that in Swedish, only Tense needs to be checked.

Conclusions

The evidence concerning the exact factors involved in the disproportional degree
to which the functional categories are affected in agrammatic aphasia and SLI
is mixed. In addition to purely structural accounts we find processing accounts.
Nonetheless, it is clear from the studies surveyed here that different inflectional systems, case endings, and determiners are affected by the two disorders
surveyed.

11 *Language attrition and death*

In this chapter I will raise the issue of whether in language attrition processes functional elements in particular are affected, and if more so than lexical elements. In a survey of the domain under discussion, Sasse (2001b: 1671) writes: 'In attrited languages, function words are often omitted (e.g. copula, Ferguson 1971) or replaced by equivalents from the dominant language (Arvanitika speakers tend to replace almost all conjunctions and many prepositions with their Greek equivalents).' I will begin by illustrating some relevant dimensions of attrition, the sociolinguistic scenarios responsible for its occurrence, and the various hypotheses about the way it is supposed to have occurred. Then I will isolate one particular linguistic topic as the focus of my discussion, case endings, to see how attrition has affected case in different contexts: Gaelic in Scotland, Dyirbal in north-eastern Australia, Hungarian in the United States, German in Jewish émigré communities in London, and Low German in western Siberia. In my conclusion I return to a slightly more general perspective.

The study of attrition

The process of language attrition is a complex one, since the term is used to refer to several different things. First of all, individuals who have left their original speech communities may forget their original language to some extent, depending on how old they were when they left, how much they kept using their language, and how long ago they left. This individual, uni-generational process is even accelerated if it is a second language that someone has learned young but then no longer speaks after leaving the second-language speech community.

A second phenomenon captured under the label of attrition concerns the gradual transformation and decay of a language in a community undergoing language shift. This process of transformation can take place in a migration setting, in which case the original language is generally spoken elsewhere in its full form, and in a setting where an indigenous minority gradually shifts to a language of wider communication, often but not necessarily the national language. In the latter case, when the language is unique to that community, we speak of language endangerment and death.

Campbell and Muntzel (1989: 182ff.) distinguish four 'types' of language death: *sudden death* (when all speakers are suddenly killed or die), *radical death* (when speakers stop using their language, as a means of self-defence), *gradual death* (very common, a gradual shift to a dominant language), and *bottom-to-top death*. In the case of bottom-to-top death, the original community language ceases to be used as a day-to-day language, and is only used for ritual purposes.

All the different sub-types of attrition, individual loss of a first or second language, language shift in a migrant community, and language endangerment and death in an indigenous community, are all extremely frequent, and in themselves by no means uniform.

Language attrition is accompanied by reduction in the structural possibilities of a language, and a gradual diminishing of the resources in the different components. In phonology, we find the disappearance of oppositions with a lower functional load and the overgeneralisation of unmarked features. In morphology we find a decreasing amount of allomorphy and of levelling of paradigms. In syntax there is the overgeneralisation of specific canonical patterns, loss of grammatical devices and of syntactic resources. These processes are most apparent in the case of gradual attrition and death, to be sure, and in addition there is wide variability between individuals in the rate at which the process takes place.

An impressive number of attrition studies have been carried out in the past decades. While traditionally descriptive linguists working on poorly described but endangered languages tended to pay little attention to the portions of their data showing considerable attrition, more recently field linguists have dedicated specific studies to this phenomenon, as it became a topic of wider academic interest and social and cultural concern. We also find a keen interest in migrant or export varieties of a number of languages, initiated by Haugen with his work on Norwegian in the United States.

The attrition of Brule Spanish in Louisiana, across various generations, as described by Holloway (1997: 197–198) is typical of the grammatical effects of the process of attrition:

(1)   (a) analytical future marking with an auxiliary
        (b) highly variable morphology
        (c) reduced allomorphy
        (d) reduction in the Tense Modal Aspect system

(e) the two copular verbs *ser* and *estar* fused, the verb *tener* used as
   an existential
(f) declarative word order in questions.

It is clear from examples such as this one that attrition has a considerable effect on the functional categories of a language. The question is of course whether all functional categories are affected at an equal rate, and if not, what causes their differentiation. As it appeared from the data available that there are different states of attrition, and various factors and hierarchies have been proposed to account for this. Some are more grammatical in nature, others more psycholinguistic. The most systematic discussion is found in Lambert and Moore (1986: 180; cf. also Smits 1996). Even if we are often considering attrition effects within communities, the constraints on it are formulated in terms of the individual speaker. Also, there is a good chance that the factors listed below will overlap in their effect on the rate of retention of particular structures:

The *recency* effect has to do with how long ago a particular item or structure was used by a speaker; the more recently used, the better retained. It is clearly something most directly relevant to individual language use.

Frequency of reinforcement has to do with the way frequent use reinforces a particular item or structure in the linguistic competence of individuals.

The *complexity* of structures likewise will play a role: highly complex structures will be subject to more rapid attrition.

The degree to which elements or structures *contrast* also influences the rate of attrition, as does their *linguistic distinctiveness*. Distinctive and contrasting elements will be retained more often.

The *irregularity* of a pattern will certainly contribute, everything else being equal, to its more rapid loss.

Another factor that may play a role is the *centrality* of a certain structure to the core of the linguistic message; more central elements will be retained longer.

Functional load concerns the idea that certain contrasts or positions in language play a more central role in distinguishing words and structures than others.

Elements with a high *pragmatic load* will be retained longer, since they are important to patterns of use.

Regression was proposed by Jakobson (1971a) originally for aphasia, but it assumes that the order of loss of functional categories is the inverse of the order of their acquisition (the last in, first out principle).

The *animacy* hierarchy is based on the idea that certain categories are more animate than others (the pronoun 'I' > nouns; nouns for humans > nouns for objects, etc.). Presumably elements high on the animacy hierarchy would be retained longer.

Keeping these various factors in mind, I will now briefly describe a number of language contact situations in which attrition has been reported, focusing on the case system. It should be kept in mind that in this survey I will generally not discuss various language contact features – which are almost invariably present – such as code-mixing, lexical and structural borrowing, and phonological changes. This is in spite of the fact that these tend to interact with the attrition phenomena in crucial ways.

Gaelic in Scotland

Dorian (1981: 147) shows that there was strong retention of nominal number, verbal tense, and verbal voice markers, but only moderate retention of case markers, of nominal gender, and verbal number. I will consider the attrition of Gaelic case marking in somewhat more detail. East Sutherland Gaelic (ESG), the variety under discussion, originally had four cases: nominative/accusative, genitive, dative, and vocative. Case marking is expressed through the form of the definite article and though mutation of the initial consonant of the noun. This mutation can take two forms: lenition and nasalisation (pp. 129–130).

Of the four cases, genitive is most affected, and moribund in ESG. Plural genitive forms are absent in the speech of contemporary speakers of all generations, and singular genitive is marked by only a few speakers. Others express nominal possession analytically with a preposition. Dative is marked only on masculine nouns with a labial or a velar stop. It is often marked after prepositions, but half the forms marked are not proper datives. There appears to be some maintenance, but possibly mostly in fixed phrases (pp. 131–132).

In the nominative/accusative there often is a form of mutation, but not always of the traditionally correct type. Dative and nominative/accusative are not always kept sufficiently distinct. The vocative case, in contrast, is often well maintained (pp. 133–134). Finally, if we want to establish a hierarchy of the different cases (pp. 135–136), we would arrive at the following:

(2)   genitive < dative < nominative/accusative < vocative

Dyirbal in north-eastern Australia

Annette Schmidt (1985: 44–126) has studied the changes occurring in Dyirbal, a highly endangered language in north-eastern Australia. Working with a translation paradigm, Schmidt elicited Dyirbal utterances from younger speakers, and she was able to contrast their production with the traditional Dyirbal that had been described by Dixon (1972). In addition to the loss of case morphology (to which I return shortly), a number of verbal affixes are lost or undergo a change in distribution. Particularly affected are the reciprocal derivational suffix, the future tense marker, the negative imperative, and switch reference subordination markers. In the pronoun paradigm the dual and plural have been replaced with forms from pidgin. A type of deictic classifier marking that a noun is invisible is also often lost. In the interrogative, the case-marked forms have been lost as well.

In traditional Dyirbal, case plays a fundamental role. There are ten cases, five of which show extensive allomorphy. There is a split ergative system, with nouns following the ergative pattern, and pronouns the nominative/accusative pattern. Given the well-known fundamental syntactic ergative alignment of Dyirbal, what has happened to the case system is of particular interest. Formal changes in the case system include (1985: 61) 'allomorphic reduction of ergative-instrumental, locative-aversive, and genitive case affixes; transference of allomorphs from genitive to dative case; generalizing a single affix to cover various peripheral case functions; loss of suffixation as a means of marking peripheral case roles'. An example is the transformation and eventual loss of the ergative case marker, which went through a number of steps. The Dyirbal ergative case marker originally had several allomorphs, as in (3) (1985: 48–52):

(3) (a) *the suffix -gu occurs with 2-syllable words:*
        girimu-gu   jugumbil   baja-n
        snake-ERG   woman   bite-NFU
        'The snake bit the woman.'

     (b) *for some speakers syllabicity has lost its role, and -gu and -ŋgu alternate*
        girimu-gu~ŋgu jugumbil   baja-n
        snake-ERG   woman   bite-NFU
        'The snake bit the woman.'

     (c) *in the next stage, the suffix -ŋgu is extended to other stems as well*
        walguy-ŋgu jugumbil baja-n
        talpan-ERG woman   bite-NFU
        'The talpan bit the woman.'

(d) *some speakers allow invariant -du after liquids*
guburr-du jugumbil baja-n
bee-ERG woman   bite-NFU
'The bee bit the woman.'

(e) *this -du is then extended to post-nasal contexts*
midin-du   guda bura-n
possum-ERG dog see-NFU
'The possum saw the dog.'

(f) *a few speakers generalise -gu to all contexts*
gugar-gu   guda bura-n
goanna-ERG dog see-NFU
'The goanna saw the dog.'

(g) *finally some speaker leave out ergative case altogether and change the word order*
gugar baja-n   ban jugumbil
goannabite-NFU she woman
'The goanna bit the woman.'

When case marking is gone, sometimes English prepositions come in, and fixed word order also plays an important role. All these morphological changes have had a profound grammatical correlate as well. While morphological ergativity is present for about half of the young Dyirbal speakers, syntactic ergativity in non-purposive clause conjunctions and relative clauses is lost much earlier (1985: 124). However, in purposive clauses, syntactic ergativity (and the use of the anti-passive) survives.

Hungarian in the United States

There has been intensive study of changes occurring in Hungarian in the diaspora, both in the countries surrounding the present-day republic of Hungary, and in Australia and the United States. Fenyvesi (1995/6; 2005) has focused on the development of the Hungarian case system in McKeesport, Pennsylvania. Hungarians have emigrated to the US since the nineteenth century and there are over a million Americans who claim Hungarian descent. Limiting myself to the domain of morpho-syntax, the Hungarian of the US shows a number of special features (Fenyvesi 2005: 289–303). The sharp distinction between the definite (with a definite object) and the indefinite conjugation of the verb has disappeared to some extent. Pre-verbs, a typical feature of Hungarian grammar, have been restructured. Nominal possessive suffixes are sometimes omitted, as well as nominal number markers. Verbal mood and the marking of habitual have been affected, as have different kinds of agreement in the clause. The complex Hungarian system of stress, word order, and focus-movement likewise has been affected.

Hungarian has a very rich case system, with between 17 and 27 cases, depending on how one counts. This system has undergone considerable changes in American Hungarian. First of all, in about half the cases, the suffix has simply been lost, as in (4) (Fenyvesi 2005: 294):

(4)　　a　magyar-0　nehezeb　　vona　　　óvas-ni
　　　　the　Hungarian　more.difficult　be.COND.3s　read-INF
　　　　'It would be more difficult to read the Hungarian [papers].'

Here the accusative marker is lacking (cf. *magyar-t* 'Hungarian-AC'). Around 30% of the case omissions concern the accusative case in American Hungarian. Other cases lost include the essive and other locative cases (around 40% of all omissions), the instrumental, and the dative. For many speakers, the loss of case is accompanied by a shift towards SVO word-order and no focus-movement.

Second, there are quite a number of case substitutions, generally involving the locative cases system: elative > ablative; illative > sublative; delative > illative; sublative, allative, essive > superessive. On the whole, the movement/non-movement distinction in the case system is maintained, but the precise location (*in*, *at*, *on*) is blurred, particularly when no influence from English can be detected. Examples would be (5), where elative (*in*) case is used instead of delative (*on*) (cf. *Magyarországról*), and (6), where superessive (*on*) (cf. *ligeten*) instead of inessive (*in*) is used (Fenyvesi 1995/6: 396):

(5)　　mi　MagyarországboL　jötünk
　　　　we　Hungary-ELAT　　　come-PST-3p-IND
　　　　'We came from Hungary.'

(6)　　ött　a　Ligeten　　dougozot　　　sokig
　　　　she　the　park-SUPER　work-PST-3s-IND　much.term
　　　　'She worked in the park for a long time.'

With placenames, the pattern is quite complicated. In native Hungarian, each placename has a fixed case: 80% have an (on)-case, 20% an (in)-case. In Fenyvesi's data (1995/6: 401), all first-generation speakers replicate this pattern (either (in)- or (on)-case) for US placenames, but second generation speakers are much more variable, tending to use either (in)- or (on)-case with any given placename. This pattern resembles, of course, what was observed above, with blurring on the locative specifications.

The pattern of substitutions is surprising in the sense that in other attrition contexts, involving e.g. American Polish and American Russian, substitution leads to fewer case distinctions, and towards convergence between nominative and accusative (Fenyvesi 1995/6: 391).

German in London

Schmid (2002) studies the attrition, use, and maintenance of their native German by German Jews in Anglophone countries, and focuses on nominal inflection, verbal inflection, and clausal syntax. She discusses (pp. 90–93) the developments in German case in L1/L2 attrition processes and cites Jordens *et al.* (1989), who contrastively test two hypotheses: Jakobson's (1971a) regression theory (which they dub the Linguistic Hypothesis) and the Cognitive Hypothesis, which relies on different cognitive principles, such as IMPL (Implied Person) and DEF (definiteness), to explain the order of attrition.

The Linguistic Hypothesis would predict that dative and accusative conflate in attrition, but this was not found. Still, the order in which German inflection is acquired also predicts the order of attrition, roughly confirming the regression theory:

(7)   Gender/Agreement < Case/Auxiliaries < Agreement

Low German in western Siberia

Nieuweboer (1998) has studied the Plautdiitsch (Low German) of the Mennonite communities in the Altai district of western Siberia. This district was founded in 1907 by Low German speaking Mennonites who moved there from southern Russia, while their origin lies in the Gdansk or Danzig area. These communities have preserved their language, in addition to learning Russian, of course, but the language has undergone some changes. First of all, the semi-auxiliary 'to do', which has a variety of functions in various Low German dialects, has undergone considerable extension in its use and meaning. The case system has also been affected. While most Low German varieties retain the dative/accusative distinction, this has been blurred for many speakers in Altai Plautdiitsch. For these, the original distinction, as in (8) for '(with) a good friend', is replaced by a variety of options, as illustrated in Table 11.1:

Table 11.1. *Variability in case marking in varieties (A–D)*
of the Altai dialect of Plautdiitsch (Nieuweboer 1998: 163)

	A	B	C	D
met öinem (DA) göuden frint	+	+	+	+
öinem (DA) göuden frint		+	+	+
öinen (AC) göuden frint	+	+	(+)	

(8)   (a) mit   einem   guten   Freund
           with a.DA.m   good.DA/AC.m friend

      (b) einen   guten   Freund
           a.AC.m   good.AC/DA.m   friend

Conclusions

After outlining the beginnings of an analytical framework and surveying some
of the factors that have been adduced as contributing to the attrition of functional
categories, this chapter turns to a series of case studies, focusing on the fate of
case systems in East Sutherland Gaelic, Dyirbal, Hungarian in the US, German
in London, and Low German in Siberia. While there are reductions in all case
systems, often leading to the loss of the more specialised cases, particularly if
these have variable realisations, certain core cases tend to be more stable, while
peripheral case endings tend to be more easily lost.

Language contact and bilingual speech

12 *Sign languages*

Deaf speakers all over the world have developed their own sign languages, with elements from already existing sign languages, spontaneous new creations, and rather independently from the spoken languages of the area. As these languages develop, and become the stable languages of Deaf communities, they develop complex systems of functional categories as well, the subject of this chapter. I begin by outlining some of the relevant issues in the study of sign languages, before turning to two concrete issues: mouthing and grammaticalisation in sign languages, and two specific functional domains in the study of these languages: reference tracking and agreement, and classifiers.

[The following sign languages will be referred to in this chapter: AdaSL = Adamarobe Sign Language (Ghana); ASL American Sign Language; DGS = German Sign Language; GSL = Greek Sign Language; ISL = Israeli Sign Language; LIS = Italian Sign Language; KSL = Korean Sign language; LIU = Jordanian Sign Language; NGT = Dutch Sign Language; TSL = Taiwanese Sign Language.]

The study of sign languages

I will not even begin to try and summarise the findings in the rapidly growing field of sign language studies, but will limit myself to highlighting only a few issues. A first question is: are sign languages, deep down inside, like spoken languages? Many sign researchers will answer this question in the positive. However, then the question is: like which spoken languages? In the book by Neidle *et al.* (2000) the position is taken that American Sign Language exhibits the exact range of functional categories that we find in a language like English, such as [Wh], [Neg], [φ-features], [Tense], and [Def]. One of the major conclusions in the study by Neidle *et al.* (2000: 151) is 'the expression of particular features in ASL in more than one syntactic position, thus indicating that the feature is present both as part of an inflected lexical item and as part of a functional head'. Thus there is Specifier-Head agreement within both TP and in DP. In ASL the functional category of Tense dominates Agreement (2000: 152). In the perspective taken here, the differences between ASL and English were of the same nature as those between the different western European languages studied within the generative framework.

Other authors, including Aronoff *et al.* (2003) and Sandler and Lillo-Martin (2006), take a more nuanced view, arguing that universal features of the human language capacity interact with specific properties of the visual/gestural modality of sign languages. This becomes clear for example in the analysis of agreement and classifiers.

Mouthing

Several researchers have studied the role of mouthing in sign languages (cf. Boyes Braem 2001). *Mouthings* is a term for those mouth patterns derived from the spoken languages, while mouth patterns not derived from the spoken languages are often termed *mouth gestures*. There is some disagreement about the relation between the two phenomena; some researchers try to describe them in the same framework and stress possible common features, while others argue that mouthings are not really part of the sign language as such, but the product of interference, borrowing, or code-mixing from the spoken language. Hohenberger and Happ (2001) argue that 'the use of mouthings is best accounted for by a comprehensive psycholinguistic theory of language contact and language change'. In line with this assumption there is also claimed to be a lexical/functional distinction. Functional categories or closed-class elements are shown to typically resist mouthings, whereas lexical categories, or open-class elements, tolerate them.

Grammaticalisation

A good way to start considering the functional categories in sign languages is through their development. Pfau and Steinbach (2006) explore various cases of grammaticalisation in a wide variety of sign languages. Since historical evidence is lacking, the authors had to rely on the method of historical reconstruction. In their extensive overview, the authors distinguish between sign language internal grammaticalisation (which resembles the processes that we find in spoken languages) and processes by which gestures turn into functional categories in sign language. With respect to the first category, they conclude that there are cases of grammaticalisation involving tense and aspect markers, modals and auxiliaries,

Table 12.1. *Instances of grammaticalisation within the sign languages*
themselves reported on in Pfau and Steinbach (2006)

Source	Target	Sign languages
FINISH	COMPLETIVE	ASL, LIS
READY, ALREADY	COMPLETIVE	ISL, DGS, NGT
GO-TO	FUTURE	ASL
STRONG/POWER	CAN	ASL
DEBT/OWE	MUST	ASL
LOCUS INDEX	INDEX	VARIOUS
GO-TO	AGR AUX ACT-ON	NGT
SEE	AGR AUX	TSL
MEET	AGR AUX	TSL
PERSON	AGR AUX	DGS
ONE PERSON	SOMEONE	DGS, NGT
PERSON	OBJECT MARKER	ISL
REASON	BECAUSE	DGS
UNDERSTAND	PROVIDED THAT	ASL
FOLLOW	AS A CONSEQUENCE OF	NGT
TRUE	VERY	ASL
STRONG	PREDOMINANTLY, MAINLY	DGS
HIT	VERY MUCH	AdaSL
EMPTY	NEG EXISTENTIAL	LIU
SLOWLY	NOT YET	LIU
REFUSE	INTRANSITIVE	AdaSL
GIVE	CAUSATIVE	GSL

complementisers, agreement, serial verbs, negative existentials, etc. As such,
sign languages are no different from spoken languages, which show the same
range of grammaticalisation phenomena. An example of grammaticalisation
would be the use of GIVE as a causative marker in GSL. Compare (1a) and
(1b):

(1)   (a) INDEX$_1$ TEACHER BOOK $_1$GIVE$_3$
            'I give the book to the teacher.'
       (b) INDEX$_2$ $_2$GIVE-AUX$_3$ BURDEN END
            'Stop being a burden to her.'

In (1a) the verb GIVE is used as a main verb, while in (1b) it modifies the lexical
verb END as a causative marker.

In Table 12.1 an overview is given of the grammaticalisations covered in the
analysis of Pfau and Steinbach.

There are also a few affixes in sign languages, which have developed out of separate lexical elements. One example is the ASL word ZERO, which has developed into an affix meaning NOT AT ALL. Likewise the DGS Person Agreement Marker is developing into a clitic on the verb and possibly even an affix, and in several sign languages the noun PERSON has developed into an agentive suffix.

Pfau and Steinbach conclude by stressing the similarities between grammaticalisation processes in spoken and in signed languages. Indeed some of the processes are strongly reminiscent of what we find in the grammaticalisation literature surveyed in chapter 6. However, the number of differences is striking as well. The auxiliaries developing out of nouns are unusual, as noted by the authors, but the specific semantic choices made in the grammaticalisation paths in sign languages are certainly not always very typical of what we find in spoken languages. Perhaps when a more complete comparative survey has been done, it will be possible to state how similar or different the processes really are.

There may be modality-specific aspects of grammaticalisation in sign languages as well, however. These have to do with manual and non-manual gesticulation entering sign language grammars as functional elements. A case in point is head shaking, which has been grammaticalised in DGS and ASL as a negation marker, and may replace the manual sign for negation. Raised eyebrows have come to be interpreted as question and topic marker in a number of sign languages. Also we find a palm-up gesture in clause final position as a question particle, as in (p. 37):

(2)   (a) $\overline{\text{CHILD ANGRY G-WH}}^{\text{wh}}$
            'Why is the child angry?

       (b) $\overline{\text{INDEX}_2 \text{ AGE G-WH}}^{\text{wh}}$
            'What is your age?'

The most important sets of functional categories related to gestures, however, are the agreement and the classifier systems. They will be treated below.

Another way to approach the issue of grammaticalisation is through studying the evidence from village sign systems. In contrast with the sign languages of relatively large signer communities, such as ASL or DGS, there are also sign languages used in small village signer communities, many of which have a proportionally high number of deaf signers, but also hearing signers. Nyst (2007: 22) lists a few of the features characteristic of such systems, on the basis of the available literature:

(a)   Relatively few, and also rather unmarked, hand shapes
(b)   A large number of locations for signing
(c)   A large signing space
(d)   A high degree of iconicity
(e)   Extensive use of different channels and non-manual elements.

By and large, Nyst's own fieldwork on AdaSL in Ghana confirms these tendencies for the village sign language that she studied.

Reference tracking and agreement

Zimmer and Patschke (1990) explore the pointing signs in American Sign Language, arguing that these can function both as determiners (combined with a noun sign) and as pronouns (by themselves). Pronouns in sign language involve 'the indexing of a particular area in signing space' (1990: 202). They are not marked for gender and case, but can refer to signer, addressee, and third referents. When pointing signs are combined with a noun they can precede it (3), follow it (4), or be signed simultaneously (5) (1990: 205).

(3)   SEE DET GIRL
      'He saw a girl.'

(4)   OTHER SISTER DET COME
      'The other sister came over.'

(5)   SAME MAN/DET CLI:ONE PERSON-MOVES-TOWARD-ANOTHER
      'The same man was walking towards her.'

Determiners in ASL are only used with 'concrete nouns that refer to specific entities' (1990: 207) and are impossible for example with generic expressions.

There has been considerable discussion about the status of these elements. Lloyd McBurney (2002: 365) argues that signed personal pronouns may in fact be demonstratives, if you consider all their typological characteristics in a cross-linguistic perspective.

In their chapter on Tense and Agreement, Neidle *et al.* (2000: 63–85) argue that Agreement can be established both manually and non-manually. The projection of Tense is external to that of Agreement. There are locations in space to represent referential entities, and there is joint articulation of the signing space with respect to third person referents (2000: 30). Verbs are divided into different classes regarding their agreement capacities. Subject agreement is prefixal, and object agreement is suffixal (2000: 33). There is also marking of definiteness:

definite objects occupy a point in space, and indefinite objects an area in space (2000: 34). Given the variety of positions in signing space, the agreement system is not really a system in terms of person features (2000: 36). The non-manual marking of agreement involves head tilt and eye gaze, which are 'manifestations of abstract agreement features located in the heads of functional projections', according to Neidle *et al.* (2000: 33–4), also occurring with verbs that show no manual agreement. With transitive verbs, head tilt marks subject agreement and eye gaze marks object agreement (2000: 65), while with intransitive verbs either device may be used (2000: 69). From the perspective of the pro-drop parameter, the rich agreement system of ASL licenses null-arguments in both subject and object positions (2000: 71).

Liddell (2000: 318) argues that in ASL, when entities referred to are present, signs indicating verbs and pronouns are simply directed at these entities, and thus cannot be viewed as grammatical agreement in the proper sense. He thus takes a less grammatical view of the agreement properties of ASL.

Aronoff *et al.* (2003: 55) claim that sign languages have agreement involving classifiers because they represent the objects agreed with directly and iconically. The abstract representation for a verb in sign language is as in (6):

(6)

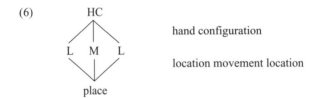

All sign languages use a system that represents the location and movement of objects in space (p. 63). In addition, the hands can be used to mark the nature of the objects. Aronoff *et al.* (2003: 65) distinguish between size and shape classifiers (the semantic classifiers), entity classifiers (delineating broad classes of objects), and handling classifiers. These will be the subject of the next section.

Lillo-Martin (2002) also argues against Liddell's position. The first person and plural agreement markers do have a specific shape (p. 249). Furthermore, the agreement process in sign languages is heavily constrained syntactically (p. 250), which is unexpected if it were simply a pointing system. Only a sub-set of verbs mark agreement at all. Finally, agreement in sign language interacts with different syntactic phenomena, e.g. in the licensing of null arguments (p. 251).

Classifiers

In their careful summary of the research literature Sandler and Lillo-Martin (2006: 77) argue that with the dominant hand in sign language three kinds of classifiers can be signalled: Size and Shape Specifiers (SASSers), entity classifiers, which refer to 'general semantic classes', and handling classifiers. The non-dominant Hand expresses properties of secondary objects, and the ground in Figure/Ground relations (2006: 83). They cite Talmy (2001a, b), and argue that thirty semantic properties in ASL are expressed through classifier constructions:

(7)   Entity properties   5 types
        Orientation   3
        Locus   1
        Motion   4
        Path   10
        Manner   2
        Relation of Figure/Path to Ground   5

Sandler and Lillo-Martin also link the discussion of classifiers in sign languages to verbal classifiers.

Citing Glück and Pfau (1998: 62) they argue that in DGS classifiers are agreement markers, since they cannot occur without an overt noun present. Thus (8) is ungrammatical.

(8)   *MAN-IND$_1$ WOMAN-IND$_2$ THREE $_1$GIVE$_2$-CL$_{FLOWER}$

The ungrammaticality of (8) constitutes an argument against noun incorporation.

According to Zwitserlood (2003), who studied classifiers in Sign Language of the Netherlands (NGT), classifiers in sign language have two functions in the system: a grammatical function, as agreement markers, and a lexical function, as roots. This raises the question, of course, of grammaticalisation: how are these two functions related? In Zwitserlood's research, two types of classifiers, viz. entity classifiers and handling classifiers, are systematically linked to arguments of verbs of motion and location. The classifier on the verb can be used to signal referents that have been left unexpressed but were introduced in the preceding discourse. Classifiers can also be used both in 'frozen' signs and in productively created signs, the components of which (hand shape, movement, location) can be morphemes. Frozen signs are analysed by Zwitserlood as compounds formed from two or more roots. Classifiers in sign languages are thus multi-functional. On location and motion verbs they function as agreement markers. Elsewhere they are lexical and function as compound roots. This link between classifiers and agreement is confirmed by data from KSL, since according to Hong (2001), KSL agreeing verbs occur with person classifiers.

Schembri (2003) questions the close link between classifiers in signed and spoken languages, given that many of the loci referred to in the signs are based on non-linguistic gestures (p. 9). He cites Supalla (1982) on the point that the forms in the signed classifier verbs are fairly late in the development of children's sign languages. Thus he prefers the term 'polycomponential verbs', which again can be roughly divided into verbs of motion and location, handling verbs, and verbs of visual/geometric description.

Indeed, following Aikhenvald (2000) and Grinevald (2000), Zwitserlood (2003: 175) argues that verbal classifiers in spoken languages have the following features:

(9)   (a) they are overt, bound morphemes;
         (b) they are always linked to an argument of the predicate, usually the
              subject of an intransitive and the object of a transitive verb;
         (c) the argument may be overtly realised as a DP or not;
         (d) not all nouns are related to a classifier, and some nouns may be
              associated with more than one classifier;
         (e) they are semantically motivated, and their use is often limited to
              certain semantic verb classes, and they categorise the element in their
              scope in terms of animacy, shape, position, etc.;
         (f) they constitute a morpho-syntactic sub-system;
         (g) they are not obligatory, subject to discourse/pragmatic conditions of
              use, and the classifiers are used for reference tracking in discourse.

According to Zwitserlood (2003: 179), the only class of verbal classifiers in sign languages that resemble those of spoken languages are those modifying verbs of location, motion, and existence.

Conclusions

In sign languages the lexical/functional distinction plays a role in various domains: mouthings can involve only lexical, not functional elements. Grammaticalisation in sign languages parallels that in spoken languages, although there are some interesting differences as well. The reference tracking and agreement system in sign languages interacts closely with the classifier system. There is no agreement as yet to what extent the classifier system in sign languages is like that in spoken languages.

13 *Code-switching and code-mixing*

An asymmetry between lexical and functional categories is also found in the type of language mixing that we find in bilingual usage. Many bilinguals will use two languages when speaking to other bilinguals in in-group conversations. Sometimes they will even mix their languages within the same sentence, often by introducing an element from a second language into a first language utterance. In many cases of this particular sub-type of this mixing process, that is referred to as insertional mixing, grammatical elements tend to come from the base language they are speaking, and only lexical elements can come from the inserted language. The chapter will explore the different explanations that have been given for this phenomenon, as well as carefully reviewing the evidence presented for the restriction just mentioned. Given the fact that fragments from both of the languages are really interspersed in most of the utterances discussed in this chapter, I will use the term 'code-mixing' here (cf. Muysken 2000), even if in the general literature often 'code-switching' is used.

The basic phenomenon

I will start out by giving a number of examples of code-mixing involving Dutch and one of the minority languages in the Netherlands. The bold elements in the glosses reflect elements from the base languages, often functional in nature; the italicised elements are the inserted words. These tend to be lexical elements; lexical elements can but need not be from the non-base language, grammatical elements need to be from the base language, as can be seen in the examples.

(1) *Sranan/Dutch* (Bolle 1994: 75)
     wan heri *gedeelte* de ondro *beheer*   fu *gewapende machten*
     one whole part   **be under** control **GE/BEN** armed forces.'
     'One whole part is under the control of the armed forces.'

(2)   *Chinese/Dutch* (Tjon 1988: 8)
Ngai yew *krampen in* nga *buik.*
1s have cramps in **1s.PO** stomach
'I have cramps in my stomach.'

(3)   *Moroccan Arabic/Dutch* (Nortier 1990: 138)
9end-na bezzaf bezzaf *moeilijkheden* u *problemen met . . .*
have-1p much much difficulties **and** problems with
'We have many many difficulties and problems with . . .'

The type of mixing process illustrated in (1) to (3) is uni-directional: the base language tends to be the community language of the migrant group, and the inserted language the dominant national language. While in most of the cases illustrated the distinction between the categories is fairly clear, there are some examples of indeterminacy: while in (1) the preposition *ondro* 'under' is realised in the base language Sranan, in (2) the preposition *in* is realised in the inserted language Dutch. Notice also that plural marking can easily come from the inserted language.

Similar examples of code-mixing are given in (4) and (5):

(4)   *Turkish/Dutch* (Backus 1992)
ben *kamer*-Im-I *opruim-en* yap-ar-ken
1s room-**1s-AC** tidy-INF **do-PR-while**
'while tidying my room'

In example (4) the italicised content words *kamer* 'room' and *opruim-en* 'tidy' are from Dutch, and the functional categories, some of which are affixes, are from Turkish. Notice also the Turkish auxiliary or light verb *yap-* 'do', which is combined with the Dutch infinitive *opruim-en* 'tidy'. Note, however, that *opruim-en* contains the Dutch infinitive marker *-en*, which is a functional category, at least in monolingual Dutch.

The next, highly complex, example comes from the mixed language, often termed Melayu Sini, of second generation Moluccan Malay speakers in the Netherlands.

(5)   *Moluccan Malay/Dutch* (Huwaë 1992)
aku *nog steeds vind-en* akan *raar* [kata koe *bell-en* aku *twee keer* [*zonder* dapat *gehoor*]]
1s still find-INF **it** strange **that** 2s call-INF **1s** two time without **get** response
'I still find it strange that you called me twice without finding anyone home.'

Again we note that in (5), there is a division of labour between Dutch and Moluccan Malay. The words from the two languages are given in (6):

(6)   (a) *Dutch*   (b) *Malay*
            nog steeds 'still'   aku 'I'
            vind-en 'find-INF'   akan 'it'
            raar 'strange'   kata 'that'
            bell-en 'call-INF'   koe 'you'
            twee keer 'two times'   dapat 'get'
            zonder 'without'
            gehoor 'response'

Although Malay is typologically very different from Turkish, we get a very similar division of labour: Malay provides the functional category elements (all of them words here), Dutch the content words.

Again, we have to treat the infinitive ending as an exception. In fact, in both (4) and (5) it is best analysed as part of the Dutch stem. Hence it is not a counter-example to the generalisation in (7a), drawn up on the basis of examples (1–5). The formulation given by Myers-Scotton (1993: 83), who proposed the System Morpheme Principle, with a similar purpose, is given in (7b):

(7)   Basic lexical/functional assymmetry
        (a) In code-mixed sentences, functional category elements come from one language, while lexical categories may come from the other one.
        (b) In Matrix Language + Embedded Language constituents, all system morphemes which have grammatical relations external to their head constituent (i.e. which participate in the sentence's thematic role grid) will come from the Matrix Language.

Examples 1–5 were specially chosen because they contain a large proportion of the content words from the second, inserted, or embedded, language. In other cases, there will be many fewer inserted content words. However, these cases are also covered by the generalisation in (7).

The wider phenomenon

If the generalisation in (7) were correct, all cases of code-mixing would be like the examples in (1–5). This is not the case. We find a number of exceptions, and indeed, (1–5) may not be typical. Consider a fairly typical example such as (8) from a South African township (from Finlayson *et al.* 1998: 408):

(8)   *So*   i–*language*   e-khuluny-w-a   a-ma-*gangs*
        so   CL9-language   CL9/REL-speak-PASS-FV   P-CL6-gangs

        it differs from one gang to another   si-ngeke
        it differs from one gang to another   1p-never

si-thi   a-ya-fan-a   *because it depends*
1p-say   CL6-PRE1-like-FV   because it depends

ukuthi le-ya   i-*involved*   ku   *which activity*
COMP CL9-DEM   CL9-involved   LOC.CL16   which activity

'So the language which is being spoken by gangs differs from one gang to another, we never say they are alike because it depends as to which one is involved in which activity.'

In this example we find a number of deviations from the examples given in (1–5) above.

First, some content words are in Sotho rather than English, like *khuluny* 'speak'. As noted, this is very general in code-mixing; often just a few elements in a mixed sentence come from a different language.

Second, there are longer English fragments, such as *it differs from one gang to another* and *because it depends*. In these fragments content elements, functional elements, and grammar are entirely English. The fragments are termed 'EL (embedded language) islands' by Myers-Scotton (1993).

Third, there are some English functional categories present, like plural *-s* on *gang-s* and participle *-ed* in *involv-ed*, contrary to what is predicted in generalisation in (7). Notice that these are part of English words, pied-piped along with the content word. For *involv-ed* it is possible and perhaps even plausible to claim that this is a fixed lexical item. For plural *gang-s* this is likewise an option, but the form does have a plural meaning and there are numerous cases of pied-piped English plural *-s* examples in the data.

The example of *which activity* is likewise a bit problematic. It could be treated like an island, or as a case of pied-piping where a functional question word, adjectival *which*, is introduced along with a content word.

Thus a more complex account of code-mixing is evidently needed than is embodied in principle (7), and a number of proposals have been made, in a still rapidly growing literature. My own interpretation of the rich tapestry of mixing patterns is Muysken (2000). Other recent monographs are Myers-Scotton (2002) and Clyne (2003). An excellent more introductory overview is given in Winford (2003).

In principle (7) the functional/lexical distinction is brought into bearing again. Earlier approaches to insertional mixing had already underlined the phenomenon of retained function words in code-mixing. It has been known for some time now (Lehtinen 1966; Joshi 1985; Myers-Scotton 1993) that in the mixing process, grammatical elements tend to come from the base language they are speaking, and only lexical elements can come from the inserted language. We have already seen the evidence for this in (1–5). In the sections to come I will further evaluate this evidence.

Language distance and equivalence

Before continuing with the evaluation of principle (7), it may be important to stress that the equivalence that speakers construct between their utterances almost surely plays a role in language contact, and in constraining mixing possibilities between languages.

Consider as an example the case of pronouns, elements that should be taken from the matrix language in code-switching and are resistant to borrowing. Giesbers (1989) has shown in his study on Ottersum (northern Limburg) dialect contact that a number of pronouns can be switched as separate elements in his corpus of Dutch dialect/standard contact (cf. the discussion in Muysken 2000):

(9)   personal   74
         reflexive   4
         possessive   4
         indefinite   22

An example is (10), where the switch takes place between the finite verb and the subject clitic *ie* 'he' (Dutch fragment in italic) (Giesbers 1989: 96):

(10)   . . . ik zei mossele da [mag-*ie*] *toch helemaal nie*
          I said mussels that may-he still completely not
          '. . . I said mussels he is not allowed them, is he?'

Similarly we find separate Spanish pronouns in Catalan/Spanish code-mixing, as studied for example by Vila i Moreno (1996). Notice that in these cases the pronouns are not in topic or focus position, in contrast with the examples to be discussed below (from Vila i Moreno 1996: 393, 419).

(11)   (a) això *a el* a ell no li i(m)porta
              this to PN.3.m to PN.3.m not CLI.3 matters
              'This he, he doesn't care (about).'

          (b) i *el* va taller el cap
              and PN.3.m PST.3 cut the head
              'and he cut his head'

Examples such as these suggest that in cases of related language varieties, the lexical/functional asymmetries that are the topic of this chapter are weaker or absent altogether.

Problem areas

I now turn to a number of problems, at first sight at least, for the principle in (7). These involve doubling, leaking, noun phrase insertion, pronouns, and prepositions.

Problem 1: Doubling.   A frequent phenomenon in code-switching involves the doubling of a functional category from the embedded language with one from the matrix language. Doubling involves particularly plurals (12), adpositions and case markers (13–14), and sometimes conjunctions (15).

The doubled plural case has often been noted. The embedded language plural ending occurs next to the embedded lexical noun stem, and external to it is the matrix language plural. The following two plural nouns occurred in Papiamentu texts (Muysken 2000: 173):

(12)   (a)   muiz-**en-nan**
                mouse-p_{Du}-p_{Pap} 'mice'
         (b)   muis-je-**s-nan**
                mouse-DIM-p_{Du}-p_{Pap} 'little mice'

All cases of plural doubling, as far as I know, involve affixes, particularly suffixes.

Less common is the combination of a post-nominal case marker and a preposition. This combination, as in (13a), was shown to be very rare in Finnish/English code-mixing by Poplack *et al.* (1987: 54), and it is not mentioned in other sources for Finnish/English code-mixing. Nishimura (1986: 139), in contrast, reports several cases from Japanese/English code-mixing (as in (13b)), and there are reports of this phenomenon for other language pairs (including Persian/Turkish and Spanish/Quechua) as well:

(13)   (a)   **to** aorta-**an**
                to aorta-IL   'to the aorta'
         (b)   **for** Sean **ni**
                for Sean-DA   'for Sean'

In Muysken (2000) this doubling is analysed in terms of adjunction, but it could be analysed in term of concord as well, where the preposition further specifies the meaning of the matrix language case marker.

There are also a few cases mentioned where the doubling involves two prepositions, as reported in the work by Hekking (1995: 159) on Spanish elements in Otomí:

(14)   När   hyu-o<u>ku</u>-ngú bi hok<u>u</u> 'nar   ngú   pa **dige** ar   nzöyö
       DET.s RC-make-house PRE.3 make in.s house for for   DET delegate
       'The mason builds a house for the delegate.'

Since the Spanish preposition has been clearly adapted to Otomí, this is probably a case of an established borrowing.

The same pattern is found with some conjunctions in Otomí, as in (15) (Hekking 1995: 168):

(15)   Ja '<u>bu</u>war   när   sei   **ke   nä'ä**   ngi ödi
       be be-LOC.CIS DET.s pulque that   that PRO.2 ask
       'Here is the pulque that you asked for.'

In Muysken (2000: 108–109) the Spanish elements in (14) and (15) are analysed as alternations, that is to say, as basically adjunct to the Otomí-determined grammatical structure.

Problem 2: Affix leaking.   Muysken (2000) points out that there is some leaking of affixes that goes against the principle in (7). These are, again, some cases of plural markers (16), but also past particles (17), and present participles (18).

In the examples in (16), French plural forms appear in an Alsatian German context. The plural markers cannot be heard and are only present in writing, but the words appear in clearly plural contexts (Gardner-Chloros 1991: 165):

(16)   photocopie**s**   'copies'
       carotte**s**   'carrots'

This phenomenon is by no means rare, and in some cases has lead to the borrowing of plural markers, as noted in chapter 17.

More striking perhaps is the appearance of past participle forms of the verb from one language in the other. This is unremarkable in adjectives derived from past participles, but it also occurs with real passives. The examples given in (17) again come from French words in Alsatian German (Gardner-Chloros 1991: 167–168):

(17)   (a) Sie sind *condamnés* worre.
           they are convicted been
           'They have been convicted.'

       (b) Noch schlimmer, wenn de *client recalé* wird am *permis*.
           still worse, when the client failed is at.the licence
           'Still worse when the client is failed on the test.'

Similar examples have been reported for German/English code-mixing in Australia and even Swahili/English mixing in Kenya.

Finally, present participle leaking has been reported particularly in the Spanish/English code-mixing literature. The examples in (18), cited from Muysken (2000: 175), show clearly non-adjectival use:

(18) (a) Mi marido está *working on his master's.*
           'My husband is working on his master's.' (Lipski 1978: 263)

      (b) Siempre está *promising* cosas.
           'He is always promising things.' (Poplack 1980: 596)

Again, this phenomenon, cited by various authors, may be by no means infrequent in Spanish/English code-mixing.

Problem 3: Noun phrase insertion and determiner leaking.   A special type of leaking problem, which has lead to a considerable discussion in the literature, is noun phrase insertion. In some code-mixing settings, for example in Moroccan Arabic/French code-mixing, we find French inserted noun phrases, including the French determiners.

(19)   *Moroccan Arabic/French* (Nait M'Barek and Sankoff 1988: 146)
        ža   *un copain* gallik   yallah nšarbu   *un pot*
        come.PERF a friend   2s.say.PERF let's.go let's.have a drink
        'A friend has come and has told us to go and have a drink.'

(20)   *Moroccan Arabic/French* (Nait M'Barek and Sankoff 1988: 150)
        l wah.ed *une certaine classe* h.ant walla *le luxe*   bezzaf f *les hotels*
        To one   a certain class   has.become   the luxury   more in the hotels
        'Especially for a certain class there is more luxury in the hotels.'

There is a very extensive discussion on these noun phrases, starting with Nait M'Barek and Sankoff (1988), and including Boumans and Caubet (2000), Muysken (2000), and Myers-Scotton (2002), with as yet no real consensus. Some of the relevant observations are:

(a) It is characteristic of Moroccan Arabic/French but not Moroccan Arabic/Dutch code-mixing.

(b) The fact that it is the regular pattern in Moroccan Arabic/French code-mixing precludes an analysis in terms of Embedded Islands.

(c) However, there may be adjectives involved as well, as with *certaine* in (20), and hence an account only in terms of the determiners is not complete.

(d)   A factor to be considered is the obligatoriness and enclitic nature of the French determiner *le/la*, which we also see appearing as a component of the French noun in many French-lexicon creoles.

(e)   There is a superficial similarity between French *le* and the Arabic article *l*.

Muysken (2000: 86) and Myers-Scotton (2002: 119–124) agree in assuming that there must have been some kind of bilingual equivalence established between determiner-like elements in the two languages for the leaking to occur. So far, neither account can explain the presence of other elements, such as French adjectives, within these inserted noun phrases.

Problem 4: Pronouns.   It has frequently been noted that strong pronouns can be inserted as separate elements, even in unrelated languages (cf. the discussion in Muysken 2000: 177–181). Consider the following examples from Moroccan Arabic/Dutch code-mixing (21, from Nortier 1990: 216) and Moroccan Arabic/French code-mixing (22, from Bentahila and Davies (1983: 313):

(21)   Eh *ana* ik heb gewoon . . .
          'Eh I_{Ar} I_{Du} have just . . . '

(22)   *moi* dxlt
          I_{Fr} 1s-went in
          'I went in.'

The best way to deal with these cases is by assuming that strong pronouns fall outside the range of functional categories subject to the principle in (7). Notice that they are often doubled with pronouns from the other language, as in (21), or with agreement markers, as in (22). This type of pronoun insertion is not infrequent; in a similar vein, inserted indefinite pronouns and independently used quantifiers have been reported.

Problem 5: Prepositions.   A final phenomenon that should be mentioned involves independently inserted prepositions. This occurs in various data sets, although not particularly frequently. Poplack (1980: 602) mentions two cases in her Spanish/English corpus from New York (out of 659 switches in total), while no cases are mentioned in Myers-Scotton's Nairobi Swahili/English corpus (1993). Chan (2003) also cites the occurrence of lone English prepositions in Cantonese discourse in his study of English/Cantonese code-mixing.

Nortier (1990: 144–145) likewise reports several cases for Moroccan Arabic/Dutch code-mixing. There are three lone Moroccan Arabic prepositions in Dutch expressions, involving the prepositions *dyal* 'of', *9la* 'on, about', and *fe* 'in'. An example is (23):

(23)   Zijstraat   *dyal* Amsterdamsestraatweg
        Side street of   Amsterdamsestraatweg

In addition, there are five cases of Dutch prepositions inserted into Moroccan Arabic expressions, of which two are used adverbially (*via via* 'through connections' and *boven* 'upstairs'), and the other three all involve the Dutch preposition *als* 'like', as in (24):

(24)   als   muslima   ma-ta-t9iš-š
        like Moslem.f   3.f-be-not-living
        'She does not live like a Moslem woman.'

In Backus' (1992; 1996) corpus of Turkish/Dutch, this type of mixing is not reported and neither can we find it in the Finnish/English data to be discussed below.

Notice that Spanish, English, Moroccan Arabic, and Dutch all have prepositions. It can be concluded that prepositions can only be inserted as separate elements in language pairs where word order is the same in both language pairs, thus falling under the equivalence constraint. Admittedly, in no code-mixing corpus, prepositions are a frequently inserted category.

I conclude that there are five problem areas for principle (7). This has led to further refinements in the definition of functional categories, in the work of Myers-Scotton and Jake (2000). This will be discussed below.

The proper definition of functional categories

For the purposes of the System Morpheme Principle, Myers-Scotton (1993: 99–102) formally defines function elements in terms of quantification and theta-theory: (a) if an element is a potential assigner or receiver of a thematic (semantic) role within the clause it is a content word; (b) if an element quantifies over a certain domain (reminding one of Jakobson's shifters; 1971b) it is a system morpheme. Thus quantifiers are system morphemes in her model, as are elements that are neither theta-role assigners nor theta-role receivers.

These criteria for distinguishing system from content morphemes are problematic for a number of reasons: (1) The [+ Quantifier] feature is not necessary for making the distinction between system and content morphemes, since the features [+ <th> assigner] and [+ <th> receiver] make the relevant distinctions, and hence it is redundant. (2) It is not easy to see how the classification into system and content morphemes can be generalised across languages. In

English the benefactive is expressed by the preposition *for* (thus a theta-role assigning content morpheme), while in Swahili it is an applicative affix, fully part of the grammatical system, and hence a system morpheme. (3) It is not always clear whether an element theta-marks a complement or not. The role of prepositions as thematic role assigners is often not independent from the verb. English *to* theta-marks an object, but often in conjunction with the verb. (4) The criteria conflict with well-established traditional criteria: bound morphemes can be theta-markers, e.g. applicative affixes in Bantu; paradigmatically structured morphemes can be theta-markers, e.g. Finnish case markers.

In more recent work Carol Myers-Scotton and Janice Jake (2000) have developed the 4-M model, which differentiates the class of 'system morphemes' into three sub-classes, which together with content morphemes yield a total of four morpheme classes, hence the name '4-M model'. The three classes are primarily defined as in Myers-Scotton (1993), but additional criteria to distinguish them stem from the level in the speech production process at which they are selected: Content morphemes are directly selected at the lemma/mental lexicon level, while Early system morphemes are indirectly selected at the lemma/mental lexicon level. Bridge late system morphemes are selected at the formulator/functional level, as are Outsider late system morphemes. The two classes of late system morphemes are differentiated in terms of the type of grammatical information they refer to: inside (Bridge) or outside (Outsider) the maximal projection of the head. The four classes are systematically presented in Table 13.1.

A more differentiated view of system morphemes allows Myers-Scotton to respond to earlier criticisms that the System Morpheme Principle did not always make the correct predictions. However, there are some conceptual problems with the 4-M model. There is a major discrepancy between the syntactic definitions and the level of access or selection. There are two levels of access or selection: the mental lexicon and the formulator, but four grammatically defined morpheme types. There is nothing in the production model as such which forces a distinction into four classes of morphemes rather than two. There may be good reasons to distinguish them, but the production model itself does not force the distinction.

In addition, Early system morphemes are a bit of a garbage category: some are featural in content, like gender, number, definiteness, and tense, while others are part of a collocation or fixed combination, and triggered by the more specific lexical item that they are associated with. Thus they fall into two classes: (a) selected through their co-occurrence with another lexical item (*look for*, *make headway*); and (b) selected because they have independent featural content.

Table 13.1. *The four morpheme classes defined in the 4-M model*

Type of morpheme	Syntactic definition	Level of access or selection	Examples
Content morpheme	Assigns or receives thematic roles; does not involve quantification over variables	Directly selected at the lemma/mental lexicon level	horse, walk, busy, under, but
Early system morpheme	Does not assign or receive thematic roles	Indirectly selected at the lemma/mental lexicon level	The, listen **to**, plural -s, my
Bridge late system morpheme	Refers to grammatical information inside the maximal projection of head	Selected at the formulator/functional level	of, possessive -s,
Outsider late system morpheme	Refers to grammatical information outside the maximal projection of head	Selected at the formulator/functional level	third person -s, grammatical case markers

Only a few items, such as *pluralia tantum* (e.g. 'scissor-s'), belong to both classes. Thus, five classes can be distinguished, as in Table 13.2.

It is clear that leaking is only possible with Bridge early system morphemes; this takes care of some of problems (1) and (2). However, the past and present participles in (17) and (18) cannot be treated in this way in Myers-Scotton's model, since they depend for their featural specification on an outside auxiliary, passive or progressive respectively.

Muysken (2000) deals with these cases in terms of lexical equivalence, claiming that when bilingual language users establish specific equivalence correspondences between categories, functional or otherwise, in different languages, code-mixing involving those categories becomes possible. Thus English *-ing* would be viewed as equivalent to Spanish *-ndo*, and French past participles would be viewed as equivalent to German past participles. This equivalence account would be rather immediately linked to the issue of (perceived) language distance. The perception of short language distance may be enhanced by real historical (structural and etymological) relationship, but this relationship is not a necessary condition, as the creole evidence suggests.

Table 13.2. *Revised grammatical classification of five morpheme classes*

	Lexical content	Linked to element with lexical content	Independent semantic contribution	Participates in local feature checking	Participates in feature checking
cheval	+	+	+	+	+
count on	−	+	+	+	+
plural -*s*; diminutive	−	−	+	+	+
Attributive adjective	−	−	−	+	+
Sequence of tenses; long-distance number agreement in anaphora	−	−	−	−	+

Conclusions

While the lexical/functional distinction plays a crucial role in constraining insertional code-switching or -mixing, the precise definition of 'functional' in this area is still a matter of discussion. Problematic in any case are pronouns and prepositions, as well as determiners and affixes closely associated with a lexical noun or verb.

14 *Lexical borrowing*

Not all words are borrowed with equal ease and frequency. A noun such as French *automobile* could be borrowed more easily into English than a conjunction such as *que*. It is possible to formulate constraints on the process of borrowing, and in the literature on lexical borrowing we can find a number of proposals to this effect. There is a tradition of trying to establish borrowability hierarchies and implicational universals of borrowing (e.g. Whitney (1881), Haugen (1950), Moravcsik (1978); for a summary, cf. van Hout and Muysken 1994 and Winford 2003). The traditional observation, with long roots in language contact research, is that different categories can be, or at least are, actually borrowed more or less easily. This observation, which had a somewhat shaky empirical base until recently, has received massive support from the work reported in Poplack *et al.* (1988) for English borrowings in Ottawa French. The finding that nouns are the most frequently borrowed element is confirmed for many other language pairs as well (Nortier and Schatz 1992). For borrowing, constraints can then be formulated in terms of a categorial hierarchy: words of one specific lexical category can be borrowed more easily than those of another. An example of such a hierarchy is (1), partly based on Haugen (1950):

(1)   nouns > adjectives > verbs > coordinating conjunctions >
        adpositions > quantifiers > determiners > free pronouns >
        clitic pronouns > subordinating conjunctions

The problem, however, with a hierarchy such as (1) is that there is no explanation given for the order of the lexical categories in the hierarchies. In addition, it turns out that there are striking language-specific deviations from it.

We find differences between languages in borrowing patterns, for instance, with respect to verbs (Nortier and Schatz 1992); in Ottawa French, English verbs are relatively rare, while in some varieties of Quechua 35% of all Spanish borrowed items are verbs (37.6% of the tokens).

In my view this type of finding should not be taken as negating the value of borrowability hierarchies, but rather as suggesting that they should be treated as diagnostic yardsticks: given overall general patterns, deviations call for specific explanations. In French, verbal morphology hinders the integration of English verb roots. In Quechua, the highly regular agglutinative morphology facilitates incorporation. For the purpose of this study, it is important to note that the hierarchies published concur in having functional categories as less easily borrowed than lexical categories.

I will begin this chapter with an overview of the earlier work on borrowing hierarchies. Then I will present two case studies of particularly intensive language contact: Spanish borrowings in Bolivian Quechua, and Romance borrowings in Maltese Arabic, before concluding with the desiderata for further research in this area.

Spanish borrowings in Bolivian Quechua

The variety of Quechua which has probably undergone most influence from Spanish without undergoing a process of accelerated language shift towards the dominant language is Bolivian Quechua, particularly as spoken in the province of Cochabamba. Quechua/Spanish language contact in the region has been studied by a number of researchers, including Albó (1975), and van Hout and Muysken (1994). On the basis of a small parallel corpus of short Quechua texts (Aguiló 1980) and the translations of these into Spanish done by members of the same community, van Hout and Muysken (1994) developed a model, which can predict, for each class of Spanish words in the Spanish translated corpus, the probability of that word recurring in the Quechua corpus as a borrowing. Through regression analysis, they isolated a number of factors which contributed to that probability. While some factors yielded a significant effect when analysed separately, such as function word status, transitivity, and inflection in the recipient language, the regression analysis revealed that certain factors had a strong independent effect: paradigmaticity and inflection in the donor language. Using the spoken informal 19,000-word Quechua corpus collected by Urioste (1964) in Bolivia in the early 1960s, I have studied the incidence of Spanish elements of various kinds. The starting point is that there has been an extreme amount of lexical borrowing, of both nouns and verbs, as well as of some other word classes and even affixes.

Very striking is the adoption of the Spanish nominal plural marker -*s*, which is extremely frequent and has lead to a restructuring of the Quechua plural marking system. With Quechua roots, ordinarily -*s* occurs after nouns ending in a vowel (123 times in the part of the corpus studied for this purpose), and the original Quechua plural suffix -*kuna* after consonants (10 times). With

Spanish-origin roots, *-es* occurs after consonants (20 times), and *-s* after vowels (175 times). Thus both phonotactics and etymology play a role. Furthermore, we find that two important restrictions on the original use of plural *-kuna* in Quechua have been much less absolute. Originally, nouns could not be pluralised after numerals, and inanimate nouns could not be pluralised. These constraints are present as a tendency though not in absolute terms. We also find occasional double plurals, both N-*s-kuna* and N-*kuna-s*.

A second highly frequent Spanish element in Bolivian Quechua is the diminutive. Its shape in Spanish is determined both by gender (e.g. *-ito* (m) versus *-ita* (f), and by phonotactics (e.g. *-ito* versus *-(e)cito*). In Bolivian Quechua the choice is primarily based on the vowel ending: *-itu* for words ending in *-u*, *-ita* for words ending in *-a*, and *-situ* for words ending in *-i*. Furthermore, other derivational affixes, such as agentive *-dur*, are borrowed occasionally. The large majority of the Quechua affixes, which do most of the morpho-syntactic work of the language, are intact, however.

When we look at lexical roots, the first thing to note is that many elements belonging to categories in the functional domain have been borrowed, but that these involve mostly the more peripheral elements. No personal pronouns have been borrowed, nor copulas or existentials such as the Spanish verbs *haber*, *estar*, and *ser*. There is one borrowed quantifier in the entire corpus, *nada* 'nothing'. Of the deictic pronouns, there are 16 occurrences of *este* .... 'this ...' as a hesitation marker, and two cases of *este* 'this' as a prenominal demonstrative. No other pronominal elements are borrowed. Special mention should be made of the Spanish emphatic negator *ni*, which has been borrowed quite productively.

A number of prepositions have been borrowed, but these do not include basic ones such as *para* 'for', and other basic prepositions are rare, often followed by a pause, and in many cases doubled with a Quechua case marker, such as associative *nin* with *con* 'with', the enclitic *jina* 'like' with *como* 'like', and *-kama* 'until' with *-hasta* 'until'.

(2)   *borrowed prepositions*

en X	'in X'	1
por	'by'	1
sin	'without'	1
con	'with'	5
con X-*nin*	'with X-ASS'	1
como X	'like X'	8
como X-*jina*	'like X-like'	4
como que	'like that'	1

hasta X	'until X'	11
hasta X-*ta-wan*	'until X-AC-WI'	1
hasta X-*kama*	'until X-until'	5
hasta que ..*kama*	'until that .. –until'	1
hasta (Adv)	'until'(Adv)	14

It is clear from (2) that the two prepositions productively borrowed as such are the more peripheral forms *hasta* 'until' and *como* 'like'. The big surprise in this respect is the preposition *a* 'dative, goal, animate accusative'. As shown in (3) it is very often introduced into Bolivian Quechua:

(3)	a ...	'to ...'	53
	a X	'to X'	41
	a na ...	'to HES ...'	7
	al	'to.ART.m'	2

While there are many cases with a pause (53) or a hesitation marker (7), there are also no fewer than 41 cases where the Spanish preposition *a* is directly followed by a nominal complement. This is completely unexpected, both in terms of the form (a single vowel) and the meaning (abstract and in Spanish subject to an animacy restriction) of *a*. The precise meaning and use of *a* in the corpus remains to be studied.

Turning to the borrowed conjunctions, listed in (4), we notice that the Spanish argument-introducing conjunction *que* is present, although relatively infrequent, while the adverbial conjunctions *cuando* 'when', *porque* 'because', and *si* 'if' are productively borrowed. Sometimes, but by no means in the majority of cases, these adverbial conjunctions are accompanied by the Quechua indefinite dubitative marker -*chus*, which has come to function as a subordination marker in southern varieties of Quechua.

(4)	*borrowed simple conjunctions*		
	que	'that'	13
	cuando	'when'	75
	cuando-*chus*	'when-DUB.SUB'	2
	porque	'because'	145
	porque-*chus*	'because-DUD.DUD'	9
	si	'if'	166
	si-*chus*	'if-DUB.SUB'	5
	si X-*chus*	'if X-DUB.SUB'	6
	como si	'as if'	5
	no sé si X-*chus*	'I don't know if X-DUB.SUB'	3

The conjunction *que* 'that' is also sometimes borrowed in combination with a preposition, another conjunction, or a fixed expression, as shown in (5). None of these elements has become productive, however.

(5)　　　*borrowed complex conjunctions involving **que***

para que	'so that'	1
de que	'(of) that'	1
ya que	'now that'	1
ni que	'nor that'	1
y que	'and that'	1
mas que	'for all that'	1
con tal que	'under the condition that'	1
que ni que	'that nor that'	1
donde que	'where that'	1
a punta de que	'at the point that'	1
siempre que	'always when'	2
hasta que	'until that'	2
ña que	'now that'	2
a que	'so that'	3
sino que	'but rather'	4
a pesar de que	'in spite of that'	5

The borrowed adverbs and adverbial expressions are not easy to classify. In (6) I list adverbials modifying the verb phrase. Only *qué tal* 'how', often accompanied by Quechua *-ta* 'accusative', is productive. A basic adverb such as *así* 'thus' does not appear in the corpus.

(6)　　　*borrowed adverbial expressions*

para abajo	'downward'	1
al aire	'to the air'	1
con todo cariño	'affectionately'	1
por algo	'for something'	1
a la mierda	'in the shit'	3
que tal(-ta)	'how(-AC)'	21

Basic temporal adverbs such as *siempre* 'always' and *nunca* 'never' do not occur. From the list in (7) it can be gleaned that only the interchangeable expressions *por/al último* and *por/en fin* 'finally' are somewhat productive.

(7)　　　*borrowed temporal adverbs*

al fin	'finally'	1
al fin y al cabo	'so at the the end'	1
en punto	'sharp'	1
a veces	'some times'	2

tal hora	'at such and such an hour'	2
por último	'at last'	3
al último	'finally'	5
por fin	'finally'	6
en fin	'finally'	13

Of the degree or quantity adverbials, only *casi* 'almost' is productive, as shown in (8). Basic forms such as *mucho* 'much' or *muy* 'very' do not occur.

(8)   *degree or quantity adverbials*

casi-*rajta*	'almost still'	1
casi-*puni*	'almost for sure'	1
casi-sito	'almost (DIM)'	1
al menos	'at least'	1
por igual	'equally'	1
en grandes	'in large part'	2
por una parte	'in part'	2
por lo menos	'at least'	2
sobre todo	'especially'	7
casi	'almost'	25

While Quechua has an elaborate system of evidentials, briefly sketched in chapter 2, only a few Spanish clausal modifiers are productively borrowed, as illustrated in (9): *tal vez* 'perhaps', and *es que* 'it is [the case] that'. These may correspond to Quechua *-cha* 'dubitative' and *-mi* 'affirmative', respectively. Forms involving *acaso* 'perhaps' are never borrowed.

(9)   *borrowed clausal modifiers*

por ejemplo	'for instance'	1
en cambio	'in exchange'	1
en primer lugar	'in the first place'	1
a lo mejor	'at most'	1
más bien	'rather'	1
a lo *astawan*	'to the most'	1
así es que	'thus it is [the case] that'	3
sin embargo	'nonetheless'	3
es que	'it is [the case] that'	5
tal vez	'perhaps'	11

A few interjections are productively borrowed: *a ver* 'let's see', *pues* 'well, then', *claro* 'clearly', and others occur as well, but less frequently. Obviously, some of these elements are difficult to classify, because they occur in the Quechua texts in a 'looser' structure than their syntactic role would have been in Spanish.

(10)   *borrowed interjections*

claro que	'clearly that'	1
por favor	'please'	1
resulta que	'it turns out that'	1
entonces que	'then that'	1
arí que	'yes that'	1
con razón	'with [good] reason'	1
cosa de que	'the thing [is] that'	1
y todo	'and all'	2
por Dios	'by God'	2
a pero	'ah but'	7
pues entonces	'well then'	7
o bien	'or rather'	8
claro	'clearly'	12
pues	'well, then'	20
a ver	'let's see'	85

Summarising the borrowing of Spanish functional elements in Cochabamba Quechua, we can state that a wide variety of elements has been borrowed, including two affixes: plural and diminutive. In addition several prepositions occur, among which the as yet not exhaustively analysed borrowed *a* 'AC/DA animate'. A number of adverbs and clausal modifiers have been borrowed, a few of which are used productively, as well as three adverbial conjunctions. In contrast, the core of the Quechua morpho-syntactic skeleton, including most of the deictic, agreement, and the TMA system, has not been affected by the borrowing process. Another striking finding is that for those categories where we do find borrowing, a number of basic Spanish forms have not been borrowed, while more elaborate but more peripheral forms do occur in the Quechua texts.

Romance borrowings in Maltese Arabic

Maltese Arabic is a variety of Arabic brought to the island of Malta during Muslim rule, which lasted from around 870 to 1090. It is related to Tunisian varieties of Arabic. Since about 1300, the dominant cultural influence has come from the north, Sicily, and the Italian mainland. The Maltese are Roman Catholics and write their language with the Latin alphabet. It is in itself surprising perhaps that the population of Malta has not shifted to Sicilian or Italian, but certainly their language has undergone a number of changes during the last seven centuries. Thus it is an interesting case for the study of language contact, and, due to the typological differences between Arabic and Romance, for the study of functional/lexical asymmetries in borrowing (cf. also Haase 2002).

Although more than 50% of the lexicon of Maltese is of Romance origin, only three of the words on the Swadesh 100 word list are from Romance (Drewes 1994: 83), and six according to Stolz (2003). Stolz (2003) argues that Maltese (Malti) does not quite qualify as a mixed language, in Matras and Bakker's sense (2003b), although it has been subject to extensive borrowing.

Nonetheless, there are many Italian-derived and English-derived nouns and verbs in frequent use. In addition Drewes (1994) shows that there has been considerable less visible European lexical/semantic influence, for example in the form of calques and light verb constructions.

There is some Italian morphological influence on Maltese. English verbs are part of the *-are* class, the largest for Italian-derived verbs, and in addition to infinitives in *-ar*, verbal participles in *-at/-ata* appear (Drewes 1994: 92, 96), as in (11):

(11)   . . . ipparkjata   '[the car turned up] parked'
        . . . inxurjat   '[he was] insured'
        . . . appruvat   '[the decree was] approved'

In addition, there is productive use of the Italian nominaliser *-tura*, as in *kraxxatura* 'a crash', and of the Italian nominal suffix *-ata*, as in *nervjata* 'a fit of nerves'. Finally, a number of other Italian-derived affixes are mentioned, such as agentive *-tur* (< It *-tore*), and adjectival *-uż* (< It *-oso*) and *-azz* (< It *-azzo*), as well as a few other affixes. Stolz (2003: 272) shows that there are Italian feminine adjectival endings: *tond-a* 'round' f and *lixx-a* 'smooth' f.

Mifsud (1995) shows that large parts of the Maltese verbal morphological system appear to be based on Arabic, and that Italian verbs were borrowed inasmuch as they fitted into the Arabic root-and-pattern system. However, Hoberman and Aronoff (2003) argue that more recent borrowings, including the verbs from English, do not fit into the Arabic pattern and are characterised by affixal morphology, so that the most productive morphological patterns in the language are currently not based on the root-and-pattern model. Nominal morphology traditionally was also based on Arabic, including 'broken plurals' for Italian-origin words such as *kamra* 'room'/*kmamar* 'rooms', and *ġurnata* 'day'/*ġranet* 'days', as well as the Arabic plural marker *-(ij)iet*, as in *kundizzjonijiet* 'conditions'. Notice incidentally that the broken plural *ġurnata/ġranet* 'day/days' shows that the *-ata* affix is not always recognised as a separate morpheme. However, we frequently encounter Italian (12) or English (13) nominal plural endings, in contexts which sometimes are perhaps cases of code-mixing rather than borrowing (from Drewes 1994: 85–96).

(12)   mil-l-karattarestič-i   'of the characteristics'
        l-individw-i   'the individuals'
        ta' l-aryuplan-i   'of aeroplanes'

(13)   on the spot fines
        goals
        in-nurses   'the-nurses'

Apart from the verb endings mentioned, all grammatical categories in Maltese are based on Arabic, even though their grammatical functioning and interpretation may sometimes be clearly influenced by Italian and sometimes even English. There is for example no Italian indefinite article (Stolz 2003: 283), and definite articles are from Arabic.

While almost all Maltese pronouns are from Arabic, a few forms have been borrowed from Italian and have been added to the pronominal system, including *stess* 'self, same' (Aquilina 1959: 321, spelling maintained), as in (14):

(14)   yien *'stess* raytu 'yaqra li-*stess* 'kotba ma-li-*stess*   'ra:jel
       I   self   saw   read   DET-same   books   with-DET-same   man
       u   ma-li-*stess*   'mara
       and   with-DET-same   woman
       'I myself saw him read the same books with the same man and the same woman.'

Other forms related to the pronominal domain are *'certu* 'a certain', *kwalsi'vo:lya* 'whatever', and *kwa'lunkwe* 'whoever, any' (Aquilina 1959: 321).
   While the basic prepositions in Maltese are from Arabic (Aquilina 1959: 299–300), some more peripheral prepositions have been borrowed from Italian (Aquilina 1959: 322):

(15)   'kontra   'against'
        'versu   'towards, for'
        skont   'according to'
        per'metts   'by means of'
        'sotta + possessive pronoun   'subject to'

A similar picture emerges for conjunctions. Most conjunctions are derived from Arabic, but in addition there are some borrowed conjunctions from Italian (Aquilina 1959: 322; Stolz 2003: 289), as listed in (16):

(16)   o   'or'
       'antsi   'not only, what more'
       pe'ro   'however'
       cyo'e   'that is to say'
       'mentri 'whilst'
       allura   'then, therefore'

Basic strategies for subordination and complementation are based on Arabic elements, however.

The lexical influence from Italian has been considerable in the domain of adverbs, including time adverbs, different manner adverbs (often formed with the productive suffix -*ment*), and adverbs of quantity:

(17)   *time adverbs* (Aquilina 1959: 321–322)
       'zobtu   'suddenly'   (< Sc subito)
       'kmieni   'early'   (< It or Sc con la mane)
       in'tant   'in the meanwhile'
       frat'tant 'in the meanwhile'

(18)   *adverbs of manner, affirmation, negation, doubt* (Aquilina 1959: 321–322)
       serya'ment   'seriously'
       probabil'ment   'probably'
       intorta'ment   'uselessly, wrongfully, unjustly'
       preci:za'ment   'precisely'
       certa'ment   'certainly'
       ap'puntu   'precisely'
       proprya'ment   'properly (speaking)'
       vera'ment   'truly'
       'forsi   'perhaps'
       in'fatti   'as a matter of fact'

(19)   *adverbs of quantity* (Aquilina 1959: 322; Stolz 2003: 289)
       al'me:+nu   'at least'
       'kwa:zi   'nearly, almost'
       tant   'so much'
       ferm   'very much' (< Sc fermu, It fermo)
       'cirka/in'cirka 'about'
       anki   'too, also'
       anzi   'nay, at least, and more than that'
       basta   'enough'

Two examples of the use of adverbs of quantity are given in (20) and (21), showing the degree of their integration into the language:

(20)   talab   'tant   u-taytu   'tant
3.asked   so much   and-1.gave   so much
'He asked so much and I gave so much.'

(21)   'cirka   γoʃriːn   'ruːh
'about twenty people'

Finally, a large number of interjections, exclamations, etc., has been taken from Italian:

(22)   interjections
'ayma   'alas'
'aybu   'pooh'
ad'diyu   'goodbye'
arrive'derci 'au revoir'
etc.

Summarising the borrowing situation for Maltese, we can state that in spite of the extensive borrowing of both verbs and nouns and the partial restructuring of Maltese verbal morphology, the influence of Romance and subsequently English on the functional category system of the language has been marginal.

Conclusions

These typologically and historically very different language pairs, Cochabamba Quechua/Spanish and Maltese Arabic/Italian show a rather similar picture, which I will dare to claim to be characteristic of processes of intensive lexical borrowing:

(a)   Very extensive borrowing in the lexical domain
(b)   Very limited borrowing, if any, in the domain of the functional categories associated with the syntactic skeleton, like tense, agreement, and case
(c)   Borrowing of nominal number, often together with the associated nouns
(d)   Borrowing of (mostly coordinating or adverbial) conjunctions, some peripheral adpositions, and adverbs.

15 *Pidgin and creole genesis*

While in regular language change we find a pattern of stability at least with some classes of grammatical elements, as documented in chapter 7, in the more disruptive case of language change involved in pidgin and creole genesis there has been a radical restructuring of the overall inventory of functional categories, while the content lexicon has been retained, even if sometimes in reduced form. In fact the restructuring of the functional category system of a language may be taken as criterial for the process of creolisation.

Considering the very basic question word 'what', we find it in a few of the creoles with English lexicon forms such as the ones in (1):

(1)   'what' in some selected English lexicon pidgins and creoles (Muysken and
       Smith 1990)
       Chinese Pidgin English   wat-ting
       Cameroon Pidgin English   wéting/húskayn/ting
       Krio   wât
       Sranan   (o) san
       Saramaccan   andí
       Jamaican Creole   wat/we/wara

There are a few direct reflexes of English 'what', but also some new forms have come in, based with one exception (Saramaccan *andí*, which goes back to the African language Fongbe), on English words: 'thing', 'which kind', 'something' (Sranan *san*), 'where'. No doubt these new forms are plausible semantically, as has been argued by Seuren and Wekker (1986), but they indicate that the transmission of grammatical elements has been interrupted in the process of creole genesis.

Contrast this with a number of verbs involving movement in the English-lexicon creole Sranan:

(2)   walk   waka (<E walk)
       crawl   kroipi (<Du kruipen)
       run   lon (<E run)

swim   swen (<Du zwem)
jump   dyompo (<E jump), dyorku, maska
fall   fadon (<E fall down)
float   dribi (<Du drijven), drifi (?<E drift), flowt (<E float)
climb   kren (E< climb, Du klimmen)
dance   dansi (<E/Du dance/dans), yanga
fly   frei (<E fly)

While there are some words taken from Dutch and a few of uncertain origin, on the whole there is a reasonable link in form/meaning pairings between English and Sranan. This does not mean that these movement verbs are used in exactly the same way in Sranan as in English, just that their shapes and meanings are similar. This is why we speak of an English-lexicon creole. The issue I want to investigate is whether this holds for the European functional categories as well.

I will begin by very briefly presenting some of the main features of pidgins and creoles, and some central issues in the study of their genesis. Then I will examine the asymmetry between lexical and functional categories from the perspective of one pidgin (and developing creole), Tok Pisin, and two Caribbean creoles, Saramaccan and Negerhollands. While Tok Pisin has a predominantly English-derived lexicon, Saramaccan has had lexical input from two European languages, Portuguese and English, which yields an additional issue of whether either language contributed most function words. Negerhollands primarily has words from varieties of Dutch.

Pidgins and creoles

Pidgins and creoles are languages for which we can specify roughly when they emerged, in contrast with other languages, which emerged very slowly and do not have a specific time (decade or even century) of origin. They emerged because there was an interruption in the chain of ordinary intergenerational language transmission, as a result of language contact and often of social upheaval. The origin of most known pidgins and creoles can be linked to the period of Western colonial expansion, slavery, and contract labour. However, there must have been pidgins and creoles throughout human history. Pidgins and creoles are not sharply defined categories. Is Afrikaans in South Africa a creole? Is the second-language Arabic spoken by many immigrant workers in the Gulf States a pidgin? No clear answers can be provided for these questions. However, it is also clear that some languages are undoubtedly pidgins or creoles.

Pidgins are distinct from creoles in not having a community of native speakers associated with them. They are by no means a unified group, and differ among themselves on a number of dimensions:

- **(a)symmetry**: have the languages involved in the language contact setting contributed lexicon and other linguistic elements in roughly equal amounts, or is there clearly one single dominant language?
- **degree of elaboration**: is it a rudimentary pidgin or a much more elaborate one, structurally hard to distinguish, if at all, from a creole?

We don't have space here to classify individual pidgins in terms of these dimensions. Below I will just discuss the well-documented asymmetric elaborate Tok Pisin, which actually has acquired native speakers in addition to being used as a pidgin.

Creole languages, then, always have native speaker communities. They may revert to pidgin status, when the native speakers readopt earlier non-creole languages as their native languages, as might have happened in parts of West Africa. They may also die out, just as with any other language, as has been the case with the Dutch lexicon creole Negerhollands, to be discussed below.

A number of processes have played a role in the formation of pidgins and creoles. The four most important ones are (taking the perspective of the native speakers of subordinate languages, like the slaves taken to Africa, who are confronted with dominant European languages):

- attempts to acquire the patterns of the dominant language, which often belong to an informal vernacular register, as a **second language**
- reliance on **universal** linguistic (phonological, grammatical, semantic) principles in the creation of new forms
- **convergence** between patterns in the native and in the dominant languages
- **relexification** of native language lexical concepts and semantic patterns with phonetic shapes taken from words in the dominant language.

To what extent different pidgins and creoles have relied on these four strategies depends greatly on the specific circumstances (languages present, demographic characteristics, etc.) under which they emerged. I will discuss the status of functional categories in pidgins and creoles in terms of these four processes.

A first perspective is that incomplete second-language learning (in part due to limited exposure to the target) has led to loss of functional categories in the pidginisation phase (Mühlhäusler 1975; Schumann 1978). In this paradigm the question is raised of how the break in the transmission chain due to incomplete (second)-language learning led to the loss of specific morphemes, particularly verbal and nominal inflections, and which morphemes may have been acquired and then retained in the resulting new variety.

In the universalist perspective (Bickerton 1981, 1984; Carden and Stewart 1988), functional categories may have been initially lost, but are then reconstituted due to pressures from the bioprogram. In Bickerton's research, the question focused upon is how properties of our innate linguistic capabilities (the language bioprogram) determine which functional items lost due to incomplete learning will be reconstituted automatically and quickly, and which items may take a long time to be reconstituted, if this happens at all. This Language Bioprogram Hypothesis assumes that there is a set of core notions and categories (certain Tense-Mood-Aspect (TMA) distinctions, pronominal reference, nouns, and verbs) that are part of the core human linguistic structures, while others (other Tense Mood Aspect distinctions, anaphoric reference, adpositions) are more peripheral or indeed superfluous.

Earlier work by Labov (1990 [1971]) on Hawaiian Creole English is also part of this more universalist perspective, but has a different slant to it. Labov has argued for stylistic adequacy as the primary motor for the development of the preverbal TMA particles, on the basis of a contrast between Hawaiian pidgin and creole. In the pidgin phase, Hawaiian English had the characteristics exemplified in (3):

(3)   *Hawaiian Pidgin English* (1930)
        My husband house kau-kau no good – cheap kind and too li-li. I kau-kau junk
        kind den keep good kind kau-kau for my mada-in-law and all da man . . . By-
        'm-bye my husband he go Honolulu. Sometime he send letta, sometime he
        send money. . .

However, in the creole phase, it has changed its character considerably, now including some verbal inflections and some pre verbal particles.

(4)   *Hawaiian Creole English* (1970)
        . . . And that thing was coming and something black on top the horse, riding,
        never have head. So she wen go hug him like that. Horse wen go pass them,
        eh. . . .

On the basis of texts such as these, Labov distinguishes several phases – from (a) to (e) – in the development of Hawaiian Creole English:

    (a) jargon: no tense marking
    (b) pidgin: tense marking with adverbs and temporal expressions on the
         discourse level

(c) *wen* preterite / *gon* future auxiliary
(d) *wen go* preterite
(e) rules of phonological contraction (compare: English *will* → *be going to*)

To explain this sequence, and particularly the transition from (b) to (c), Labov (1990 [1971]: 44–45) writes with respect to the development in Hawaiian English:

> There is no basis for arguing that tense markers express the concepts of temporal relations more clearly than adverbs of time. What then is the advantage that they offer to native speakers, the advantage that native speakers seem to demand? The most important property which tense markers possess, which adverbs of time do not, is their stylistic flexibility. They can be expanded or contracted to fit in with the prosodic requirements of allegro or lento style. Because tense markers are not assigned stress in the normal cycles, their vowels are reduced and contracted . . .
>
> One might say that a developing grammar serves the need of stylistic variation. But it would be more accurate to say that grammar is style. The deep and complex apparatus that has developed in English syntax and morphophonemics does not necessarily make the speakers wiser, more logical, or more analytical in their ways of talking.

Thus phonological and stylistic requirements are argued to have led to the emergence of functional categories.

Convergence between functional categories in the native and the dominant languages can be studied most fruitfully in the process of grammaticalisation. In the grammaticalisation and contact tradition (Heine and Kuteva 2002, cf. chapter 6; Bruyn 1995), the way certain creole grammatical elements have resulted from the rapid grammaticalisation of content words in the lexifier languages is explored. Thus adverbs may have developed into auxiliaries, locative expressions into adpositions, etc. The language contact perspective adds to this the idea that these grammaticalisation chains may have already existed in the contributing West-African languages (this is far from implausible) and have been relexified lock, stock, and barrel into the resulting creoles.

Finally, the relexification perspective has been taken by scholars such as Lefebvre (1998), who argues that many of the functional categories of Haitian are inherited from Fongbe, and are only superficially French in their outward phonetic shape, or may be null. In the discussion of the three languages mentioned below, I will not enter into the question about possible survivals of native functional categories in a new phonetic shape. This very fruitful area of study is currently being explored intensively (Bruyn 1995; Migge 2003a; Keesing 1988).

The possibility of null functional categories is further explored by Veenstra, in various publications. Veenstra (1994) argues that Saramaccan is a pro-drop language, containing a functional category Agr_S. Evidence comes from perception complements and from the paradigms of pronominal elements in subject position. There is good reason to suppose that some of the functional categories in creoles may be null, given their limited inflectional morphology. However, in the context of this book, I will not explore this issue further since it requires a level of detail in syntactic analysis beyond the scope of the present overview. Also, we should not overstate the role of null functional categories in elaborated pidgins and creoles.

In my survey of Tok Pisin, Saramaccan, and Negerhollands two questions are central:

- Were the functional categories of the lexifier language transmitted to the pidgin and creole?
- Can we trace the pidgin and creole functional categories back to elements in the lexifier language which show an identical or similar form/meaning pairing?

Quite obviously, these are huge questions. I will limit myself here to four groups of categories in the three languages:

(a) Pronouns
(b) Pre- and postpositions
(c) Auxiliaries, TMA-markers, copulas, and serial verbs
(d) Conjunctions, question words, and relativisers.

I will consider the inventory of elements of the three languages in this order; they have a quite healthy inventory, as we shall see.

Tok Pisin

Tok Pisin is a pidgin language spoken as a second language by roughly 50% of the four million inhabitants of (Papua) New Guinea, and by an increasing number of town-dwellers as a first language (Mühlhäusler 2003: 2). It is related to other pidgins in the region, such as Solomon Islands Pidgin English, Bislama of Vanuatu, and the Kanaka English of Queensland. However, these varieties cannot properly be said to be related as dialects of one overarching pidgin. Its earliest roots lie in English pidgins brought to the eastern Bismarck Archipelago around 1850, but it really took off when Bismarck islanders were taken to German plantations on Samoa after 1878. Around 1900 we can speak of Samoan Plantation Pidgin. From 1914 onward the pidgin spread to increasingly extensive parts of New Guinea, particularly the previously German part of the island (Mühlhäusler 2003: 5–6). In 1975 Papua New Guinea became independent and the language continues to flourish, although it is now in close contact with English.

In view of these events, the development of Tok Pisin can be viewed as having gone through four stages (Mühlhäusler 2003: 10–11):

I	1850 →	Jargon stage
II	1890 →	Stabilised Tok Pisin
III	1930 →	Expanded Tok Pisin
IV	current	Creolised Tok Pisin

In these different stages, the language gradually acquired an increasing range of grammatical structures, and, relevant to my concerns, functional categories. Other forms fell into disuse, and there is considerable variation across different regions, and often parallel with this, between different stages in the historical development of the language. The picture I will sketch below is thus an idealisation, in part based on Mühlhäusler (2003), in part on the detailed text study of Geoff Smith (2002), and in small part on Dutton (1973). The idealised composite picture presented here is bound to be incorrect for a specific variety, although I hope to avoid glaring errors. It should also be kept in mind that many developments in the language concern specific substrate languages, which again leads to more regional diversity. In spite of all this, I hope that my general conclusions will still hold.

In the case of Tok Pisin, the lexicon is taken mostly from English. An example is provided in (5):

(5)   Malaria em i namba wan sik i save bagarap-im ol man-meri bilong dispela
       kantri. Malaria 3s PM number one disease PM can kill-TR p man-woman RE
       DET-AM land.
       'Malaria is disease number one killing men and women of this country.'

The pronoun system is based on a singular/dual/trialis/plural distinction, as well as an inclusive/exclusive first person distinction, but no case marking, and no gender in the third person singular, as shown in Table 15.1. The basic elements themselves obviously derive from English (*-em* from 'him', *-pela* from 'fellow', *tu* from 'two', *tri* from 'three', *ol* from 'all'), but only *yu* and *mi* have undergone no meaning change.

Table 15.1. *The Tok Pisin pronoun system*

	1	2	3
Singular	mi	yu	em
Dual	yumi tupela	yu tupela	(em) tupela
Trialis	yumi tripela	yu tripela	(em) tripela
Plural	yumi (inc)	yupela	(em) ol
	mipela (exc)		

As for prepositions, there are basically two classes in Tok Pisin, the grammatical prepositions *long* (basically linking verbs and arguments) and *bilong* (basically linking nouns to nouns), and a reduced number of locational prepositions, only one of which links directly to an English preposition (*insait*). None of the core prepositions of English appears in Tok Pisin.

Tok Pisin prepositions

long	locative	< E along
bilong	non-locative	< E belong
antap	on	< E on top
daun	down, below	< E down
insait	inside	< E inside
olsem	like	< E all the same

While most Tok Pisin auxiliaries, copulas, TMA markers, and serial verb constructions go back to English lexical items, very few are a direct continuation of the functional inventory of English. Exceptions are *mas*, which appears to have the range of meaning of English 'must', *ken*, which has the permissive meaning of English 'can', and possibly *gat*, since English 'got' can also occur in English existential and possessive constructions. The other English etymons do not serve as semi-auxiliaries or the like in English.

Tok Pisin auxiliaries, copulas, TMA markers, and serial verb constructions

gat	possessive/existential	< E got
kisim	get/acquire	< E catch
kamap	become	< E come up
bin	past	< E been
bai	future	< E bye and bye
pinis	perfective	< E finish
stap	locational be	< E stop
laik	want to/be about to	< E like

save/sa	recurring/habitual	< P saber
wok long	continuous (active verbs)	< E walk along
klostu	about to	< E close to
maski	negative imperative	< ?P mas que
mas	must (deontic, epistemic)	< E must
ken	can (permission)	< E can
inap	can (physical ability)	< ?
kirap	get up, begin	< E get up
V... bek	back, again (resumptive)	< E back
V... i stap	durative (stative verbs)	< E stop
V... i go	directional, back/ongoing	< E go
V i kam	towards speaker	< E come

The same can be said about Tok Pisin conjunctions, question words, and relativisers. With the exception of *we* < E 'where' and *haumas* < E 'how much',
they do not correspond to English words with a similar function, and the corresponding English words like 'that', 'who', 'which', 'if' are not present in
Tok Pisin. A number of Tok Pisin prepositions, *long*, *bilong*, and *olsem*, also
function as conjunctions. Two question words double as relativisers.

Tok Pisin conjunctions, question words, and relativisers

ia	deictic, clause marker	< E here
bilong	in order to	< E belong
maski	although, even if	<?P mas que 'although'
inap long	until	< ?
haumas	how much/many	< E how much
husat	who/which person, relativiser	< E who's that
wonem	what/which thing	< E what name
we	where, relativiser	< E where
kain	what sort of	< E kind
long	relativiser	< E along
sapos	focus	< E suppose
olsem	that	< E all the same
se	that	< E say, ?Fr *c'est* 'that is'
na	and	< ?

Summarising, the Tok Pisin functional inventory can be related to English,
but by and large does not reflect the English one, and many core elements of

the English system have not survived in Tok Pisin. Nonetheless, there is good evidence that the Tok Pisin elements have been fully grammaticalised, for at least two reasons.

First, many of the functional elements in Tok Pisin can occur in phonologically reduced form, as noted by Sankoff and Laberge (1973) and documented in detail by Geoff Smith (2002) (where many forms occur, the most frequently used forms according to the text counts in Smith (2002) have been underlined).

> **olsem**: olsem > osem > ose > sem > se > s
> **husat**: husat > usat > husaet > usaet > husait > usait > huset > uset
>   > set > sat
> **dispela**: dispela > displa > disla > dsla >disa > dsa > sla > sa
> **laik**: laik, lai, la
> **wok long**: wok lo, wo lo, o lo, wo l'

This phonological reduction is evidence for extensive grammaticalisation.

Second, the elements listed are among the most frequent in Tok Pisin texts. Smith (2002: 101–102) provides a list of the 58 most frequent words found in the texts he collected. There is some variation between different regions, but basically the list is as follows:

em	3s pronoun	**meri**	woman	wantaim	when
na	and	dispela		**brata**	brother
nau	emphatic, now	**haus**	house	insait	inside
go		bai		yumi	
long	locative	save		**mama**	mother
ia	deictic	kirap		laik	
bilong		**lukim**	look, see	**wara**	water
mipela		pinis		olgeta	
kam		tasol		tru	
mi		nogat		okei	
i	he	no		**putim**	put
stap		bin		bek	
tok	speak	**kaikai**	eat	wok	work
tupela		wanem		yupela	
wanpela		liklik	little	ken	
kisim		antap	on	**slip**	sleep
olsem		tokim	say	**was**	wash
man	man	daun		narapela	other
yu		**ples**	place	karim	
				papa	father

Out of 58 elements, only the 14 in bold would not generally be analysed as functional categories.

Table 15.2. *The Saramaccan pronoun system*

	Singular				Plural			
	subj	*obj*	*emp*	*neg*	*subj*	*obj*	*emp*	*neg*
1	mi		mí/míi	ma		u		wa
2	i		i/ju	ja	un/unu	unu		wan
3	a	ën	hën	an		de		

I have not done an analysis of lexical categories in Tok Pisin, and hence cannot compare these to functional categories, but with respect to the latter, there is considerable discontinuity between the lexifier and the pidgin/creole.

Saramaccan

Saramaccan or Saamaka is the language of the descendants of one of the groups of maroons who escaped from the plantations along the Surinam river in the late seventeenth century, and went up river. Lexically it has elements from English, Portuguese, and Dutch, as well as from Fongbe and Kikongo (cf. also Daeleman 1972; Smith and Cardoso 2004). With the exception of locative *a*, with an obscure, possibly African, possibly Portuguese etymology, all elements have an English lexical base as shown in (6), from de Groot (1981: 118):

(6)   a   bi   túe   wan   sitónu   gó   a   mi   báka
       3s   PST   throw one   stone   go   LOC 1s   back
       'He threw a stone at me (from behind).'

Nonetheless, the grammatical organisation is quite distinct. Direction is indicated by a separate (serial) verb, which has a complex locative complement.

In the pronoun system, there is no gender difference, and the pronouns are distinguished in terms of subject, object (non-subject), emphatic, and negated elements. Again, the basic elements *ju* and *mi* are clearly traceable to English, as is the third person form. The Saramaccan pronoun system is shown in Table 15.2 (cf. de Groot 1981).

The Saramaccan prepositions come from various lexical sources. Only one corresponds to an English core preposition, *fu/u*, which however has a much wider use in Saramaccan. Several Portuguese prepositions have direct reflexes in Saramaccan: *ku* (which in addition to 'with' can mean 'and'), *té/téé*, and *kuma*.

Saramaccan prepositions

a	location	< ?P na 'in it'
fu/u	of, for	< E for
ku	with	< P com 'with'
té/téé	until	< P até ' until', Kikongo (na)te
kuma	like	< P como, coma 'like'
bóíti	except	< Du buiten 'outside'
sóndo	without	< Du zonder 'without'

In addition to the preposition system, Saramaccan has a complex set of locative + postposition combinations, to mark specific spatial relations. The English roots which formed the basis for some of these lexically tend to be nouns, while two of the Portuguese roots are complex prepositions originally, one an adjective/adverb, and one a noun.

Saramaccan postpositions

báka	behind	< E back
bándja	next to	< P banda 'side'
		< Kikongo mbaansya 'side'
básu, bâsu, basu	under	< P baixo 'low'
déndu	inside	< P dentro 'inside'
édi	cause	< E head 'cause'
fési	in front of, before	< E face
líba	above	< P riba de 'above'
sinkíi	stuck against	< E skin
míndi	in the middle of	< E middle

When we consider Saramaccan auxiliaries, copulas, TMA markers, and serial verbs, we find that only a minority of these corresponds directly to an English element with the same meaning and function: *bigí* 'begin', *músu* 'must', *hábi* 'have', *sa* 'shall'. For Portuguese, the relation is often more direct: *kabá* < acabar 'finish', *ké* < quer 'want', *sá* < saber 'know (how)'. Altogether, the relation between the Saramaccan functional categories in this domain and that of either of its lexifiers is rather tenuous, to say the least.

Saramaccan auxiliaries, copulas, TMA markers, and serial verbs

kabá	finish	< P acabar 'finish'
bigí	begin	< E begin
séti	set up, begin	< E set
ké	want	< P querer 'wish, want'
kó	(be)come	< E come
biá kó	turn into	< P virar 'turn', E come
mbéi	let	< E make
músu	must	< E must
nángó	go on . . .	< E stand go
sá	can	< P saber 'know (how)'
'a/ábi/hábi/há	have, possess	< E have
tán	stay	< E stand
da	identity	< E that
dé	location	< E there
bi	past	< E been
ó	future	< E go
sa	future	< E shall
tá	durative	< E stand
de a	durative	< E there, P na 'in the'
V . . . lóntu	around	< E round, Du rond
V . . . dóò/dóu	outside	< E through, Du door
V . . . kumútu	outward	< E come out
V . . . pói	(too) much	< E spoil
V . . . táa	say	< E talk
téi V	take	< E take
V . . . túe	away	< E throw away
V . . . dá	dative	< P dar 'give'
V . . . kó	toward speaker	< E come
V . . . gó	away from speaker	< E go

The same can be said about the Saramaccan conjunctions, question words, and relativisers, which generally have an English source, sometimes a Fongbe source, and occasionally a Portuguese source. It is quite exceptional for Caribbean creole functional categories to have a direct African root. In a few cases there is a direct form/function mapping: *biká, bigá* 'because', *bifó/ufó* 'before', *é/éi/ee* 'if, whether', *ma* 'but', but in most cases the relationship is much more indirect. In this domain Portuguese influence is fairly limited.

Saramaccan conjunctions, question words, and relativiser

aluási, awínsi	although	< ?P alias 'for that matter'
híi fa	although	< Du hele 'all', E fashion
híi di	although	< Du hele 'all', E this
biká, bigá	because	< E because
dí	when, because	< E this
bifó/ufó	before	< E before
té fu	before	< E time for
é/éi/ee	if, whether	< E if
fá i si, té	when	< E fashion you see
fu/u	in order to	< E for
fu di/u di	because	< E for this
ká fu	instead of	< ?, E for
ma	but	< Du maar 'but', P mais 'but'
naa	or	< ?
fa	how (after verb)	< E fashion
ambé	who	< F amɛ
andí	what	< F ani
fá, umfa	how	< E fashion
ún-	question prefix	< E which
unsè, un sè	where	< E which side
naase	where	< na, E side
un juu	when	< E which, Du uur 'hour'
un mèni	how many/much	< E which many
faándí mbéi	why	< E fashion F ani E make
andí di	what (relativiser)	< F ani 'what', E this
ká	where	< ??
dí	deictic/relativiser singular	< E this
déé	deictic/relativiser plural	< E them
te	when	< E time

Negerhollands

The now extinct creole Nederhollands was spoken by slaves and their descendants on the Virgin Islands, particularly St Thomas. Its main lexical sources are (mainly Zealandic) varieties of Dutch, but there are also elements from English and Portuguese. An example illustrating some of its features is (7):

Table 15.3. *The Negerhollands pronoun system*

	Subject	Object	Possessive
1s	mi	mi	(fa) mi
2s	ju	ju	ju
3s	(h)am	em	ši/fa am
3sn	di	di	ši
1p	ons	ons	ons
2p	jini/ju	jinni	(fa) jini/ju
3p	sini/si/sel	sini (/am)	(fa) sin(i)

(7)   from Josselin de Jong (1926)
       no šiní e:nte:n fet   it fa   bo   di   foma: ju sa mata di   kui
       not cut any   grease out of above 3s.n since 2s FU kill DET cow
       'Do not cut out any grease from on top of it, because you will kill the cow.'

The Negerhollands data were collected from a number of sources: van Diggelen (1978), the word lists in Stein (1996) and van der Voort (1996), and the
texts collected in van Rossem and van der Voort (1996). Before going on, I
should mention that there are considerable methodological difficulties, particularly because the sources cover a time span of 250 years, and reflect different varieties (slave, planter) of Negerhollands. Also, spellings are far from
consistent.

In Negerhollands, as shown in Table 15.3, in the third person a distinction is
made between subject, object, and possessive forms. In other persons, this distinction is largely absent. The Dutch third person gender distinction is lacking,
except that there is a neuter expletive element. The actual forms used generally
can be directly traced back to Dutch (often dialectal) forms.

Like Dutch, Negerhollands has a quite rich preposition system. The majority
of elements can be directly related to Dutch (again often dialectal) source prepositions. The exceptions are two prepositions from Portuguese (also present in
Saramaccan), locative *na* and *tē* 'until', as well as *kant* 'next to, beside', which
in Dutch is a noun, and *amolē* 'below', which contain the locative element *a*
(< *na*). There is a small group of complex locative prepositions, semantically
corresponding to the Saramaccan postpositions, and containing the locative
element *na*. In contrast to Saramaccan, Negerhollands distinguishes benefactive *fo* and genitive *fan*, but the Dutch dative pronoun *aan* 'to' is lacking, as are directional elements such as Dutch *naar* 'towards'. Finally
the Dutch locative preposition and non-finite marker *te* (roughly, 'to') is

lacking, as well as the infinitival complementiser/preposition *om* (roughly, 'for').

Negerhollands prepositions

fa(n)	of	< Du van 'of'
ini (rare)	in	< Du in
mi	with	< Du met 'with'
ondə	underneath	< Du onder 'underneath'
it	out of	< Du uit 'out'
de:	through	< Du door 'through, by'
o:bu	onto, over	< Du over
bu	on	< Du boven 'above'
op	on	< Du op 'on'
bi	by	< Du bij 'by, near'
te:	until	< P até 'until'
fo	for	< Du voor 'for'
sonder	without	< Du zonder 'without'
kant	next to, beside	< Du kant 'side'
rond	around	< Du rond(om) 'around'
astər	after	< Du achter 'behind', E after
gliek, liek	like	< Du gelijk 'like'
na	locative	< ?P na 'in.the(f)'
((n)a)bini (ši)	into, inside	< Du binnen 'inside'
(na)biti (ši)	outside	< Du buiten 'outside'
(na)bo(no), na bobo	above	< Du boven 'above'
afo (fa(n))	in front of	< na + Du voor 'for, before'
amolé	below	< na + ?

There is also quite a rich system of auxiliary-like elements in the language, but it cannot be directly traced back to Dutch lexical sources, as with the prepositions. There are a few English elements (*bin* 'past', and the copula *mi*), a few forms from Portuguese (*kā*, 'resultative', *lo* 'future', *kabá* 'completive'), and a few particles which are difficult to trace back to a possible Dutch source, such as *le* 'progressive, future' and *lo* 'durative, habitual'. The other forms have obvious Dutch lexical antecedents, but of these there is only a minority with a similar function, such as *sa(l)* 'future', *kan* 'possibility, iterative, habitual', *wil* 'want', and *mut* 'obligation'. Altogether, the continuities in this domain are not so evident as with the prepositions.

Negerhollands auxiliaries, copula, TMA markers, and serial verbs

(h)a/na	past	< ?Du had 'had'
sa(l)	future	< Du zal 'shall.s'
bin	past	< E been
be	'be' (local)	< ?E be
a	'be' (identity)	< Du dat 'that'
wēs	'be' (general)	< Du wees 'be.s'
mi	'be' (with adjectives)	< ?E be
kā	resultative	< ?P acabar 'finish'
le	progressive, future	< ?Du leggen 'lie, lay'
lo	durative, habitual	< ?Du lopen 'walk'
lo	future	< ?P logo 'soon'
mut	obligation	< Du moeten 'must'
kan	possibility, iterative, habitual	< Du kan
wil	'want, like'	< Du willen 'want'
mankē	'want', 'need'	< Du mankeren 'lack' (orig. Fr)
ha fo	obligation	< Du had 'had', voor 'for'
lastā, tā, da:	'let'	< Du laat staan 'let stand/be'
V . . . kabá	completive	< P acabar 'finish'
V . . . gi	'give'	< Du geef, E give
V . . . kō, kom	'come, become'	< Du komen 'come'

With respect to the main clause linkers – the Negerhollands conjunctions, question words, and relativisers – the picture is quite mixed. With the question words, there is a clear link with the Dutch forms but no direct copying of the Dutch forms; some contain the focal element *a* (*(a)wi(di)* 'who', *awamā*, 'why') typical of Caribbean creole information questions. The conjunctions show a much more direct resemblance to their Dutch historical antecedents, although there are occasional English forms as well, such as *ef* 'in case that' and *astər* 'after', and *so long* 'while'.

Negerhollands conjunctions, question words, and relativisers

awi(di)/widi	who	< Du wie 'who'
wa(t)	which	< Du wat 'what'
apē	where	< na + E place
wagut	what	< wa + Du goed 'substance'
awamā	why	< a 'FOC' + wa + Du maak 'make'
en	and (clauses)	< Du en 'and'

mi	and (noun phrases)	< Du met 'with'
maar/ma	but	< Du maar 'but'
since	since	< E since
sinds	since	< Du sinds 'since'
as	if	< Du als 'if, when'
toen	when	< Du toen 'when/then'
derwil	while	< Du terwijl 'while'
voordoor	while	< ?Du voor 'for' + door 'through'
so long	while	< E so long
maski	although	< ?P mas que 'although'
wel	although	< Du hoewel 'although'
adima	therefore	< a 'FOC' + dit maak 'this make'
ef	in case that …	< E if
leiki	like	< Du gelijk, E like
foma/fordiemaek	because	< Du voor die maak 'for this make'
weni/wani	when	< Du wanneer 'when'
dan	then	< Du dan 'then'
kan	until	< ?
te:	until	< P até 'until'
sodat	so that	< Du zodat 'so that'
astər	after	< E after
sondə	without (that)	< Du zonder 'without'

The data from the three languages discussed provide some interesting contrasts with respect to the issue at hand. The Tok Pisin system of functional elements is by and large English-derived etymologically, but the system that has developed is quite different from the English system of functional categories. Likewise, the Saramaccan systems are quite far apart from the English and Portuguese lexical sources. In contrast, the Negerhollands system shows more similarities to that of Dutch, except for basic components of clausal organisation such as the TMA markers.

Creole lexical and functional categories

The next question to be asked is how lexical categories compare with functional ones with respect to the continuity of transmission.

I was only able to compare (a sub-set of) the Saramaccan lexical categories with the functional categories. I have chosen the domain of movement and handling verbs. Although this is not easy to demonstrate conclusively, the semantic continuities in this domain appear to be much larger than in the domain of the functional categories. I have divided the verbs into groups on the basis of their most likely etymological origin. Out of a total of 68, one third (24) of the verbs were clearly English in origin. Of these, three were based on an English intransitive preposition: *aaba* 'put .. across (a river)' < 'over', *lombóto, lóntu, bóto* 'surround, encircle' < 'round about', and *hópo/ópo* 'lift' < 'up'. One appears to derive from a past participle form: *lási* 'get lost' < 'lost'. The remaining 19 derive from an English verb with a roughly corresponding meaning.

English lexicon movement and handling verbs		
aaba	put ... across (a river)	< over
béndi	bend	< bend
lombóto, lóntu, bóto	surround, encircle	< round about
djómbo	jump	< jump
dóu	arrive	< through
fáa	fell	< fell
tómbi	stumble	< stumble
sún	swim	< swim
gó/nangó	go	< (stand) go
hái	drag	< haul
héngi	hang	< hang
híti/íti	throw	< ?hit
hói	hold, stay	< hold
hópo/ópo	lift	< up
kumútu	come out	< come out
lási	get lost	< lost
logodá	roll	< ?roll go down
míti	meet	< meet
púu	take away	< pull
séki	shake	< shake
sindó	sit down	< sit down
síngi	sink	< sink
tjá	carry	< carry
wáka	walk, travel	< walk

There appear to be eight verbs which derive from Dutch. One of these goes back to a Dutch noun: *sodá* 'march' < *soldaat* 'soldier'.

Dutch lexicon movement and handling verbs

diípi	float	< drijven 'float'
dóki	dive	< duiken 'dive'
gii/gili	grate	< schuren 'grate'
jáka	chase	< jagen 'hunt'
kándi	topple over	< kantelen 'topple over'
sáka	lower	< zakken 'lower'
sodá	march	< soldaat 'soldier'
tóto	thrust, pound	< stoten 'thrust'

No fewer than 26 of the 68 verbs appear to have a Portuguese base, and in all these cases this is a verb with roughly the same meaning.

Portuguese lexicon movement and handling verbs

bajá	dance	< bailar 'dance'
baziá	descend	< baizar 'descend'
buá	fly	< voar 'fly'
bulí	shake	< bulir 'stir, flutter'
butá	put	< botar 'put'
dendá/dendáa	enter	< entrar, dentro 'enter, inside'
disá	let go	< deixar 'leave, let'
djulá	direct oneself	< ajular 'turn ship into the wind'
fiká	remain behind	< ficar 'remain'
fusí	flee	< fugir 'flee'
kaí	fall	< cair 'fall'
kóndò	push forward (of wood)	< conduzir 'lead, bring'
koogá	slip	< escorregar 'slip'
kulé	run, leak, stream	< correr, escorrer 'run, leak'
lola, lólu	roll	< rolar 'roll'
mandá	send	< mandar 'send'
paajá	spread	< espalhar 'spread'
pasá	pass	< pasar 'pass'
peeká/peká	fasten	< pegar 'fasten'
pusá	shift, move aside	< puxar 'move, push'
saí	be, find oneself	< sair 'go out'
sakpí	shake	< sacudir 'shake'
subí	climb, go up	< subir 'mount'

Table 15.4. *The contribution of different source languages to the Saramaccan inventories in the different lexical classes, in percentages (absolute figures in parentheses)*

	English	African	Dutch	Portuguese/ Unknown	Total
Prepositions	14 (1)	57 (4)	29 (2)		7
Movement and handling verbs	35 (24)	38 (26)	12 (8)	15 (10)	68
Postpositions	56 (5)	44 (4)			9
Subordinators	66 (19)	3 (1)	10 (3)	21 (6)	29
Auxiliaries	80 (23)	17 (5)		3 (1)	29

teemé	tremble	< tremer 'tremble'
tooná	turn	< tornar 'turn'
zuntá	bring together	< juntar 'join'

Finally, there are 10 movement and handling verbs with an unknown, possibly African etymological source.

Unknown, possibly African lexicon movement and handling verbs

bangulutu	push aside
bigodó	turn over (intransitive)
doodó	swing, oscillate
faáka	track (animals)
giin	make turn around
jajó	roam about
jamba-jamba/jambu-jambu	hang around
kama-dombói	turn somersault
kòndò	saunter around
sangá	stumble

The significance of these findings is brought into relief when we compare the figures for the studies of the different categories (disregarding pronouns because of their special status) on two dimensions: language of origin and restructured or not.

In Table 15.4 the etymological origin of the different categories is presented in absolute figures and percentages, and in Table 15.5 the amount of restructuring, for each category for each language, in absolute figures is shown. Table 15.4

Table 15.5. *The number of restructured items (in bold in parentheses) of the total number of items for the different source languages in the Saramaccan inventories in the different lexical classes, in absolute figures*

	English	Portuguese	Dutch	Unknown/ African	Total
Prepositions	1 **(1)**	4 **(1)**	2		7
Postpositions	5 **(5)**	4 **(2)**			9
Auxiliaries	23 **(19)**	5 **(2)**		1	29
Subordinators	19 **(16)**	1 **(1)**	3 **(2)**	6	29
Movement and handling verbs	24 **(4)**	26	8 **(1)**	10	68

shows English-origin elements are present most strongly in the auxiliaries and the subordinators, and least strongly in the prepositions and movement and handling verbs. For Portuguese and Dutch the reverse pattern holds. Under the assumption that the TMA and the subordinator systems provide the basic structural skeleton for a language, this would suggest that the basic structure of Saramaccan derives from an English-lexicon pidgin, which was supplemented lexically with elements from Portuguese and later on Dutch.

The next question then is whether the amount of restructuring differs for the different languages and different categories. A number of conclusions can be drawn from the figures in Table 15.5. First, the amount of restructuring is much higher for the functional categories (47 out of 76 items) than for the movement and handling verbs (5 out of 68 items). Furthermore, the amount of restructuring is higher in the English-origin lexicon (45 out of 71) than in the Portuguese-origin lexicon (6 out of 40). This may suggest that the Portuguese pidgin that fed into Saramaccan was closer to the target than the English pidgin; admittedly, the figures for Portuguese are not very large overall, so that this conclusion can only be tentative, but the trends are suggestive.

Conclusions

The systematic survey of the functional categories of Tok Pisin, Saramaccan, and Negerhollands in several domains – pronouns, adpositions, auxiliaries, and subordinators – confirms the hypothesis that functional categories are substantially affected by the process of pidginisation/creolisation in their transmission from the lexifier to the pidgin/creole. This is clearest for auxiliaries and subordinators. Creole pronouns tend to be based on the lexical shapes of the pronoun systems of their lexifiers, but the paradigm is often substantially restructured, in terms of the categories expressed, if not the actual morphemes used. For prepositions, the picture is mixed, while the Saramaccan postpositions are of course an innovation with respect to English and Portuguese, which lack these categories.

16 *Mixed languages*

While in most languages in the world the pair {lexicon, grammar} has the same historical origin (e.g. Romance or Turkic), there are a few dozen at most of recalcitrant linguistic varieties, in which significant parts of the grammar and the lexicon have different origins. These are called mixed, intertwined, or relexified languages. They very often show asymmetries in the origin of their lexical versus their functional categories. This is the reason for dedicating a chapter to them here.

Issues of definition and delimitation

I will define mixed languages as (a) more or less stable languages, (b) with substantial parts of their grammar and/or their basic lexicon from specific, historically different sources. This still includes a wide variety of language systems, with different types of community status as daily vernaculars. However, it excludes:

- Languages which have undergone extensive borrowing, because ordinarily large parts of their basic lexicon and their grammar will still be derivable from one source
- Bilingual code-mixed speech, since it is not stable
- Relexicalised street languages, jargons, etc., since these are not stable
- Pidgins with a mixed lexicon, because their grammar is often not traceable to specific sources.

There are always borderline cases and grey areas, but an analysis of mixed languages has to start somewhere. I will begin my discussion of mixed languages with what one might call the 'classical type', exemplified by Media Lengua. Other mixed languages, such Callahuaya, and a bit more controversially, Ma'a, are also assumed to belong to this class (cf. Bakker 1997: 192–213, who discusses this class in detail). In the classical type, the morpho-syntax and the functional categories are claimed to have one historical source, the original

Table 16.1. *Schematic overview of the four main types of mixed languages*

Type	Examples	Original community language	New or dominant language
Classical	Media Lengua, Callahuaya, Ma'a	grammar	lexicon
Split	Michif	verbal system	nominal system
Reverse split	Copper Island Aleut, Gurundji Kriol	nominal system	verbal system
Reverse	Para-Romani	lexicon	grammar

community language (Quechua in the case of Media Lengua), and (much of) the lexicon another (Spanish in the case of Media Lengua). I will then discuss the 'split type' Michif, where the nominal system (French) and the verbal system (Cree) have two different origins. If we take the verbal system to be more central to the grammar than the nominal system, then Michif is like the classical type in grammatically aligning itself with the original community language, Cree. I will go on to discuss the less known and less understood 'reverse split' type, exemplified by Copper Island Aleut and Gurundji Kriol. Here again, the nominal and the verbal systems are not from the same language source, but the verbal system does not stem from the original community language. Finally, I should briefly mention the 'reverse' type, with a basic grammar/lexicon division, but with the lexicon aligning itself with the original community language. Examples cited by Bakker (1997) are the so-called Para-Romani languages of western Europe. In Table 16.1 I summarise the four types in very schematic terms. Please bear in mind that this schematic representation is oversimplified.

Before turning to the four types in rather more detail, perhaps the issue of the social conditions under which these different mixed codes emerged should be discussed. What brings speakers to the creation of varieties which draw upon quite different sources? Disregarding less stable mixed languages which could have emerged in a process of language death through extensive borrowing, and urban youth or street languages, and disregarding trade languages created for interethnic contact, such as pidgins and jargons, we can think of the following scenarios:

- semi-shift languages: speakers give up their community language but relexicalise or relexify the new language with the vocabulary of the old one

- mixed marriage languages: in communities with substantial interethnic marriages, a new language emerges, generally with the grammar of the language of the mothers, and the lexicon of the language of the fathers
- new community languages, which owe their existence to the need to express a new ethnic identity
- secret languages, formed by relexicalising a majority language with lexical elements drawn from an older or a minority language. A special case of this may be ritual languages, such as Callahuaya.

In what follows, the different scenarios will not play a central role.

Classical mixed languages: Media Lengua

Bakker (1997: 213), the central reference for this type, gives the following recipe for a mixed or intertwined language:

(i)   Bound morphemes (always of a grammatical nature) are in language A.

(ii) Free lexical morphemes are in language B.

(iii) Free grammatical morphemes can be in either language.

(iv) The grammatical system is that in language A.

In the classical case, language A is the original community language, and language B the new, or dominant language.

One of the examples cited by Bakker (1997: 198) was noted by den Besten (1987: 26): the Griekwas or Basters language documented in mulatto communities in South Africa and Namibia. Nama Hottentot or Khoekhoen has provided the affixes and grammar, Afrikaans the roots:

(1)   *Heeltemaal*-se *natuur*-a-xu   *bedorven*-he (Basters)
       Hoaraga-se   =ûb-a-xu   gaugau-he   (Nama/Khoekhoen)
       totally-ADV   nature-CAS-P rotten-PASS
       'totally rotten in nature'
       Van nature helemaal bedorven.   (Dutch)

Unfortunately, not many examples of this Griekwas or Basters language have been documented, and it is not known whether it is still spoken. Bakker notes that Callahuaya in Bolivia, Ma'a or Inner Mbugu in Tanzania, the now extinct Island Caribs men's language of the lesser Antilles, and Peranakan Chindo on Java show roughly the same pattern. The variety I will document here in more detail is the mixed language I have worked on myself, Media Lengua in Ecuador.

Media Lengua is or was spoken in a number of highland communities throughout Ecuador. In my own work I have documented varieties from Saraguro (Loja), sub-urban Cañar, and Salcedo (Cotapaxi) (Muysken 1979, 1981, 1996), while Rendón (2005) has documented very similar varieties from the province of Imbabura. The circumstances under which Media Lengua has emerged in the different communities are not known. In the case which I have studied in most detail, Salcedo, I assume that in the 1910s and 1920s young (15-20-year-old) Quechua-speaking male workers left for the capital to work in construction, for months on end, and brought back an improvised in-group language, which may originally have been mostly used in jest or word play. In the communities nearest to the small urban centre, this language may then have gained a wider acceptance, up to converting itself into the main community language in the 1950s and 1960s. In the 1970s, when I made my recordings, it was the one variety that every generation spoke: while the middle generation was trilingual in Media Lengua, Quechua, and Spanish, the older generation mostly knew Media Lengua and Quechua, and the younger generation knew Spanish and Media Lengua. The fact that Media Lengua emerged in at least four places, widely separated from each other, and involving different Quechua dialects, suggests that its genesis relies on mechanisms easily available to Quechua/Spanish bilinguals in Ecuador. The surprising thing is that in Peru and Bolivia no similar varieties have been documented, even though there is extensive Quechua/Spanish bilingualism there as well, except in bilingual songs (Muysken 2000). It is not known yet what the special socio-cultural matrix is of Ecuador, such that these varieties can really gain community acceptance.

In Media Lengua, Quechua has provided the affixes, Spanish the lexical roots. The following (Muysken 1988b, cited in Bakker 1997: 419) is an example:

(2)
ML	*Miza*	*despwes-itu*	*kaza*-mu	*i*-naku-ndu-ga *ahí*-bi		*buda*	*da*-naku-n
Q	Miza	k'ipa	wasi-mu	ri-naku-sha-ga chi-bi		buda	ku-naku-n
	Mass	after(-DIM)	house-TO	go-p-SS-TO	there-LOC	feast	give-p-3

'Going home after Mass, they then give a feast there.'
(Sp)   'Yendo a la casa después de la Misa, ahí dan una boda.'

In Muysken (1981) I claim that the main process responsible for the emergence of Media Lengua is relexification, the grafting of new Spanish-derived phonetic shapes onto Quechua lexical entries. Thus, the postposition *k'ipa* 'back, after' appears as the Spanish-related adverb *despwesitu* 'afterwards-DIM'. The

Quechua root *ri*- 'go' is replaced by a Spanish root, *i*- (based on the infinitival form *ir* 'to go'), and the Quechua root *ku*- 'give' by *da*- (based on the Spanish form dar 'to give'). For the rest, the Quechua syntactic frame and the Quechua endings have been preserved.

However, it is not always possible to distinguish between relexification and simple lexicon replacement or relexicalisation, where the meaning from the donor lexical item is imported as well. In (2), the meaning of Quechua *ri*- 'go' is similar to that of Spanish *ir* 'go', and *wasi* 'house' is not distinct in meaning from *casa* 'house' (even if indigenous houses are different from Spanish houses). However, sometimes we can see direct evidence of relexification, as with the Quechua existential verb *tiya*-, which can also mean 'be seated, be located, live'. In (3a) it is relexified with the Spanish-derived element *sinta*- 'be seated', directly corresponding to its Quechua meaning (*huarango* is the (in the Andes quite rare) Ecuadorean variant of the Mexican cactus drink *pulque*). However, in (3b) this same existential verb appears as *abi*- 'have', in a personalised form of Spanish impersonal *hay* 'there is', which is based on Spanish *haber* 'have'. (The Quechua noun *shutichiy* ' baptism' (literally, name-cause-NOM) is one of the rare Quechua lexical items in my data that is not used in the local Spanish as well.)

(3)   (a) Chango-bi-ga   warang-itu   *sinta*-xu-n-chari
            Chango-LOC-TO   huarango-DIM   sit-3-DUB
            'Maybe there is huarango at Chango's.'

       (b) shutichiy *abi*-xu-n zi-n-mi
            baptism   have-PR-3 say-3-AF
            'There is reported to be a baptism.'

There is also a Quechua negative existential verb *illa* , which is relexified with a combination of Spanish *no* and the verb *haber* 'have', which in the impersonal form *hay* or past *había* may be existential. In (4) a brief overview of the different realisations of the existential, negative or not, is given (based on Muysken 1988b: 203):

(4)   nuway (frozen from Sp *no hay* 'there is not')   12
       nuwabi- (regularised frozen form from Sp *no haber*)   8
       abi- (regularised from Sp *haber*)   21
       abi (uninflected form of *haber*)   1
       a (from Spanish *ha*, the 3s auxiliary form of *haber*)   1
       sinta- (from Spanish *sentar* 'be seated')   4

In (3b), finally, the reportative expression *zi*-n-mi 'say-3-AF' (< *decir* 'say') replaces the Quechua enclitic evidential reportative *-shi*, and corresponds directly to Spanish *dicen* 'they say'.

Consistently, all bound forms are Quechua, with the exception of an occasional diminutive *-itu/-ita*, as in (3a) above, and the subordinator *-ndu* (Spanish gerund *-ndo*). In Quechua adverbial clauses there is switch reference, i.e. the form of the subordinator depends on the identity (*-sha*) or non-identity (*-kpi*) of the two subjects. In (5) we find both *-sha* and *-ndu* being used.

(5) *ahi*-munda   *durmi*-sha-ga   *tres*   *día*-da   *bindi*-**sha**   *lunis*,
     there-ABL   sleep-SS-TO   three   day-AC   sell-SS   Monday

     domingo,   *lunes,*   *martes*-ta   *bindi*-**ndu**   *martes*   *tarde*-ga
     Sunday   Monday   Tuesday-AC   sell-SUB   Tuesday   late-TO

     bini-lla
     come.1s-DEL
     'Then sleeping there, selling three days, selling Monday, Sunday, Monday,
     Tuesday, I come [home] late Tuesday.'

In the recorded sequence in (6) various cases of the existential appear. In (6a) we find the new relexified form *nuway* (Sp *no hay* 'there is not'). In (6b), (6d), and (6e) we see *abi*- in combination with the Quechua different subject subordinator *-kpi* and the Spanish-derived *-ndu*.

(6)   (a) *awa*   **nuway**-ga   *así*-mi   *no*   *bali*-n-ga
          water   there.is.not-TO   thus-AF   not   be.worth-3-TO
          'There is no water. Like this it is not worth it.'

      (b) *awa*   **abi-kpi**-ga   *xwirti*   *llano*-guna   *sembra*-na,   *fruta*-guna
          Water   have-DS-TO   strong   field-p   sow-p   fruit-p

          azi-na-chari,   *no,*   *papa*   *azi*-na,   *manzana*-guna,
          make-NOM-DUB   no   potato   make-NOM   apple-p

          peras-guna   *sembra*-na   *llano*-guna
          pear.p-p   sow-NOM   field-p
          'If there is water [we can] sow fields liberally, fields to plant fruit
          perhaps, no, plant potatoes, plant apples, pears.'

      (c) *aki*-bi-ga   *artu*   *xundu*   *llano,*   *ñutu*   *llano*-guna-marí
          here-LOC-TO   much   deep   field   fine   field-p-CONF
          'Here [there are] many deep fields, fine [earth] fields.'

      (d) *awa*   **abi-ndu**-ga   *lindo*   *kosecha*-ni
          water   have-SUB-TO   pretty   harvest-1s
          'If there is water, I harvest very well.'

(e) *porke   no   awa   **abi-kpi**,   no   kosecha*-nchi,   *ni   llober,*
    because   not   water   have-DS   not   harvest-1p   nor   rain.INF

   no   llobi-y-da-sh   *no   llobi*-n
   not   rain-NOM-AC-IND   rain-3
   'Because there is no water, we don't harvest, nor rain, no rain it doesn't
   rain.'

In (6e) a Spanish subordinating conjunction appears, *porke* 'because', which does not have a Quechua correspondent. I will return to such elements below, and want to refer readers to my earlier work for a more detailed perspective on Media Lengua.

The question to be posed here is how the facts of Media Lengua relate to a possible lexical/functional distinction. The facts are not exactly as in the scheme given above by Bakker. The grammar and the bound forms are from Quechua, the free lexical morphemes are from Spanish, but the free grammatical morphemes are not from either language, but exclusively from Spanish. These include in Media Lengua:

(7)   (a) pronouns: nustru 'we', el 'he/she/it'
        (b) negation: no 'not', ni 'not (emphatic)'
        (c) demonstratives: isti 'this', isi ' that'
        (d) locatives: akí 'here', ahí 'there'

However, none of these categories belongs to the Quechua functional skeleton. In Quechua, the corresponding elements function morpho-lexically as independent elements, which can be marked for case and carry other morphological endings. Negation is additionally marked by an enclitic *-chu*, which appears as such in Media Lengua. Quechua pronouns are only obligatory in emphatic contexts. Nonetheless, sometimes these category systems are relexified pretty much intact, as is the case with the pronouns. In Table 16.2 the Media Lengua pronoun system is contrasted with that of Quechua and Spanish. It is clear that it resembles the Quechua system much more than the Spanish system, with the exception of the first person non-subject form *ami*, modelled on Spanish. Its bi-syllabic nature (which conforms better to Quechua phonotactics, in which mono-syllabic roots are rare) may have contributed to its retention in Media Lengua. In Quechua and Media Lengua, but not in Spanish, case differences in the pronouns are marked by case endings, and not by suppletion, as in Spanish.

Most of the lexical items in Media Lengua correspond to lexical categories in Quechua, but there are a few sets of elements present which have no Quechua counterpart, summarised in Table 16.3.

These categories can be viewed as Spanish borrowings into Media Lengua, however. They correspond to a considerable extent to what we saw in chapter 15 with respect to Spanish loans in Bolivian Quechua.

Table 16.2. *The personal pronouns of Media Lengua contrasted with those of Quechua and Spanish (based on Muysken 1981: 58) (in parentheses, the number of cases encountered [variants which only occurred once in the corpus are excluded]; In bold, the forms which can be directly modelled on Quechua)*

	Quechua	Media Lengua	Spanish
1s	ñuka(-case)	**yo** (83) ami-case (12)	yo (NOMI) a mí (AC/DA, strong) me (AC/DA, weak) mi (GE)
2s	kan(-case)	**bos(-case)** (19)	vos (familiar) tú (intimate) usted (polite) te (AC/DA non-polite) le (AC/DA polite) tu (GE non-polite) su (GE polite)
3s	pay(-case)	**el(-case)** (20)	él (m, NO) ella (f, NO) le (AC/DA) su (GE)
1p	ñukunchi(-case)	**nustru(-case)** (35) nustrus (2) nosotros (2)	nosotros (NO) nuestro/a (GE)
2p	kan-guna(-case)	**bos-kuna(-case)** (4)	ustedes su (GE)
3p	pay-guna(-case)	**el-kuna(-case)** (20)	ellos (m, NO) ellas (f, NO) su (GE)

The existence of varieties such as Media Lengua have alerted us to the possibility of taking lexical shapes from one language and combining them with grammatical elements from another one, the process referred to by Bakker (1997) as intertwining. One of the examples cited by Bakker (1997: 200) is Senkyoshigo, the Japanese/English jargon used by American Mormon missionaries in Japan as an in-group language (Smout 1988). English provides the function words and affixes, Japanese the content words:

(8)   Hey   *dode*, have you   *benkyo*ed your   *seiten*s for our   *sukay* today yet?
         Companion   study   scriptures   meeting
         'Hey companion, have you studied your scriptures for our meeting today yet?'

Table 16.3. *Spanish borrowings into Media Lengua (based on Muysken 1981)*

Category	Examples	#
Prepositions	de 'of'	12
	a 'to, AC.AN'	12
	por 'by'	6
	para 'for'	6
	entre 'among'	4
	komo 'like'	3
	hasta 'until'	3
	sin 'without'	3
	en 'in'	2
Conjunctions	i 'and'	17
	o 'or'	6
	pero 'but'	13
	sino ke 'but rather'	1
Complementiser *ki*	ki 'that'	6
	porke 'because'	3
	aunke 'although'	3

Again, what counts as a function word may be different here from other cases. Elements like *today* and *Hey* pattern with the function words here.

Split languages: Michif

Michif, a Cree/French contact language that emerged in Canada in the nineteenth century and is now spoken in parts of western Canada and the northern United States, shows an asymmetry between the nominal and the verbal complex. The most complete account of this language is given in Bakker (1997). The predominant feature of this language is that the verbs are derived from Cree and the nouns from French. The spelling here is orthographic rather than phonemic, and French is in italic:

(9)   kî-nipi-yiwa   *son frère*   aspin kâ-*la-petite-fille*-iwi-t
      PST-die-OBV.SU   3s.PO.m brother   since COMP-the-little-girl-be-3s
      'Her brother died when she was a young girl.' (Bakker and Muysken 1994: 45)

(10)   *la*   *jument* ki:-aja:w-e:w   *un*   *petit*   *poulain*
      DET.f.s   mare PST-have-TA-3>3'   IND.m.s   little   foal
      'The mare had a foal.' (Bakker 1997: 87)

Table 16.4. *Contribution of different languages to the Michif word inventory (based on Bakker 1997: 117, Table 4.3)*

Category	Cree	French	Other
nouns	few	**83–94%**	few Ojibwe, English
verbs	**88–99%**	few	some mixed Cree/French
question words	**almost all**		
personal pronouns	**almost all**		
adverbial particles	70%	30%	
postpositions	**almost all**		
coordinating conjunctions	55%	40%	5% English
prepositions	some	**70–100%**	
numerals		**almost all**	
demonstratives	**almost all**		
negation	30%	70%	

(11)   êkwa   pâstin –am   *sa*   *bouche*   ôhi   *le*   *loup*
        and   open-he.it   his.f   mouth   this-OBV DET.M wolf

        ê-wî-otin-ât
        COMP-want-take-he.him
        'and he opened his mouth and the wolf wanted to take him.' (Bakker 1997: 6)

The asymmetry coincides with the asymmetry between function words and content words, in Bakker's analysis (1997). He argues that the verbal roots in Algonquian (the family to which Cree belongs) should be viewed as abstract functional elements, and are hence not subject to relexification. However, it remains to be established whether this explanation suffices. Table 16.4 presents an overview of the contribution of the different languages to the Michif word inventory.

This table shows the clear division, in most domains, between different categories with respect to their language source. It is clear from Bakker's description that overall, Cree has made the most important contribution to Michif grammar, except for the domain of the noun phrase. However, on the level of the sentence as a whole, there has been extensive influence from French as well, and some innovation.

In Table 16.5, the contribution of the different languages to the morpho-syntactic categories in the nominal and verbal domain are presented.

The more detailed overview of Table 16.5 gives a clearer picture of the nature of the asymmetry, in conjunction with Table 16.4. In the verbal domain, the only productive influence from French is at the sentential level. The most striking

Table 16.5. *Contribution of the different languages to the morpho-syntactic categories in Michif*

	Cree	French
Nominal	obviation marking	fem/masc gender
	demonstratives	number
	some quantifiers	definite/indefinite articles
	personal pronouns	pre-nominal adjective agreement
	question words	possessive pronouns
		numerals
		some quantifiers
Verbal	order or mode	clausal modal particles
	person agreement	conjugation *avoir* (limited distribution)
	tense	conjugation *être* (limited distribution)
	mood	
	modality	
	aspect	
	direct/inverse	
	obviation	
	verbal number	
	animate/inanimate gender	

example is a set of innovative modal particles, which have grammaticalised, such as:

(12) encore   'I wish'
       pas moyen 'it is impossible'
       ça prend 'it is necessary'

For the rest, French only plays a role in the immediate nominal domain, which we may call the 'small DP'. The large DP, linking the noun phrase to the rest of the clause, is Cree-oriented, as shown by the presence of obviative marking and the demonstratives. The clausal skeleton is solidly Cree in origin.

Can we state that Michif is like Media Lengua in being primarily the result of intertwining? Even disregarding the innovations at the level of the sentence (which, incidentally, we find in Media Lengua as well), and accepting Bakker's account for why the verbs have remained Cree (they are functional in Cree rather than lexical), the answer is still negative. The 'small DP'-internal French structure, with French gender, number, definiteness, and pre-nominal adjective agreement, is adopted as a whole, and shows only marginal Cree influence.

Table 16.6. *Overall text count (in percentages, types) of the Copper Island Aleut lexicon in terms of word classes and etymological source (based on Sekerina 1994: 29)*

	% Aleut	% Russian	Total #
Verbs	94	6	180
Nouns	61.5	38.5	150
Pronouns	33.5	66.5	18
Function words	31.5	68.5	152

Reverse split type

While Michif resembles Media Lengua in that the verbal system derives from the original community language, Copper Island Aleut provides a more complex mixture. It is currently being replaced by Russian, but contains both Aleut and Russian elements. An example of this language is given in (13) (Russian in italic), where it can be seen that verbal tense and the clitic pronouns are Russian:

(13) *ya*   *tibe*   cíbu-x   ukagla:γa:sa:-*l*
      1s.SU 2s.ob   parcel-ABS   bring-PST
      'I brought you a parcel.' (Golovko and Vakhtin 1990: 105)

Table 16.6 gives an overall text count (in types) of the Copper Island Aleut lexicon in terms of word classes and etymological source (based on Sekerina 1994: 29):

Table 16.6 shows the strong lexical presence of Aleut, and the more important role of Russian in the grammatical system, but is of limited use in that the categories distinguished are too general and no attention is paid to derivational and inflectional morphology. In Table 16.7, a more detailed overview is given of the contribution of Aleut and Russian to the morpho-syntactic categories in the nominal and verbal domain.

From Table 16.7 it is quite clear that there is an intricate mixture of the two languages, with a pronounced asymmetry between the nominal (mostly Aleut) and the verbal (mostly Russian) domain. At the clausal level both languages appear to be active, and as in the case of Media Lengua and Michif, much innovation has taken place.

As pointed out by McConvell (e.g. 2001) a number of new mixed languages are emerging in Australia which resemble Copper Island Aleut in their features. I will illustrate these very interesting new types of language with data from

Table 16.7. *Contribution of Aleut and Russian to the morpho-syntactic categories in the nominal and verbal domain (primarily based on the data in Sekerina 1994)*

	Aleut	Russian
Nominal	absolute (0) / relative (m) case	subject pronouns
	possessive nominal markers	some object pronouns replacing Aleut forms
	nominal derivational suffixes	some demonstratives
	direct object pronouns	
	oblique objects	
	comitative marking	
	local postpositions	
	demonstratives	
	question words	
	no adjectives	
	topic number agreement	
	nominal negation	
Verbal	derivational suffixes	tense (agglutinative)
	conjunctive (rare)	person (agglutinative)
	conditional (rare)	number (agglutinative)
	purposive (rare)	marginal gender (agglutinative)
	some verbal negation	no Russian aspect
		verbal negation
		negative existential

Light Warlpiri (O'Shanessy 2005). The following three sentences, taken from O'Shanessy's work, illustrate the contrast:

(14)   (a)   Warlpiri
             Yirra-rni ka-Ø-Ø *leda* watiya-ngka kurdu-pardu-rlu.
             put-NPST IMPF-3s-3s ladder tree-LOC child-DIM-ERG
             'A child is putting a ladder against the tree.'

        (b)   Aboriginal English
             Dat boi bin purr-um leda on dat tri.
             DET boy PST put-TR ladder P DET tree
             'The boy put a ladder against the tree.'

        (c)   Light Warlpiri
             Kurdu-pawu-ng *i*-m *purr-um leda* na watiya-wana.
             child-DIM-ERG 3sg-NFU put-TR ladder DIS tree-PERL
             'The child is putting the ladder against the tree.'

Reverse type: Spanish Romani or Caló

A number of mixed Romani varieties in Europe have been documented. Quite a bit is known about some of them, such as Angloromani, while very little is known about others. Here I will present some data from Spanish Romani or Caló, reported from Spanish Gitanos in Portugal by Coelho (1892) and analysed in the excellent overview article by Boretzky and Igla (1994: 55). While numerous texts in this Spanish with Romani words have survived, there is no good evidence of full Romani having been spoken in Spain, although it surely must have been spoken at an earlier stage. In the following texts, the traceable Romani items are bold, the Spanish elements italic. An occasional element has no known etymology.

(15)   **parn**-*és*   *de*   **sanacay**
       coin-p   of   gold
       'golden coins' (p. 7)

(16)   *para*   **jal**-*ar*   **terel**-*a*   **boque**
       for   ear-INF   have-3s   hunger
       'one is hungry enough to eat' (p. 7)

(17)   **mek**-*les*!   *Non*   **chingarel**-*as*   *más*   *con*   *los*   **gacho**-*s*
       leave-CLI3p.ob   not   quarrel-2s   more   with   DET.m.p   non-Gypsy-p
       'Leave them! Do not quarrel any more with the (outsider) men!' (p. 9)

(18)   *te*   **amarel**-*o*   *con*   *una*   **churi**
       CLI2s.ob   kill-1s   with   IND.f.s   knife
       'I will kill you with a knife.' (p. 8)

(19)   *qué*   **chorro**   *está*   *el*   **chibe**   *que*   *non*   *pued-en*
       what   weary   is   DET.m.s   day   that   not   can-3p
       and-ar   *los*   **chiquel**-*es*
       walk-INF   DET.m.p   dog-p
       'How weary is this day that the dogs cannot walk.' (p. 9)

(20)   *vamos*   **jun**-*ar*   **O-tebel**   *la*   **cangueri**?
       let's.go   listen-INF   DET-God   DET.f.s   church
       'Shall we go and listen to God in the church?' (p. 10)

All functional categories, including person, tense, infinitive markings, prepositions, number, articles, pronouns, the copula, and conjunctions are from Spanish. Romani-derived verbs are inflected with the -*ar* conjugation. Romani-derived nouns do retain their own gender, however. Thus we have *una churi* 'a (f) knife' and *la cangueri* 'the (f) church'. The article *o* in *O-tebel* 'God' is a frozen form. Finally it should be mentioned that in other texts the Romani copula has survived.

Table 16.8. *Possibilities for the intact preservation of source language semantic and syntactic organisation of functional categories when relexified*

Source language grammaticalised	Target language grammaticalised	Relexification outcome
yes	no	preservation
no	yes	restructuring
yes	yes	intermediate
no	no	like other lexical items

Functional categories and relexification

A final issue to be discussed is whether the process of relexification affects functional categories differently from lexical categories. In Muysken (1988b) the hypothesis is put forward that functional categories are restructured under relexification because of target language paradigmatic pressure: since the target language form is part of a paradigmatic system, its meaning plays a role in the resulting relexified item. For lexical items, there is an independent *tertium quid*, a third concept (e.g. the idea of 'hunger'), on the basis of which relexification may take place. Thus the Spanish noun *hambre* 'hunger' provided the phonetic model for a Media Lengua impersonal verb *ambri-* 'to give the sensation of hunger', modelled on the Quechua verb *yarxa-* with the same meaning. For functional categories, such a language-independent bridge concept is not available, and hence the semantic organisation of the phonetic target language always plays a role. This was argued to be true for Media Lengua on the basis of the demonstratives, which in Quechua, but not in Spanish, can also serve as locatives in combination with a case marker. Hence we have Quechua *chi-bi* 'there' (literally, 'that-LOC') and *kay-mu* 'to here' (literally, 'this-DA'). In Media Lengua we have either the Spanish demonstrative (e.g. *isi* 'that' and *isti-da* 'this-AC') but a locative adverb combined with a case marker (*ahi-bi* 'there' (literally, 'there-LOC') and *aki-mu* 'to here' (literally, 'here-DA')).

A contrasting hypothesis would be that functional categories are in fact successfully relexified, without semantic restructuring, because of source language stability. This would depend of course on the degree to which they are grammaticalised in the source language. Since the item may or may not be grammaticalised in the target either, this would give us four possibilities, as illustrated in Table 16.8.

It will require much further research to see whether indeed the interaction between source language stability and target language paradigmatic pressure really does lead to the mixed results predicted in Table 16.8, but it provides a way to explain the findings in some recent studies such as the ones of Aboh (2006), which contradict the earlier hypothesis in Muysken (1988b).

Conclusions

The picture that emerges from this survey of so-called 'mixed languages' is a very mixed one. On the one hand, we find language such as Media Lengua where the functional categories (which then need to be defined as affixes) are from the matrix language, and lexical categories (which then need to be defined as roots) are from Spanish. On the other hand, there are various types of languages where the inventory of functional categories itself is mixed in nature. It may be possible to draw up scenarios which account for these asymmetries, but this is not easy to do.

17 *Foreigner Talk*

In Foreigner Talk – the way some native speakers interact with people who barely speak their language, particularly speakers with low social status – a number of modifications occur (Ferguson 1971; Snow *et al.* 1981). These particularly affect functional categories proper, such as determiners, agreement and tense markers, and some linkers. Discourse cohesion in Foreigner Talk is established contextually rather than overtly.

Meisel (1980: 20) provides a number of typical examples of German Foreigner Talk. In (1a) the non-polite second pronoun *du* is used, the article before *Seite* is omitted, and there is an infinitive *gehen* used in an imperative context. In (1b) there is no verb, again the use of *du*, and no directional preposition. In (1c) the future time reference is lacking, the negator *nix* 'nothing' is used instead of *nicht* 'not', and a directional adverb is lacking. It cannot be established whether the verb is in the infinitive here or in the (correct) plural.

(1)   (a) Du auf andere Seite gehen.
             you on other side go.INF
             'You should go to the other side.'

       (b) Du schnell Haus.
             you fast house
             'You should go home quickly.'

       (c) Wir nix gehen hin.
             we nothing go.INF/p toward
             'We will not go there.'

These are examples of fairly impolite Foreigner Talk (see below).

The following examples from Finnish Foreigner Talk (cited by Meisel 1980: 23, from work by Manfred Pienemann) show that the phenomenon is not limited to Indo-European languages (although quite possibly culture-specific). Compare the Foreigner Talk versions in (2a–d) with the standard Finnish paraphrases for the sentences in (2a′–d′) (provided by Helena Halmari):

(2)   (a)   Mikä maa?
              'What country [are you from]?'

       (a')   Mistä maasta tulet?
              where-ELAT country-ELAT come-2S
              or more naturally:
              Mistä maasta olet kotoisin/lähtöisin?
              'What is your home country?'

       (b)   Huomenna sauna?
              '[Shall we go] tomorrow [to the] sauna?'

       (b')   Mennäänkö huomenna saunaan?
              go-PASS-Q tomorrow sauna-IL
              'Let's go to the sauna tomorrow, okay?'
              (here *mennäänkö* is a bit informal, but quite natural)

       (c)   Miksi Suomessa?
              'Why [are you] in Finland?'

       (c')   Miksi olet Suomessa?
              why   be-2S Finland-INE
              'Why are you in Finland?'
              or also:
              Minkä vuoksi/takia olet Suomessa?
              'For what reason are you in Finland?'

       (d)   Suomi hyvä.
              'Finland [is] good'

       (d')   Suomi on hyvä.
              'Finland is good.'
              more natural would be:
              Suomi on hyvä maa.
              'Finland is (a) good country.'

Foreigner Talk in Finnish involves the overuse of the nominative case (e.g. *maa* instead of *maasta* in (2a), *sauna* as opposed to *saunaan* in (2b), as well as the deletion of the copula, as in (2c–d).

Abney (1987: 66) writes: 'Words with immediacy and concreteness are those with descriptive content; they are the words that survive when language is reduced to its bare bones, as when one is attempting to communicate with a non-speaker of one's language.' However, other elements may not be affected: (strong) pronouns and deictic elements are prominent in Foreigner Talk. In this chapter, the data for Foreigner Talk in different languages will be systematically compared, and models for Foreigner Talk production will be explored. First, however, I will try to delimit Foreigner Talk in relation to other simple codes.

Simple codes

It has been known at least since the work of the Austrian Romanist Hugo
Schuchardt that in language-contact settings native speakers often adjust their
speech to accommodate to non-native speakers; this was later called 'Foreigner
Talk Register'. In Schuchardt (1909) the use of infinitives instead of finite verb
forms in the Mediterranean contact vernacular Lingua Franca was attributed to
the way speakers of Romance languages adjust their speech in this register, using
infinitives when speaking to foreigners. In Schuchardt (1921) several stages in
native/non-native interaction (involving overseers and slaves on a plantation)
are distinguished, part of the process of creole genesis in Surinam. In stage 1 the
slave tries to learn the emphatic expressions and exaggerations of the overseer. In
stage 2 there was mutual adjustment: the slave stripped away everything special
from the European languages, while the overseer kept everything special ('alles
besondere') back. They found each other in the middle.

Bloomfield (1933: 472) termed this way of speaking **Baby Talk**, and writes
in a by now classic paragraph:

> Speakers of the lower language may make so little progress in learning the
> dominant speech, that the masters, in communicating with them resort to
> 'baby talk'. This 'baby talk' is the master's imitation of the subjects' incorrect
> speech. There is reason to believe that it is by no means an exact imitation,
> and that some of its features are based not upon the subjects' mistakes but
> upon grammatical relations that exist within the upper language itself. The
> subjects, in turn, deprived of the correct model, can do no better now than to
> acquire the simplified 'baby talk' version of the upper language.

Bloomfield thus perceives Foreigner Talk as something with potentially distinct
properties, in principle, from interlanguage, the product of L2 learning. For
Schuchardt, the two might coincide in converging on the unmarked.

Foreigner Talk has a few properties in common with **Teacher Talk**, the
register used by foreign language teachers who are trying to use the target
language, new to the pupils, in class. Both use simple short sentences and
frequent pauses. However, Teacher Talk has properties of its own, dictated by
the pedagogic situation, and may be much more normative than other forms of
addressing non-native speakers.

Similarly, Foreigner Talk may resemble, or not, **Interlanguage talk**, as noted
above. Although many users of Foreigner Talk believe there is an almost exact
resemblance (see below), in fact there are many differences.

A third register to be considered here is **Caretaker Speech**, also referred to
as 'baby talk' or 'motherese'. Clearly young children are addressed in a special

way, with short, comprehensible sentences, but just as in the case of Teacher Talk, Caretaker Speech has many special features, such as high pitch, using endearing names, diminutives, etc., which make it different from Foreigner Talk. Nonetheless, there are many commonalities, and users of both registers may rely on shared capacities.

Finally, the omission of many elements and the use of short sentences make Foreigner Talk similar to **Telegraphic Style**, used when messages have to be conveyed in a succinct manner, as in a telex or telegram, and perhaps also in sms-messages, chat-messages, etc. Pragmatically, this is a very distinct way of communicating, but the abbreviation capacity may be shared.

Leaving these other simplified codes aside (and there may be many other partly similar ones, such as headline style, recipe style, some nurse/patient interactions, etc.), I now turn to Foreigner Talk proper. Broadaway (1994) distinguishes **Foreigner Talk**, 'a mode of simplification by which native speakers imitate the speech of non-native speakers for the purpose of entertainment, social distancing, mimicking, etc.', from **Foreigner Register**, 'an empathetic mode of simplification that seeks to improve communication with foreigners by simplifying surface forms'. I think this separation between 'good' Foreigner Talk (empathetic, adaptive, helpful for the learner) and 'bad' Foreigner Talk (discriminatory, distance creating, not helpful for the learner) is too absolute. Rather, Foreigner Talk must be seen as quite varied in its manifestations, varying along at least two dimensions: (a) some, but by no means all, of it is strongly influenced by (sometimes colonialist and discriminatory) transmitted cultural models, as stressed by Valdman (1977); (b) the type of Foreigner Talk also depends quite a bit on the amount of L2 competence of the non-native speaker. Perhaps culturally transmitted Foreigner Talk is particularly frequent when the non-native speaker has very limited competence, triggering an extreme response, or when there are sharp social and ethnic divisions, to which Foreigner Talk then contributes. Fully realising that reality is more complex, I will use the terms 'moderate' and 'extreme' Foreigner Talk here, occasionally turning to the issue of cultural models.

The study of Foreigner Talk

A number of sources are available for gaining insight into the various dimensions of Foreigner Talk: popular fiction, introspection studies, observations of non-routine interactions, and observations of routine interactions. The sources reported on here come from four different European languages – English,

French, German, and Dutch – and there are also reports of it with non-Indo-European languages, as noted. There are some differences between the languages involved, but these are not striking.

In popular fiction, the cultural stereotypes of Foreigner Talk are transmitted. Note that it is not the native speaker here who provides the basis for the stereotype, but the way the non-native speaker is portrayed, at worst as a case of 'Tarzanese'. A typical example is the way in which the speech of Friday in *Robinson Crusoe* is represented, at least in some editions. We studied a number of the Dutch translations of this book and noted that Friday's speech is progressively presented as more deviant in the later translations (cf. Werkgroep Taal Buitenlandse Werknemers 1978). Another example is the older editions of Tintin or other comic books. More recent editions of Tintin have been cleansed of this clearly derogatory way of portraying foreigners.

Ferguson (1975) introduced the research paradigm of 'introspection studies': asking a group of native speakers how they would transform a set of specific sentences if they had to convey their meaning to speakers with very limited knowledge of the language. Fairly consistent reactions are given by native subjects; however, these are in part based on the cultural stereotype mentioned before and do not necessarily reflect actual practice. Another interesting finding is that there is no difference between introspective judgements about the native speakers' own Foreigner Talk and about their view of what non-native speakers with limited competence would say.

More reliable information comes from recordings and observations of interactions between native speakers who do not interact with non-native speakers on a routine basis. Some of this comes from recordings where passers-by were asked where a public building like a post office was and were surreptitiously taped. Native speakers differ quite a bit in their reactions to questions of this nature, e.g. the extent to which they rely on cultural stereotypes in such a setting.

Finally, some researchers have succeeded in making observations of interactions between native speakers and non-native speakers where the native speaker interacted with L2 learners on a routine basis. Thus we recorded officials at a municipal desk for public housing distribution and for residence permit distribution (Werkgroep Taal Buitenlandse Werknemers 1978, the officials are termed 'routiniers' in that study). Here the influence of cultural stereotypes seems absent and patterns are most regular. We also found that there was a high correlation between the complexity of the speech of the officials and that of the non-native speakers.

I will begin by reporting on the features of moderate Foreigner Talk, as observed by various authors (see also Broadaway 1994). Pragmatic features of this register include:

- a focus on the here and now
- comprehension checks
- a preference for yes/no questions.

Among the grammatical features we find:

- a lower degree of subordination
- various forms of repetition
- paraphrasing, rephrasing
- an avoidance of reductions in rapid speech
- producing separate words with pauses
- the use of highly frequent and transparent words
- highlighting of specific words.

Thus speakers adjust their pace, their prosody, and their lexicon. They introduce small changes in the grammar and produce shorter sentences. However, the speech remains fully grammatical, and functional elements are not affected.

This changes when there is very little comprehension. Then native speakers may start to produce elliptic speech with VP-chunks and separate constituents, and omit specific elements. There may also be much gesturing. Extreme Foreigner Talk is interesting to me in this context because functional categories are affected, as can be seen in Table 17.1.

This table contains the features reported on in a number of studies of different types: literary sources, introspection studies, non-routine Foreigner Talk, and routine Foreigner Talk. The features are arranged in terms of the frequency with which they have been noted to occur. Notice, however, that the different types of studies have not always yielded similar results.

We may divide the features into three groups:

(A) *Features that are frequently mentioned in all studies.*
The features in this category tend not to reduce the semantic content of the message a great deal, and this category does not contain any overtly stigmatised features. They are listed in (3).

(3)   General features
        (a) Article omission is reported in a great many studies; it affects
            particularly the indefinite article.
        (b) Similarly, short sentences are highly frequent. These are probably
            general across the board although this is not always reported.

Table 17.1. *Schematic overview of findings for different grammatical variables in a number of studies of Foreigner Talk, based on Werkgroep Taal Buitenlandse Werknemers (1978)*

	Literary sources	Introspection studies					Non-routiniers			Routiniers			
	1	2	3	4	5	6	7	8	9	10	11	12	13
article omission	F	T	+	F	+	+		+	F			M	F
short sentences	T	T	+	T		+		+	F				M
copula omission	F	T	+	T	+	+	A		M	M	T	M	M
no question inversion		T	F	F		+			+	T	F	F	F
subject pronoun omission	A	F	M	F		+	A	+	F	F	F		M
strong pronouns	+	F		T	+	+						F	F
auxiliary omission	F	T		F		+	A		M	T	F		F
finiteness omission	F		F	F	F	F		F	M				M
juxtaposition			T	T		+						M	M
negative simplification		F	T	M		+			A	F	F	M	
you *in imperatives*	M	F	T	M		+							
past tense omission	+	T		M			A			T	F		
possessive omission		M								M	M		T
adpositional genitive		M	+								F		
polite form omission		T	M			F		+	A				A
plural omission		F	+	A						A	A	T	A

Note: M = marginal, less than 30% of the cases; F = frequent, between 30% and 80% of the cases; T = typical, more often than 80% of the cases; + = mentioned, no indication of frequency; A = absent
Literary sources: 1 = Robinson Crusoe and Tintin
Introspection studies: 2 = Ferguson (1975); 3 = Meisel (1975); 4 = Amsterdam group (1978), 5 Valdman (1977); 6 – Meisel (1977)
Empirical studies with non-routiniers: 7 = Campbell *et al.* (1977); 8 = Clyne (1968); 9 = Amsterdam group (1978)
Empirical studies with routiniers: 10 = Hatch *et al.* (1978) Rina; 11 = Hatch *et al.* (1978); 12 = Katz (1977); 13 = Amsterdam group (1978)

(c) Apparently, questions need not be inverted, with pragmatic intent signalled in other ways.
(d) Copula omission is very often reported as well, although it is sometimes claimed to be absent or marginal, possibly because it is stigmatised somewhat as a 'pidgin' feature.
(e) Subject pronoun omission is often mentioned, and indeed in many contexts it will be neither stigmatised nor lead to loss of meaning.

(B) *Features frequently mentioned in the literary sources and in the introspection studies, but not in the recorded interactions.*
The features in this category, listed in (4), tend to be part of the stereotypical view of Foreigner Talk, but are stigmatised as impolite and pidgin-like, and may hinder communication:

(4)   Frequent only in literary and introspection studies
    (a) Strong pronouns are often assumed to be part of Foreigner Talk, but may be stigmatised to some extent.
    (b) Finiteness omission, i.e. speaking in infinitives, and auxiliary omission, which often leads to the same result, are part of the intuitive Foreigner Talk repertoire for many speakers, but also quite stigmatised as 'pidgin'.
    (c) Juxtaposition, the combining of constituents without apparent cohesion, likewise will occur particularly in extreme settings, but is considered quite impolite.
    (d) The same holds for the emphatic use of 'you' in imperatives.
    (e) Past tense omission again can be seen as pidgin-like, and sometimes may lead to communication problems.

(C) *Features that are not particularly frequently mentioned in any kind of study.*
This category contains features that are either highly stigmatised, concern constructions relevant only to particular languages, or seriously impede communication.

(5)   Infrequent features
    (a) Possessive omission leads to semantic loss.
    (b) The adpositional genitive, e.g. Dutch *huis van mij* 'house of me' instead of *mijn huis* 'my house' is relevant only for some languages, and considered impolite.
    (c) Polite form omission, e.g. a *du* form in stead of a *Sie* form in German, is highly stigmatised, and often mentioned as a feature of Foreigner Talk by non-native speakers.
    (d) Plural omission, finally, leads to information loss, and does not really present a simplification.
    (e) Negative simplification.

Various attempts have been made to relate the incidence of these three groups of features to more general accounts of Foreigner Talk. These are discussed in the next section.

Maxims, strategies, and models for Foreigner Talk

There are various ways to bring the discussion of Foreigner Talk to a slightly more abstract level, although so far no altogether theoretically coherent account has emerged. Possibly this is due to the diffuseness of the phenomenon under consideration. I will discuss an approach in terms of maxims, and a second and third approach in terms of strategies and models. A first possibility is that we assume that the incidence and shape of Foreigner Talk is constrained by a number of maxims, which may compete or operate conjointly:

(6)   Be **polite**. Show respect for the status of the interlocutor.

As already alluded to above with the distinction between Foreigner Talk and Foreigner Register and in the discussion of individual features, simplified forms of speech are subject to considerable stigmatisation in certain cultures. Hence (6) blocks a number of reductions.

(7)   Be **informative**: Try to convey your message as accurately as possible.

This maxim blocks extreme reductions in meaning, leading to a preference for those forms of simplification which affect only the surface realisation of information.

(8)   Pay **attention** to the hearer.

This maxim stresses the degree of adaptation to the interlocutor's speech.

(9)   Try to present the information as **comprehensibly** as possible.
(10)   Be as **brief** as possible.

These maxims, which build on the maxims in the work of Grice (e.g. 1989), depart from the intention of the speaker, which is culturally and situationally grounded, to be sure. Notice that these maxims may conflict with each other.

   A second possibility is in terms of psycholinguistic strategies. Meisel (1980: 14) distinguishes five strategies of simplication, which may be operant in Foreigner Talk as well.

(11)   Meisel's simplification strategies
        (a) Simplification of surface structure and deletion of morphological
            information;
        (b) Derivational simplification and fewer transformational rules between
            deep and surface structure;
        (c) Simplification of underlying structure;
        (d) Psychological simplification, in terms of processing time, reliance
            on memory span, etc.;
        (e) Perceptual simplification, in terms of the non-violation of perceptual
            strategies.

These strategies are not mutually incompatible, but address simplification from different perspectives.

Finally, we can consider Foreigner Talk in terms of a number of models, which are the result of these strategies (Werkgroep Taal Buitenlandse Werknemers 1978: 78–82). The first one would be the **adaptation model**: native speakers adjust their production to features of the interlanguage (IL) grammar of their interlocutors:

(12) $NS_{Gn} \leftrightarrow IL_i \ldots IL_j \ldots IL_l$

In such a model native speakers would have some kind of copying capacity, allowing them to model the features of their own speech on those of their interlocutor.

A second possibility would be an **earlier grammar model**, in which the native speaker reverts to earlier stages in her/his own grammatical development when addressing foreigners:

(13) $NS_{Go} \ldots NS_{Gi} \ldots NS_{Gn} \leftrightarrow IL$

In this model speakers have unconscious access to properties of their own earlier language development, which they can reproduce.

An entirely different possibility would be a parataxis, **juxtaposition**, or non-grammar model, in which native speakers rely on non-grammatical strategies in concatenating simple utterances when addressing foreigners:

(14)   ----------- $NS_{Gn} \leftrightarrow IL$
        ---- juxtaposition

The idea behind this model is that speakers have various modes of chaining together words at their disposal, particularly syntax and juxtaposition or parataxis. These modes have different properties:

(15)   (a) *Syntax*
             language specific, even if constrained by universal (UG) principles
             grammaticised, i.e. rich in functional categories
             automatised

        (b) *Juxtaposition or parataxis*
             universal
             non-grammatical, no specific functional categories
             not automatised, improvisational

Notice that in the second mode, functional categories are not there as part of the operating system.

A model which takes cultural norms explicitly into account would be a cultural filter model. Here the full native grammar output would be subject to various culturally determined omission procedures, which then yield the Foreigner Talk utterance:

(16) NS_{Gn} + omission procedures $\leftrightarrow$ IL

This model would work best if mere reduction of specific features is what is at stake, and possibly register-specific grammatical sub-features or lexical items are required.

Finally, we could conceive of a reduced processor model, in which part of the procedures of the formulator (Levelt 1989) are not carried out.

(17)   ----------------------------------   NS $\leftrightarrow$ IL
          conceptualizer > lexicon > (formulator)

I am not able at this point to derive the precise predictions that these different models would make in such a way that they could be reliably tested.

Conclusions

Whether conceived of in terms of maxims, strategies, or models, it is clear that Foreigner Talk is not a single, invariant, and universal pattern. It is subject to choice by individual speakers, and part of culturally determined modes of interethnic communication. Thus, Dutton (1983) shows that there were two varieties of a Hiri trading language, used in Eleman and Koriki village ports, respectively, in Papua New Guinea, and with separate adaptations of the Hiri forms to non-speakers.

Universal principles are operant in the formation of Foreigner Talk utterances, but the actual form that they take is highly culture specific. In any case, it is clear that functional categories play an important role in the specific features of Foreigner Talk, although we cannot assume a blanket putting out of action of the functional category-specific language production component.

18 Conclusions: towards a modular and multi-dimensional perspective

In this book I have surveyed the role of functional categories in a wide variety of sub-domains, and in this chapter I will try to draw some conclusions. After a summary of the main findings from these different sub-disciplines, the question is raised of how to reconcile the apparent logical independence of the syntactic, semantic, phonological, and morpho-lexical dimensions of functional categories with the fact that they so frequently converge to define what appear on the surface as unitary entities. A multi-factorial model is proposed, where optimalisation strategies lead to further convergence of items on the phonological, morphological, semantic, and syntactic dimensions. I then go on to sketch the issue of functional categories from the perspective of language evolution, the topic of the last section.

Before turning to the general discussion it is useful to summarise the main findings of the different sections of the book: grammar, historical linguistics, psycholinguistics, and language contact studies. As I pointed out in the introductory chapter 1, the concept of 'functional category' is multi-dimensional; it can be viewed from the perspective of syntax, semantics, pragmatics, morphology, the lexicon proper, and phonology. In different chapters, different dimensions of functional categories are stressed.

The syntactic dimensions of functional categories play a role particularly in the studies of psycholinguistics and language contact, as well as in grammaticalisation theory. Semantic aspects play a role in the latter domain as well, both in spoken and in signed languages. Pragmatic aspects play a role in the discussion of language typology, grammaticalisation, code-switching, and Foreigner Talk. Basically, the morphological dimension, the role of inflection, is ubiquitous. It plays a particularly important role in agrammatic aphasia, SLI, language attrition, and language death. Lexical aspects are central of course to linguistic reconstruction, speech production, and many domains of language contact. Phonological aspects are particularly important in historical linguistics and language borrowing. The focus on different sets of categories in different chapters is summarised in Table 18.1.

Table 18.1. *Features of functional categories focused upon in the different chapters*

	Syntax	Semantics	Pragmatics	Morphology	Lexicon	Phonology
Grammar						
2 Language description and typology		X	X	X		
3 Lexicon, morphology, phonology				X	X	X
4 Semantics and pragmatics		X	X			
5 Theoretical syntax	X					
Historical linguistics						
6 Grammaticalisation theory	X	X	X	X		X
7 Linguistic reconstruction				X	X	X
Psycholinguistics						
8 Speech production	X			X	X	
9 Language development	X			X		
10 Agrammatic aphasia, SLI	X			X	X	
11 Language attrition and language death				X		
Language contact						
12 Sign languages	X	X		X	X	
13 Code-switching and code-mixing	X		X	X		
14 Lexical borrowing				X	X	X
15 Pidgin and creole genesis	X			X	X	
16 Mixed languages	X			X	X	
17 Foreigner Talk	X		X	X	X	

Main findings from grammar

In the section on Grammar a number of issues were reviewed: studies in language description and typology, the study of morphology, the lexicon and phonology, and the study of semantics, pragmatics, and theoretical syntax.

In the chapter on **language description and typology** it was shown that the structural description of hitherto undocumented languages had helped refine the notional classification of functional categories and extend the range of categories, including various types of classifiers and deictics, nominal tense markers, etc. The links between the notions embodied in different functional categories have become more diverse, and the absolute separation between the nominal and the verbal domain has disappeared. The existence of widespread polysemy of functional items, often on a concrete/abstract scale, has triggered the study of grammaticalisation processes, discussed separately in chapter six.

The chapter on **morphology, the lexicon, and phonology** concludes from the survey that indeed there is an overall correspondence between the functional status of an element and its form, but that this correspondence cannot be captured by structural principles in an absolute sense. Rather, the tendential nature of the correspondence should be captured by optimalisation procedures at the syntax/lexicon interface. While the study of the phonology/syntax interface has shown that functional categories often show special phonological behaviour, we cannot conclude that the notion of functional category as such needs to be invoked in the study of this interface.

In the chapter on **semantics and pragmatics** a number of semantic and pragmatic aspects of functional categories were surveyed. I conclude that very few semantic features, if any, unambiguously characterise a class of elements that may reasonably be termed functional categories. In the domain of semantics, the absence of sense relations among functional categories and the fact that functional category features sometimes remain uninterpretable at the syntax/semantics interface (since they participate in agreement) are among the clearest properties not found in the domain of lexical categories. As to discourse markers and interjections, these are generally found at the lexical/functional divide.

Finally, the chapter on the **generative syntax tradition** with respect to functional categories points to the fact that these provide the structural skeleton for the main constituents of the sentence, namely the clause and in some languages also the noun phrase and possibly other types of phrases. Skeletal elements are complementisers, agreement and tense markers, and in some languages also case markers and determiners.

Other elements may share some semantic, morphological, and phonological properties with these skeletal elements, and hence resemble syntactically functional categories, but they do not have the central properties of unique categorical selection and non-modifiability of functional categories from the perspective of syntactic processing. There are clear differences between the ways in which adpositions are realised as a lexical class in different languages. Nonetheless, nothing is accomplished by claiming that this class of elements is functional in nature.

Main findings from historical linguistics

From the brief survey of processes of **grammaticalisation theory** in the first chapter of this section it can be concluded that the extent to which different dimensions are involved in the process of grammaticalisation differs somewhat from case to case; often semantic changes are involved, but phonological and morpho-lexical changes may lag behind. Many different categories are involved in grammaticalisation processes. In particular, auxiliaries, adpositions, and conjunctions are categories that often result from grammaticalisation processes. Generative models of syntactic change have successfully incorporated the notion of grammaticalisation, and in some cases have given some of the properties of this process a stronger theoretical foundation.

From the survey of Indo-European, Proto-Uralic, Afro-Asiatic, and Amerind in the chapter on **linguistic reconstruction** it is clear that among the possibly reconstructable items we find many functional categories, which can be expected given the stability of some of these. However, this stability only holds for some categories, notably for pronominal and gender systems.

Main findings from psycholinguistics

In the chapter on **speech production** it is shown that the lexical/functional distinction plays an important role in the psycholinguistic and neurolinguistic study of language processing. However, the definition of what counts as lexical and functional needs further elaboration, since neuro-imaging studies tend not to make the fine distinctions that can be possible in the analysis of the speech error data. Furthermore, it is not clear to which factors the distinct behaviour of the different types of categories must be attributed. Thus, the idea that there is a clear neural functional distinction between the category types as such needs further confirmation. Differences are gradient between the different category types; the fact that prepositions rank high in these studies on the functional scale but not in other domains of analysis also suggests that a more systematic analysis of the available data is needed. Finally, word length, frequency, and abstract meaning may play a separate independent role.

The chapter on **language development** illustrates that in development studies the lexical/functional distinction plays an important role. In first language development, many researchers distinguish between a first phase, in which only a specific set of functional items is present, and a second phase, in which the other categories are gradually acquired. However, the idea that the functional skeleton is completely absent in the earliest stage finds little support. In bilingual child language development there is still disagreement about the degree to which the different languages influence each other. In those cases where interlingual influence is claimed, it seems that the interface between the functional categories and either the lexical representations or the semantics/pragmatics is central to the process of mutual adjustment. Functional categories are acquired in L2 development in a much more gradual fashion; the L1 functional skeleton often plays a central role here.

In the chapter on **agrammatic aphasia and SLI** a number of clinical studies and analyses based on overview surveys are reviewed. The evidence concerning the exact factors involved in the disproportional degree to which the functional categories are affected in agrammatic aphasia and SLI is mixed. In addition to purely structural accounts we find processing accounts. Nonetheless, it is clear from the studies surveyed here that different inflectional systems, case endings, and determiners are affected by the two disorders surveyed.

The chapter on **language attrition and death**, after outlining the beginnings of an analytical framework and surveying some of the factors that have been adduced as contributing to the attrition of functional categories, turns to a series of case studies, focusing on the fate of case systems in East Sutherland Gaelic, Dyirbal, Hungarian in the United States, German in London, and Low German in Siberia. While there are reductions in all case systems, often leading to the loss of the more specialised cases, particularly if these have variable realisations, core cases are often maintained.

Main findings from language contact studies

In this book a number of language contact phenomena have been analysed from the perspective of the role that the lexical/functional distinction plays in them: sign languages, code-switching and code-mixing, lexical borrowing, pidgin and creole genesis, mixed languages, and Foreigner Talk.

In **sign languages** the lexical functional distinction plays a role in various domains of analysis; thus, the phenomenon of mouthing can involve only lexical, not functional elements. Grammaticalisation in sign languages parallels that in spoken languages, although there are some interesting differences as well. The reference tracking and agreement system in sign languages interacts closely with the classifier system. There is no agreement as yet as to what extent the classifier system in sign languages is like that in spoken languages.

The chapter on **code-switching and code-mixing** surveys a number of recent studies in this area. While the lexical/functional distinction plays a crucial role in constraining insertional code-switching or -mixing, the precise definition of 'functional' in this area is still a matter of discussion. Problematic in any case are pronouns and prepositions, as well as determiners and affixes closely associated with a lexical noun or verb.

In the chapter on **lexical borrowing** two typologically and historically very different language pairs, Cochabamba Quechua/Spanish and Maltese Arabic/ Italian were analysed. The two data sets show a rather similar picture: (a) there is very extensive borrowing in the lexical domain; (b) in contrast, we find very limited borrowing, if any, in the domain of the functional categories associated with the syntactic skeleton, like tense, agreement, and case; (c) frequent is the borrowing of nominal number, often together with the associated nouns; and (d) borrowing of (mostly coordinating or adverbial) conjunctions, some peripheral adpositions, and adverbs also occurs.

The chapter on **pidgin and creole genesis** presents a systematic survey of the functional categories of Tok Pisin, Saramaccan, and Negerhollands in several domains: pronouns, adpositions, auxiliaries, and subordinators. It confirms the hypothesis that functional categories are substantially affected by the process of pidginisation and creolisation in their transmission from the lexifier to the pidgin/creole. This is clearest for auxiliaries and subordinators. Creole pronouns tend to be based on the lexical shapes of the pronoun systems of their lexifiers, but the paradigm is often substantially restructured, in terms of the categories expressed, if not the actual morphemes used. For prepositions, the picture is mixed, while the Saramaccan postpositions are of course an innovation with respect to the English and Portuguese, which lack these categories.

In the chapter on **mixed languages** the picture that emerges is a very complex one. On the one hand, we find language such as Media Lengua where the functional categories (which then need to be defined as affixes) are from the matrix language Quechua, and lexical categories (which then need to be defined as roots) are from Spanish. On the other hand, there are various types of languages where the inventory of functional categories itself is mixed in nature. It may be possible to draw up scenarios which account for these asymmetries, but this is not easy to do.

Similarly the chapter on **Foreigner Talk** suggests that the Foreigner Talk register is not a single, invariant, and universal pattern, whether conceived of in terms of maxims, strategies, or models. It is subject to choice by individual speakers, and part of culturally determined modes of interethnic communication. Universal principles are operant in the formation of Foreigner Talk utterances, but the actual form that it takes is highly culture specific. In any case, it is clear that functional categories play an important role in the specific features of Foreigner Talk, although we cannot assume a blanket putting out of action of the functional category-specific language production component.

A differentiated perspective on functional categories

Altogether, the results of the different chapters present us with a double message. On the one hand, the lexical/functional distinction consistently plays an important role in a large variety of domains of language behaviour. On the other hand, there is no single definition of functional category that satisfactorily splits up the domain under consideration into two distinct classes. There are at least a number of elements that fall under the loose definition of 'functional category', a class of elements which is relatively limited in size and does not readily admit new members. The elements typically have a fairly abstract meaning and serve to link different expressed notions, such as predicates and arguments. In (1) seven sets are distinguished, arranged in terms of their degree of integration into the clause:

(1)   *Rough classification of functional categories*
   (a) Interjections are not at all integrated into syntactic structure, and often have deviant morpho-phonological shapes;
   (b) Discourse markers and adverbs are only loosely integrated into the clause;
   (c) Evidential markers, conjunctions, and adpositions;
   (d) Classifiers generally fit into more or less closed classes, but these are often not paradigmatically structured;
   (e) Pronouns are generally tightly organised in paradigms, but often play a relatively independent role, and often do not have special morphology;
   (f) Modals and auxiliaries are often closely linked to tense markers, but vary somewhat in their morpho-phonological features;
   (g) Tense and agreement markers, case markers, and determiners tend to have reduced phonological shapes and are tightly linked to the syntactic skeleton of the clause.

The classification in (1) could be made more or less fine-grained. However, it is clear that we are not dealing with a unified phenomenon here. Rather, it seems that lexical elements are 'recruited', to a greater or lesser extent, into syntactic processing.

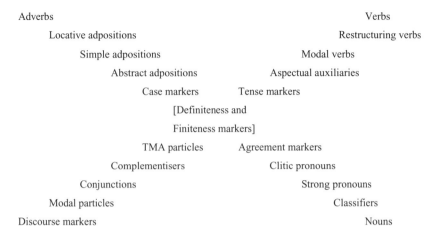

Figure 18.1 *Chains of related categories, arranged from lexical to functional from the outside inwards*

The core of the functional system is constituted by the notions of definiteness (in the nominal domain) and finiteness (in the clausal domain). Verbs, adverbs, discourse markers, and nouns are the lexical elements that correspond to four of the chains linked to these core elements, as shown in Figure 18.1. Obviously, there may be other chains as well.

The syntactic processing achieved with the aid of the functional categories is linked to some kind of semantic map involving functional notions. A first approximation of such a map is given in Figure 18.2.

The map sketched here involves six 'anchor points': entities, properties, locations, predicates, actions, and events, and is indicative of the richness of the concepts expressed in the functional domain.

Functional categories from an evolutionary perspective

In this book I have shown that functional categories play an important role in the languages of the world, the centrality of which is reflected by the fact that the lexical/functional distinction is relevant in grammar, in historical linguistics, psycholinguistics, and in language contact studies.

How can we explain the presence of functional categories in human language from an evolutionary perspective? We need to ask ourselves what the specific advantage of functional categories would be in human language. In the following sections, which are as speculative as the previous chapters were grounded in

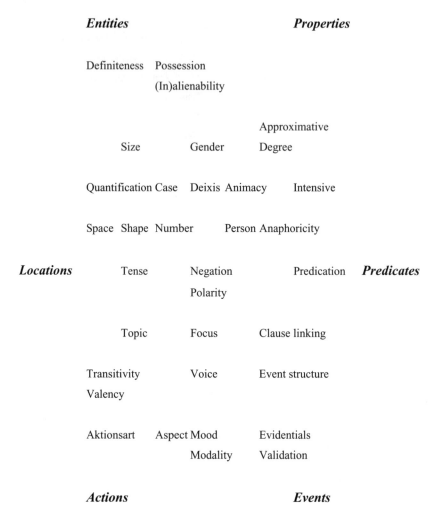

Figure 18.2 *Rough semantic map of a number of notions likely to be expressed by functional categories*

empirical evidence, I will explore various ideas, with reference to proposals by researchers such Bickerton (1990) and Jackendoff (2002), in general elaborating on the possibility that in the course of language evolution, language went from a functional category-free to a category-rich system.

An alternative would be that language started out as a system consisting mostly of functional categories (albeit of a different nature), and only then acquired a rich content lexicon. It is true that its extremely rich vocabulary is as much a feature setting human language apart from possibly antecedent animal communication systems as its rich syntax and inventory of functional categories. However, if we take functional categories to be the original set of elements, we probably must assume these to the continuation of the limited set of alarm calls, etc., of animal communication systems, something which is quite unlikely given their highly abstract and category-bound nature. Furthermore, the above discussion has shown that the functional categories are linked to various lexical categories through chains and contiguity in semantic maps.

Before continuing I should stress I will adopt the preliminary assumptions of scholars like Jackendoff (2002: 236–237), namely that language evolution involved a number of steps towards a more adequate communicative system, and involved the evolution of language-specific cognitive abilities.

From a functional element-free to a system rich in functional elements. The primary proponent of the 'functional expansion' scenario is Bickerton (1990), who proposed an early protolanguage, with little syntax, followed by a qualitatively very different stage with full language. Bickerton assumes that with *homo erectus*, about one million years ago, protolanguage emerged, a system with a lexicon, but without a syntax. Clausal organisation would be in term of pragmatic principles first, then semantic principles, and finally syntactic principles. There would be flat structure rather than layered structure, and no agreement markers instead of the complex agreement characterising some natural languages. Finally, there would be no recursion.

As to the lexicon, there would be only lexical categories, rather than lexical and functional categories as in full languages. There would be no morphology, not the complex morphology of full languages. Also, protolanguage would show little diversity in categories, rather than the high diversity in categories of at least some full languages, and vocabulary would be poor.

As far as the pragmatics of information processing is concerned, interpretation would be context dependent rather than context independent, processing would not yet be fully automatic, as with full languages.

As regards the phonology, protolanguage would have purely syllabic articulation, rather than the articulation based on more complex phoneme combinations. Phoneme inventories would be simple rather than the complex inventories of some modern languages, and likewise syllables would be simple. There would be no lento/allegro styles, presumably, rather than the complex lento/allegro and sandhi rules of modern languages.

Bickerton adduces the evidence (p. 180) that whatever vocabularies primates manage to acquire in human captivity they only involve content words. However, Bickerton (1990: 181–185) assumes that certain functional pre-syntactic categories developed during the protolanguage period, since certain abstract notions are central to any basic communicative system. These would include:

(2)   negation
       wh-words
       possibly pronouns
       modal operators such as *can* and *must*
       aspectual operators to indicate completed or earlier actions, or later actions
       direction and location markers
       quantifiers such as *many* and *few*

For Bickerton, following his work on pidgin and creole genesis in Bickerton (1981), it is crucial to adopt a non-gradualist position: in his view, the transition between protolanguage and full language was radical and did not involve any intermediary stages. However, the evidence from pidgin/creole genesis for this position is weak, and in other domains, such as child language and aphasia, adduced by Bickerton (1990: 105–129), the evidence for a sharp break is not very strong either, if existent at all.

Jackendoff (2002), building on Bickerton's work, assumes a much more complicated pattern of incremental development, involving a number of logically independent and in part logically subsequent separate steps. There is generally no independent evidence for these steps, but certainly they correspond to mostly separate phenomena, and they are logically ordered in a certain progression. I will first present them and then turn to the question of how these interact with the possible emergence of functional categories. The steps are (2002: 238–260):

(3)   (a)   Pre-existing primate conceptual structure
       (b)   Use of symbols in non-situation-specific fashion
       (c)   Use of an open, unlimited class of symbols
       (d)   Development of a phonological combinatorial system
       (e)   Concatenation of symbols
       (f)   Use of symbol position to convey basic semantic notions
       (g)   Hierarchical phrase structure
       (h)   Symbols that explicitly encode abstract semantic relations
       (i)   Grammatical categories
       (j)   System of inflections to convey semantic relations
       (k)   System of grammatical functions to convey semantic relations

After phase (3f), something like Bickerton's protolanguage may have been arrived at, and after the final phase, (3k), we can speak of modern language. The sequence of different developmental steps can be portrayed as in Figure 18.3.

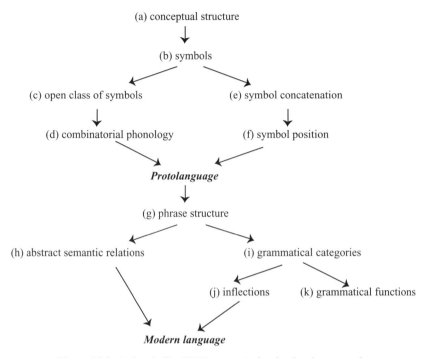

(a) conceptual structure

(b) symbols

(c) open class of symbols

(e) symbol concatenation

(d) combinatorial phonology

(f) symbol position

Protolanguage

(g) phrase structure

(h) abstract semantic relations

(i) grammatical categories

(j) inflections

(k) grammatical functions

Modern language

Figure 18.3 *Jackendoff's (2002) scenario for the development of grammar*

One type of functional categories is introduced in step (3h). Here Jackendoff mentions notions similar to those suggested by Bickerton in (2), enumerating the following types of elements (pp. 253–254):

(4)   (a) Spatial relation terms: *up, towards, behind*
       (b) Time terms: *now, yesterday, before*
       (c) Markers of illocutionary force or modality: *if, may, can*
       (d) Markers of discourse status: definite and indefinite determiners
       (e) Quantification: *some, all, always*
       (f) Purposes, reasons, intermediate causes: *for ... to, with, because*
       (g) Discourse connectors: *but, however, and so forth*

A second type of functional category is introduced in step (3j), referring to case markers, agreement markers, etc., elements whose interpretation is strictly grammatical rather than notional.

Thus Jackendoff splits the functional categories into two sets: elements with more semantic content, often realised as separate words, and more purely formal elements, often realised as inflections.

Evolutionary advantages of functional categories. Assume that there was an earlier stage in the evolution of language in which there were no functional categories. Rather, this language would have only the equivalent of content words. What would be the advantage that the emergence of functional categories would confer upon a language?

Surprisingly perhaps, this question was first posed, as far as I am aware, in Labov ([1971] 1990), already cited in chapter 15, 'The adequacy of natural language I: The development of tense'. Here Labov contrasted the English pidgin of Hawaii with the later creole, in terms of the marking of tense. In the pidgin, temporal reference was marked with adverbs like 'yesterday' and 'later', in the creole with particles like 'been' and 'go'. Claiming that there is no inherent semantic reason to have 'been' rather than 'yesterday', Labov argues that a system with tense particles allows greater stylistic possibilities. Citing the English example of the huge range of variability accompanying the pronunciation of 'I am going to go', which can be reduced to [angnego], but with many intermediary forms, Labov argues that there at least 27 ways of pronouncing this sequence, and this variability makes a language with a future marker of the 'be going to'-type more attractive than one only with adverbs like 'later'. The problem is of course that theoretically, adverbs might also show the same possibility of being shortened, yielding stylistic options. This is precisely what has happened with the Tok Pisin tense marker 'bye and bye', which is ultimately pronounced like [bə] (Sankoff and Laberge 1973). However, the reduction of 'bye and bye' went in parallel with its shift to the pre-verbal position.

While Labov's answer focuses on the stylistic dimension, Bickerton (1990: 55) assumes that functional categories provide a cognitive advantage: 'They constitute, as it were, the coordinates of the linguistic map, a kind of topological grid whereby the positions of objects and events can be plotted relative to the observer and to one another.' Bickerton bases himself on work by Talmy in this respect, who contrasts (2001a: 32–33) the open-class system, which is engaged in conveying conceptual content, with the closed-class system, which conveys conceptual structure. Thus we can think of the emergence of functional categories as the result of the emerging need to provide conceptual structure to messages as they became more complex. Even though the same meaning can be expressed with adverbs as with tense markers, there may be semantic advantages as well to more abstract meaning-carrying elements. It may not always be relevant to indicate that something happened 'yesterday' or 'last week', and in such a case a more generic marker like 'before' would be preferable.

Other researchers have sought answers in the domain of formal syntactic patterning. One syntactic possibility, following the work by Hauser *et al.* (2002), was that functional elements emerged because of the development of recursion in the syntax: functional elements would help to make the links between the constituents visible in structures that were growing to be progressively more complex. The types of elements that could fulfil this task would primarily be complementisers, as in (5a), and adpositions or case markers, as in (5b):

(5)　　(a) I told you already **that** I had seen **that** Mary had left.
　　　　(b) my cousin**'s** neighbour**'s** cat

A second possibility was that functional categories emerged to facilitate efficient marking of head/complement dependencies. As syntactic structures became more complex, there was an increasing need to clearly delineate the relation between the predicate and its arguments, as well as that between a head noun and its dependents. Consider a sentence such as (6) from Cuzco Quechua:

(6)　　Mariya-**man** Pedru-**q**　wasi-**n**-**ta**　riku-**chi**-**rqa**-**ni**.
　　　　Mary-DA　　Peter-GE house-3-AC see-CAU-PST-1
　　　　'I showed Peter's house to Mary.'

In (6) there are agreement markers indicating subject (*-ni* 'first singular') and possessor (*-n* 'third singular'), and case markers indicating indirect object (*-man* 'dative'), possessor (*-q* 'genitive'), and direct object (*-ta* 'accusative'). These elements generally allow unambiguous identification of the various interactants.

A third possibility is that the functional categories actually define the categorical status of the content words. Consider the words from Quechua in (7a):

(7)　　(a) wasi　'house'　(b) wasi-**yki**　'your house'
　　　　　　rumi　'stone'　　　rumi-**yki**　'your stone'
　　　　　　riku-　'see'　　　　riku-**nki**　'you see'
　　　　　　puri-　'walk'　　　puri-**nki**　'you walk'
　　　　　　puka　'red'　　　　puka-**yki**　'*you(r) red/your red one'
　　　　　　yana　'black'　　　yana-**yki**　'*you(r) black/your black one'

While the lexical forms of Quechua nouns, verbs, and adjectives are non-distinct or very similar, the endings make clear what kind of element is used. Verbs receive forms like *-nki* for the second person, and nouns forms like *-yki*. Adjectives can be marked only with *-yki* when they denote a noun. It is the functional categories that give the lexical ones their clear categorical status.

Thus various syntactic explanations may be given for why functional categories are useful in a slightly more complex grammatical system. However, these various explanations, and other imaginable ones, suffer from two deficiencies, at least.

(A) They each only cover certain sets of cases, not all functional categories. Roughly the following relations hold between these three functions and specific sets of categories:

(8)   (a) *recursion marking*   complementisers, adpositions, and case markers
        (b) *head/complement marking* agreement markers, adpositions, and case markers
        (c) *categorical distinctions*   determiners, inflections, and case markers

Thus, different explanations would hold for different categories.

(B) Languages considerably differ in the extent to which these different syntactic functions are realised by functional categories. Everett (2005) claims that the Brazilian language Pirahã has only very limited sentential recursion, if any. Similarly, in some languages head/complement is indicated by strict word order, rather than with agreement and case marking. Finally, some languages show clear lexical distinctions between, for example, nouns and verbs. Even if the claims about Pirahã by Everett and similar claims by others about different languages cannot be fully maintained, it remains clear that the role of functional categories in non-configurational languages (cf. Hale 1983 and subsequent literature) may be quite different from that in configurational ones.

Thus, the syntactic processing advantages of functional categories cannot easily be stated in terms of a single aspect of syntax. Rather, it is syntactic processing overall that is facilitated by functional categories. Levelt (1999: 86) writes: 'Syntax develops as "the poor man's semantics" for the child to systematize the expression of semantic roles, just as phonology is "the poor man's phonetics", a lean system for keeping track of the subtle infinitude of articulatory patterns.' In the same vein, we may suggest that functional categories are the poor man's lexicon – that part of the lexicon involved in morpho-syntactic patterning. Automaticity of processing is what is involved in the use of highly frequent markers, and automaticity of retrieval of functional elements from the mental lexicon.

Claims of the linguistic fossil analysis In Bickerton's work discussed above, two or more parallel processing systems were postulated, available for language use, which are a syntactic system A and a fossil paratactic system B. The syntactic processing system A uses functional categories as part of the functional skeleton, is highly automatised, and has recursion. The primary syntactic structure building takes place through the selection of a specific complement by a specific head, like of NP by D(eterminer), or VP by I(nflection).

The paratactic processing system B uses various principles for ordering – iconicity, information structure – is only partially automatised, and has no recursion. There are no functional categories, and there is no functional skeleton. The primary syntactic structure building takes place through adjunction.

Evidence for processing system A is provided throughout this book. Relevant evidence includes the lexical/functional asymmetries in insertional code-mixing, borrowing, creole genesis, and mixed languages that we saw in the previous chapters. We may also refer to patterns of L1 development versus L2 development, and the results from speech error research.

Evidence for system B includes the possibility for paratactic speech in Foreigner Talk and other restricted registers, the emergence of early pidgins, the Basic Language Variety that emerges in early L2 learning, and the possibility of agrammatic speech by patients with aphasia. In Muysken (2000) I discuss the capacities of bilinguals to create structures in alternational code-mixing and the acquisition of complex structures in early L1 through adjunction, as examples of this paratactic processing capacity.

While system B is always available as a fall-back system, system A is dominant in actual language production for acquired languages, because it is more efficient, rapid, etc. It is tempting to assume that system B is anterior, in evolutionary terms, to system A, making pidgins, etc., special windows on biologically earlier stages of human language.

However, the route by which B developed into A is not clear. A first scenario would be that automatisation of frequently used forms would lead to internal restructuring, while a second scenario would be that another system (phonology, motor control) was co-opted to provide the functional skeleton.

Prospects

The picture that I have tried to sketch in this overview is a mixed one: on the one hand it is clear that functional categories play a central and defining role in the way humans use language. Perhaps they constitute the single most distinctive feature of human language. On the other hand, it is clear that they constitute a multi-dimensional phenomenon, with converging but autonomous semantic, pragmatic, phonological, and lexical properties. The range of functional categories, and their role in the system, also differ widely from one language to another. In trying to bring together the material from the wide range of sub-disciplines covered here I realise that in some cases I have only barely scratched the surface, but that is not a plea for a book twice this size. More promising is setting up interdisciplinary research teams, consisting of both general linguists and researchers in psycholinguistics and the other areas discussed here, to try to establish whether the more differentiated picture of functional categories sketched here yields clearer results.

References

Abney, S. (1987) The English noun phrase in its sentential aspect. Doctoral dissertation, MIT.

Aboh, Enoch (2006) The Left Periphery in the Surinamese Creoles and Gbe: on the modularity of substrate transfer. Ms., to appear in Pieter Muysken and Norval Smith (eds.) *The Surinam – Benin Sprachbund.*

Abu-Akel, Ahmad, Alison L. Bailey, and Yeow-Meng-Thum (2004) Describing the acquisition of determiners in English: a growth modelling approach. *Journal of Psycholinguistic Research* 33, 407–424.

Adelaar, Alexander and Nikolaus P. Himmelmann (eds.) (2005) *The Austronesian languages of Asia and Madagascar.* London: Routledge.

Aguiló S.J., Federico (1980) *Los cuentos. ¿Tradiciones o viviencias?* Cochabamba: Editorial Amigos del Libro.

Ahlsén, Elisabeth and Christina Dravins (1990) Agrammatism in Swedish: two case studies. In Menn and Obler (eds.) (1990a), pp. 545–622.

Aikhenvald, Alexandra Y. (2000) *Classifiers: a typology of noun categorization devices.* Oxford: Oxford University Press.

Albó, Xavier (1975) *Los mil trostros del quechua.* Lima: Instituto de Estudios Peruanos.

Albó, Xavier (1988) Bilingualism in Bolivia. In Christina Bratt Paulston, *International Handbook of Bilingualism and Bilingual Education.* New York: Greenwood Press, pp. 85–108.

Alpatov, Vladimir M. (1979) *Struktura grammatičeskix edinic v sovremennom japonskom jazyke.* Moskva: Nauka.

Ameka, Felix (1992) Interjections: the universal yet neglected part of speech. *Journal of Pragmatics* 18, 101–118.

Anderson, Stephen A. (1982) Where's morphology? *Linguistic Inquiry* 13, 571–612.

Aquilina, Joseph (1959) *The structure of Maltese: a study in mixed grammar and vocabulary.* Valletta: The Royal University of Malta.

Arends, Jacques, Pieter Muysken, and Norval Smith (eds.) (1994) *Pidgins and Creoles. An introduction.* Amsterdam: Benjamins.

Aronoff, Mark (1976) *Word formation in generative grammar.* Cambridge, MA.: MIT Press.

Aronoff, Mark, Irit Meir, Carol Padden, and Wendy Sandler (2003) Classifier construction and morphology in two sign languages. In Emmorey (ed.), pp. 53–84.

Auger, Julie (1994) Pronominal clitics in Québec colloquial French: a morphological analysis. Doctoral dissertation, University of Pennsylvania.

Austerlitz, Robert (1987) Uralic languages. In Comrie (ed.), pp. 569–576.

Award, Jan (2001) Parts of speech. In Haspelmath *et al.* (eds.), pp. 726–735.

Backus, Ad (1992) *Patterns of language mixing. A study in Turkish/Dutch bilingualism.* Wiesbaden: Otto Harassowitz.

Backus, Ad (1996) Two in one. Bilingual speech of Turkish immigrants in the Netherlands. Doctoral dissertation, Katholieke Universiteit Brabant, Tilburg. Studies in Multilingualism 1, Tilburg University Press.

Badecker, William and Alfonso Caramazza (1991) Morphological composition in the lexical output system. *Cognitive Neuropsychology* 8, 335–367.

Badecker, William and Alfonso Caramazza (1998) Morphology and aphasia. In Spencer and Zwicky (eds.), pp. 390–405.

Baerman, Matthew, Dunstan Brown, and Greville G. Corbett (2005) *The syntax-morphology interface. A study of syncretism.* Cambridge: Cambridge University Press.

Baharav, Eva (1990) Agrammatism in Hebrew: two case studies. In Menn and Obler (eds.), pp. 1087–1190.

Bailey, N., C. Madden, and Stephen Krashen (1974) Is there a 'natural sequence' in adult second language learning? *Language Learning* 24, 235–243.

Baker, Mark C. (1988) *Incorporation: a theory of grammatical function changing.* Chicago: Chicago University Press.

Baker, Mark C. (2003) *Lexical categories: verbs, nouns, and adjectives.* Cambridge: Cambridge University Press.

Bakker, Peter (1994) Michif, the Cree/French mixed language of the Métis buffalo hunters in Canada. In Bakker and Mous (eds.), pp. 13–33.

Bakker, Peter (1997) *A language of our own. The genesis of Michif, the mixed Cree/French language of the Canadian Métis.* Oxford: Oxford University Press.

Bakker, Peter and Maarten Mous (eds.) (1994) *Mixed languages. 15 case studies in language intertwining.* Amsterdam: IFOTT.

Bakker, Peter and Pieter Muysken (1994) Mixed languages and language intertwining. In Arends *et al.* (eds.), pp. 41–55.

Bates, Elisabeth, Angela Friederici, and Beverly Wulfeck (1987) Grammatical morphology in aphasia: evidence from three languages. *Cortex* 23, 545–574.

Batllori, Montse, Maria Lluïsa Hernanz, Carme Picallo, and Francesc Roca (eds.) (2005) *Grammaticalization and parametric variation.* Oxford: Oxford University Press.

Beekes, Robert S.P. (1995) *Comparative Indo-European linguistics. An Introduction.* Amsterdam: Benjamins.

Beghelli, Filippo and Timothy A. Stowell (1997) Distributivity and negation: the syntax of each and every. In A. Szabolcsi (ed.) *Ways of Scope Taking.* Dordrecht: Kluwer, pp. 71–107.

Bender, M. Lionel (1990) A survey of Omotic grammemes. In P. Baldi (ed.) *Linguistic change and reconstruction methodology.* Berlin: Mouton de Gruyter, pp. 661–695.

Bennis, H., R.S. Prins, and J. Vermeulen (1983) Lexical-semantic versus syntactic disorders in aphasia: the processing of prepositions. Ms., Universiteit van Amsterdam.

Bentahila, Abdelâli and Eileen D. Davies (1983) The syntax of Arabic/French code-switching. *Lingua* 59, 301–330.

Besten, Hans den (1987) Die Niederlandischen Pidgins der alten Kapkolonie. In Norbert Boretzky *et al.* (eds.) *Beiträge zum 3. Essener Kolloquium uber Sprachwandel und seine bestimmenden Faktoren, vom 30.9–2.10 1987 [sic: 1986] and der Universitat Essen*. Bochum: Studienverlag Dr. N. Brockmeyer, pp. 9–40.

Bhatnagar, Subhash C. (1990) Agrammatism in Hindi: a case study. In Menn and Obler (eds.), pp. 975–1012.

Bickerton, Derek (1981) *The roots of language*. Ann Arbor, MI: Karoma.

Bickerton, Derek (1984) The language bioprogram hypothesis. *Behavioral and Brain Sciences* 7, 173–188.

Bickerton, Derek (1990) *Language and species*. Chicago: University of Chicago Press.

Binder, J.R., C.F. Westbury, K.A. McKiernan, E.T. Possing, and D.E. Medler (2005) Distinct brain systems for processing concrete and abstract concepts. *Journal of Cognitive Neuroscience* 17, 905–917.

Binnick, Robert I. (2001) Temporality and aspectuality. In Haspelmath *et al.* (eds.), pp. 557–567.

Bishop, D.V.M. and C. Adams (1989) Conversational characteristics of children with semantic-pragmatic disorder II. What features lead to a judgment of inappropriacy. *British Journal of Disorders of Communication* 24, 241–263.

Blakemore, Diane (2004) Discourse markers. In Laurence R. Horn and Gregory Ward (eds.) *The handbook of pragmatics*. Oxford: Blackwell, pp. 221–240.

Bloomfield, Leonard (1933) *Language*. New York: Holt Rinehart and Winston.

Blutner, Reinhard, Helen de Hoop, and Petra Hendriks (2006) *Optimal communication*. Stanford, CA: CSLI Publications.

Boas, Franz (1938) *The mind of primitive man*. New York: Macmillan.

Bock, Kathryn and Willem Levelt (1994) Language production: grammatical encoding. In M.A. Gernsbacher (ed.) *Handbook of Psycholinguistics*. San Diego: Academic Press, pp. 945–984.

Bolle, Jette (1994) Sranan Tongo – Nederlands. Code-wisseling en ontlening. M.A. thesis in linguistics, Universiteit van Amsterdam.

Boretzky, Norbert and Birgit Igla (1994) Romani mixed dialects. In Bakker and Mous (eds.), pp. 35–68.

Borsley, Robert D. (ed.) (2000) *The nature and function of syntactic categories*. Syntax and semantics 32. New York: Academic Press.

Boumans, Louis and Dominique Caubet (2000) Modeling intra-sentential code-switching: a comparative study of Algerian/French in Algeria and Moroccan/Dutch in the Netherlands. In Jonathan Owens (ed.) *Arabic as a minority language*. Berlin: Mouton de Gruyter, pp. 113–180.

Boyes Braem, Penny (2001) The function of the mouthings in the signing of Deaf early and late learners of Swiss German Sign Language (DSGS). In Penny Boyes Braem and Rachel Sutton-Spence, eds. (2001) *The hands are the head of the mouth: the mouth as articulator in sign languages*. International Studies on Sign Language and Communication of the Deaf 39. Hamburg: Signum GmBH, pp. 99–132.

Bradley, David C., Merrill F. Garrett, and Edgar B. Zurif (1980) Syntactic deficits in Broca's aphasia. In D. Caplan (ed.) *Biological studies of mental processes*. Cambridge, MA: MIT Press, pp. 269–286.

Bradley, David C. and Merrill F. Garrett (1983) Hemispheric differences in the recognition of open- and closed-class words. *Neuropsychologica* 21, 155–159.

Broadaway, Rick (1994) The simplified speech of native speakers living abroad: foreigner talk, foreigner register, and AIDS. *Journal of Kanazawa Women College* 8.

Brown, Colin M. and Peter Hagoort (eds.) (1999) *The neurocognition of language.* Oxford: Oxford University Press.

Brown, Colin M., Peter Hagoort, and Mariken ter Keurs (1999) Electrophysiological signatures of visual lexical processing: open and closed class words. *Journal of Cognitive Neuroscience* 11, 261–281.

Brown, Roger (1973) *A first language.* Cambridge, MA: Harvard University Press. Cited from the 1976 Penguin edition (Harmondsworth: Penguin Books Ltd).

Bruyn, Adrienne (1995) Grammaticalization in creoles. The development of determiners and relative clauses in Sranan. Doctoral dissertation, Universiteit van Amsterdam, IFOTT.

Butterworth, Brian (1989) Lexical access in speech production. In William Marslen-Wilson (ed.) *Lexical representation and process.* Cambridge, MA: MIT Press, pp. 108–135.

Bybee, Joan (1985) *Morphology: a study of the relationship between meaning and form.* Amsterdam: John Benjamins.

Bybee, Joan and Östen Dahl (1989) The creation of tense and aspect systems in the languages of the world. *Studies in Language* 13, 51–103.

Campbell, C., K. Schlue, and S. Vander Brook (1977) Discourse and second language acquisition of yes-no questions. In C.A. Henning (ed.) *Proceedings of the Los Angeles Second Language Research Forum.* UCLA, pp. 73–87.

Campbell, Lyle (1997) *American Indian languages: the historical linguistics of Native America.* Oxford: Oxford University Press.

Campbell, Lyle and Martha C. Muntzel (1989) The structural consequences of language death. In Nancy Dorian (ed.) *Investigating obsolescence.* Cambridge: Cambridge University Press, pp. 181–196.

Cann, Ronnie (2000) Functional versus lexical: a cognitive dichotomy. In Robert D. Borsley (ed.), pp. 37–78.

Caramazza, A. and R. Sloan Berndt (1985) A multi-component deficit view of agrammatic Broca's aphasia. In Mary-Louise Kean (ed.) *Agrammatism.* New York: Academic Press, pp. 27–63.

Carden, Guy and William A. Stewart (1988) Binding theory, bioprogram, and creolization: evidence from Haitian Creole. *Journal of Pidgin and Creole Languages* 3, 1–67.

Chan, Brian (2003) *Aspects of the syntax, the pragmatics and the production of code-switching: Cantonese and English.* New York: Peter Lang.

Chomsky, Noam (1957) *Syntactic structures.* The Hague: Mouton.

Chomsky, Noam (1965) *Aspects of a theory of syntax.* Cambridge, MA: MIT Press.

Chomsky, Noam (1970) Remarks on nominalization. In R.A. Jakobs and P.S. Rosenbaum (eds.) *Readings in English transformational grammar.* Waltham, MA: Ginn, pp. 184–221.

Chomsky, Noam (1981) *Lectures in government and binding.* Dordrecht: Foris.

Chomsky, Noam (1986a) *Knowledge of language.* New York: Praeger.

Chomsky, Noam (1986b) *Barriers.* Cambridge, MA: MIT Press.

Chomsky, Noam (1995) *The Minimalist Program*. Cambridge, MA: MIT Press.

Cinque, Guglielmo (1994) On the evidence for partial N-movement in the Romance DP. In G. Cinque, J. Koster, J.-Y. Pollock, L. Rizzi, and R. Zanuttini (eds.) *Paths towards universal grammar*. Washington, DC: Georgetown University Press, pp. 85–110.

Cinque, Guglielmo (1999) *Adverbs and functional heads: a cross-linguistic perspective.* New York: Oxford University Press.

Clahsen, Harald (1989) The grammatical characterization of developmental dysphasia. *Linguistics* 27, 897–920.

Clahsen, Harald and Martine Pencke (1992) The acquisition of agreement morphology and its syntactic consequences. New evidence on German child language from the Simone-Corpus. In Meisel (ed.), pp. 181–224.

Clyne, Michael (2003) *Dynamics of language contact. English and immigrant languages*. Cambridge approaches to language contact. Cambridge: Cambridge University Press.

Coelho, Adolpho F. (1892) *Os ciganos de Portugal*. Lisbon: Imprensa Nacional.

Collinder, Björn (1960) *Comparative grammar of the Uralic languages*. Stockholm: Almqvist and Wiksell.

Comrie, Bernard (ed.) (1987) *The world's major languages*. London: Croom Helm.

Comrie, Bernard (1988) General features of the Uralic languages. In Sinor (ed.), pp. 451–477.

Comrie, Bernard (1990) Word order in the Germanic languages – Subject-verb or verb-second. Evidence from aphasia in Scandinavian languages. In Menn and Obler (eds.), pp. 1357–1364.

Comrie, Bernard (2001) Different views of language typology. In Haspelmath *et al.* (eds.), pp. 25–39.

Corbett, Greville G. (2001) Number. In Haspelmath *et al.* (eds.), pp. 816–831.

Corder, S.P. and E. Roulet (eds.) (1977) *Actes du 5ème colloque de linguistique appliquée de Neuchâtel. The notion of simplification, interlanguages and pidgins and their relation to second language pedagogy*. Geneva: Droz.

Corver, Norbert and Henk van Riemsdijk (2001a) Semi-lexical categories. In N. Corver and H. van Riemsdijk (eds.) (2001b) *Semi-lexical categories*. Berlin: Mouton de Gruyter pp. 1–21.

Corver, Norbert and Henk van Riemsdijk (eds.) (2001b) *Semi-lexical categories*. Berlin/New York: Mouton de Gruyter.

Costa, João and Anabela Gonçalves (1999) Minimal projections: evidence from defective constructions in European Portuguese. *Catalan Working Papers in Linguistics* 7, 59–69.

Craats, Ineke van de, Norbert Corver, and Roeland van Hout (2000) Conservation of grammatical knowledge: on the acquisition of possessive noun phrases by Turkish and Moroccan Arabic learners of Dutch. *Linguistics* 38, 221–314.

Craats, Ineke van de, Roeland van Hout, and Norbert Corver (2002) The acquisition of possessive HAVE-clauses by Turkish and Moroccan learners of Dutch. *Bilingualism: Language and Cognition* 5, 147–174.

Croft, William (1991) *Syntactic categories and grammatical relations*. Chicago: Chicago University Press.

Cruse, Alan (2000) *Meaning in language. An introduction to semantics and pragmatics.* Oxford: Oxford University Press.

Cusihuamán, Antonio (1976) *Gramática del quechua de Cuzco.* Lima: Instituto de Estudios Peruanos.

Cutler, Anne and D.M. Carter (1987) The predominance of strong initial syllables in the English vocabulary. *Computer Speech and Language* 2, 133–142.

Cutler, Anne and D.G. Norris (1988) The role of strong syllables in segmentation for lexical access. *Journal of Experimental Psychology: Human Perception and Performance* 14, 113–121.

Daeleman, Jan (1972) Kongo elements in Saramacca Tongo. *Journal of African Linguistics* 11, 1–44.

De Vogelaer, Gunther and Johan Van der Auwera (2006) When typological rara become productive: the extension of grammatical agreement in Dutch dialects. Paper presented at Rara & Rarissima. Collecting and interpreting unusual characteristics of human languages. Leipzig (Germany), 29 March – 1 April 2006.

Décsy, Gyula (1990) *The Uralic proto-language: a comparative reconstruction.* Bloomington, IN: Eurolingua.

Demuth, Katherine (1994) On the 'underspecification' of functional categories in early grammars. In Barbara Lust, Margarita Suñer, and John Whitman (eds.) *Syntactic theory and first language acquisition: cross-linguistic perspectives.* Hillsdale, NJ: Lawrence Erlbaum Associates, pp. 119–134.

DeVilliers, Jill (1974) Quantitative aspects of agrammatism in aphasia. *Cortex* 10, 3–54.

DeVilliers, Jill (1992) On the acquisition of functional categories: a general commentary. In Meisel (ed.), pp. 423–443.

Diggelen, Miep van (1978) Negro-Dutch. *Amsterdam Creole Studies* II. University of Amsterdam, pp. 69–100.

Dikken, Marcel den (1995) *Particles. On the syntax of verb-particle, triadic, and causative constructions.* Oxford: Oxford University Press.

Dixon, R.M.W. (1972) *The Dyirbal language of north Queensland.* Cambridge: Cambridge University Press.

Dorian, Nancy C. (1981) *Language death. The life cycle of a Scottish Gaelic dialect.* Philadelphia: The University of Pennsylvania Press.

Drewes, A.J. (1994) Borrowing in Maltese. In Bakker and Mous (eds.), pp. 83–111.

Dulay, Heidi and Marina Burt (1974) Natural sequences in child second language acquisition. *Language Learning* 24, 37–53.

Dutton, Thomas E. (1973) *Conversational Tok Pisin.* Canberra: Pacific Linguistics, D12.

Dutton, Thomas E. (1983) Birds of a feather: a pair of rare pidgins from the Gulf of Papua. In Ellen Woolford and William Washabaugh (eds.) *The social context of creolization.* Ann Arbor, MI: Karoma, pp. 77–105.

Ellis, Rod (1994) *The study of second language acquisition.* Oxford. Oxford University Press.

Emmorey, Karen (ed.) (2003) *Perspectives on classifier constructions in sign languages.* Mahwah, NJ: Lawrence Erlbaum Associates.

Emonds, Joseph E. (1973) *A transformational grammar of English.* New York: Academic Press.

Emonds, Joseph E. (1985) *A unified theory of syntactic categories.* Dordrecht: Foris.

Evans, Nicholas (1995) *A grammar of Kayardild. With historical-comparative notes on Tangkic.* Berlin: Mouton de Gruyter.

Everett, Dan (2005) Cultural constraints on grammar and cognition in Pirahã: another look at the design features of human language. *Current Anthropology* 46, 621–646.

Faller, Martina (2003) The evidential and validational licensing conditions for the Cusco Quechua enclitic *-mi. Belgian Journal of Linguistics* 16, 7–21.

Fenyvesi, Anna (1995/6) The case of American Hungarian case: morphological change in McKeesport, PA. *Acta Linguistica Hungarica* 43, 381–404.

Fenyvesi, Anna (2005) Hungarian in the United States. In Anna Fenyvesi (ed.) *Hungarian language contact outside Hungary.* Amsterdam: Benjamins, pp. 265–318.

Ferguson, Charles A. (1971) Absence of copula and the notion of simplicity: a study of normal speech, baby talk, foreigner talk, and pidgins. In Dell Hymes (ed.) *Pidginization and creolization in language.* Cambridge: Cambridge University Press, pp. 141–150.

Ferguson, Charles A. (1975) Towards a characterization of English foreigner talk. *Anthropological Linguistics* 17, 1–14.

Finlayson, R., K. Calteaux, and Carol Myers-Scotton (1998) Orderly mixing: code-switching and accommodation in South Africa. *Journal of Sociolinguistics* 2, 395–420.

Finocchiaro, Chiara and Alfonso Caramazza (2006) The production of pronominal clitics: implications for theories of lexical access. *Language and Cognitive Processes* 21, 141–180.

Foley, William (1986) *The Papuan languages of New Guinea.* Cambridge: Cambridge University Press.

Francis, Elaine J. and Stephen Matthews (2005) A multi-dimensional approach to the category 'verb' in Cantonese. *Journal of Linguistics* 41, 269–305.

Friederici, Angela (1982) Syntactic and semantic processes in aphasic deficits: the availability of prepositions. *Brain and Language* 15, 249–258.

Friederici, Angela, Paul W. Schönle, and Merrill F. Garrett (1982) Syntactically and semantically based computations: processing of prepositions in agrammatism. *Cortex* 18, 525–534.

Friederici, Angela D. and Douglas Saddy (1993) Disorders of word class processing in aphasia. In G. Blanken *et al.* (eds.) *Handbücher zur Sprach- und Kommunikationswissenschaft*, Band 8: *linguistic disorders and pathologies: an international handbook*, Berlin: Mouton de Gruyter, pp. 169–181.

Friedmann, N. and Y. Grodzinsky (1997) Tense and agreement in agrammatic production: pruning the syntactic tree. *Brain and Language* 56, 397–425.

Fromkin, Victoria J. (ed.) (1980) *Errors in linguistic performance: slips of the tongue, ear, pen, and hand.* New York: Academic Press.

Froud, Karen (2001) Prepositions and the lexical-functional divide: aphasic evidence. *Lingua* 111, 1–28.

Fukui, Naoki (1988) Deriving the difference between English and Japanese. *English Linguistics* 5, 249–270.

Fukui, Naoki and Margaret Speas (1986) Specifiers and projections. *MIT Working Papers in Linguistics* 8, 128–172.

Gardner-Chloros, Penelope (1991) *Language selection and switching in Strasbourg.* Oxford: Clarendon.

Garrett, Merrill F. (1975) The analysis of sentence production. In G. Bower (ed.) *The psychology of learning and motivation,* vol. 9. New York: Academic Press, pp. 133–177. Reprinted in Gerry T.M. Altmann (ed.) (2002) *Psychology and Linguistics. Critical concepts in psycholinguistics V.* London: Routledge, pp. 34–75.

Garrett, Merrill F. (1980) Independent processing levels in sentence production. In Fromkin (ed.), pp. 263–71.

Garrett, Merrill F. (1982) Production of speech: observations from normal and pathological language use. In A.W. Ellis (ed.) *Normality and pathology in cognitive functions.* London: Academic Press, pp. 19–76.

Gelderen, Elly van (2004) *Grammaticalization as economy.* Amsterdam: Benjamins.

Genesee, Fred (1989) Early bilingual development: one language or two? *Journal of Child Language* 16, 161–179.

Giesbers, Herman (1989) *Code-switching tussen dialect en standaardtaal.* Amsterdam: Publicaties van het P.J. Meertens-Instituut, 14.

Gil, David (2001) Quantifiers. In Haspelmath *et al.* (eds.), pp. 1275–1294.

Gijn, Rik van (2006) A grammar of Yurakaré. Doctoral dissertation, Radboud University Nijmegen.

Glück, Susanne and Roland Pfau (1998) On classifying classification as a class of inflection in German Sign language. In T. Cambier-Langeveld, A. Lipták, and M. Reford (eds.) Console VL Proceedings. *Sixth Annual Conference of the Student Organization of Linguistics in Europe.* Leiden: HIL Publications, pp. 59–74.

Goldsmith, John A. (ed.) (1995) *The handbook of phonological theory.* Oxford: Blackwell.

Golovko, Evgeniy V. and Nicolai B. Vakhtin (1990) Aleut in contact: the CIA enigma. *Acta Linguistica Hafniensia* 22, 97–125.

Goodglass, Helen (1968) Studies on the grammar of aphasics. In S. Rosenberg and J.H. Kaplan (eds.) *Developments in applied psycholinguistic research.* New York: Academic Press, pp. 177–208.

Greenberg, Joseph H. (1987) *Language in the Americas.* Stanford: Stanford University Press.

Grice, Herbert Paul (1989) *Studies in the way of words.* Cambridge, MA: Harvard University Press.

Grimshaw, Jane (1990) *Argument structure.* Cambridge, MA: MIT Press.

Grimshaw, Jane (1991) Extended projections. Ms., Brandeis University.

Grinevald, Colette (2000) A morphosyntactic typology of classifiers. In Gunter Senft (ed.) *Systems of nominal classification.* Cambridge: Cambridge University Press, pp. 50–92.

Groot, A.H.P. de (1981) *Woordregister Saramakaans-Nederlands.* Paramaribo, Surinam: Vaco Press.

Guéron, Jacqueline and Teun Hoekstra (1988) T-chains and the constituent structure of auxiliaries. In A. Cardinaletti, G. Cinque, and G. Giusti (eds.) *Constituent structures.* Venice: Annali di Ca' Foscari, pp. 35–99.

Gumperz, John J. (1982) *Discourse strategies.* Cambridge: Cambridge University Press.

Haase, Martin (2002) Mehrschichtiger Sprachkontakt in Malta. In Michael Bommes, Christina Noack, and Doris Tophinke (eds.) *Sprache als Form. Festschrift für Utz Maas*. Opladen: Westdeutscher Verlag: I, pp. 101–107.

Hagiwara, H. (1995) The breakdown of functional categories and the economy of derivation. *Brain and Language* 50, 92–117.

Hagoort, Peter, Colin M. Brown, and Lee Osterhout (1999) The neurocognition of syntactic processing. In Brown and Hagoort (eds.), pp. 273–316.

Hale, Kenneth L. (1983) Warlpiri and the grammar of non-configurational languages. *Natural Language and Linguistic Theory* 1, 5–47.

Halpern, Aaron L. (1998) Clitics. In Spencer and Zwicky (eds.), pp. 101–122.

Hamann, Cornelia, Zvi Penner, and Katrin Lindner (1998) German impaired grammar: the clause structure revisited. *Language Acquisition* 7, 193–245.

Haspelmath, Martin (1994) Functional categories, X-bar theory, and grammaticalization theory. *STUF – Sprachtypologie und Universalienforschung* 47, 3–15.

Haspelmath, Martin, Ekkehard König, Wulf Oesterreicher, and Wolfgang Raible (eds.) (2001) *Language typology and language universals I, II*. Berlin: Mouton de Gruyter.

Hatch, Evelyn, R. Shapira, and J. Gough (1978) 'Foreigner talk' discourse. *ITL Review of Applied Linguistics* 39/40, 39–60.

Haude, Katharina (2006) A grammar of Movima. Doctoral dissertation, Radboud University, Nijmegen.

Haugen, Einar (1950) The analysis of linguistic borrowing. *Language* 26, 210–231.

Hauser, Mark D., N. Chomsky, and W. Tecumseh Fitch (2002) The faculty of language: what is it, who has it, and how did it evolve? *Science* 298, 1569–1579.

Heine, Bernd and Tania Kuteva (2002) *World lexicon of grammaticalization*. Cambridge: Cambridge University Press.

Hekking, Ewald (1995) El otomí de Santiago Mexquititlán. Desplazamiento lingüístico, préstamos y cambios gramaticales. Doctoral dissertation, University of Amsterdam.

Herschensohn, Julia (2001) Missing inflection in second language French: accidental infinitives and other verbal deficits. *Second Language Research* 17, 273–305.

Hetzron, Robert (1987) Afro-Asiatic languages. In Comrie (ed.), pp. 647–653.

Hetzron, Robert (1990) Dialectal variation in Proto-Afroasiatic. In P. Baldi (ed.) *Linguistic change and reconstruction methodology*. Berlin: Mouton de Gruyter, pp. 577–597.

Hinzelin, Marc-Olivier (2003) The acquisition of subjects in bilingual children: pronoun use in Portuguese/German children. In Natascha Müller (ed.) *(In)vulnerable domains in multilingualism*. Amsterdam: Benjamins, pp. 107–138.

Hoberman, Robert D. and Mark Aronoff (2003) The verbal morphology of Maltese. From Semitic to Romance. In Joseph Shimron (ed.) *Language processing and language acquisition in a root-based morphology*. Amsterdam: Benjamins, pp. 61–78.

Hoekstra, Teun and Nina Hyams (1998) Aspects of root infinitives. *Lingua* 106, 81–112.

Hohenberger, A. and D. Happ (2001) The linguistic primacy of signs and mouth gestures over mouthings: evidence from language production in German Sign Language (DGS). In Penny Boyes Braem and Rachel Sutton-Spence (eds.) *The hands are the head of the mouth: the mouth as articulator in sign languages*. International Studies on Sign Language and Communication of the Deaf, 39 Hamburg: Signum-Verlag. pp. 153–190.

Hohle, Barbara, Jürgen Weissenborn, Dorothea Kiefer, Antje Schulz, and Michaela Schmitz (2004) Functional elements in infants' speech processing: the role of determiners in the syntactic categorization of lexical elements. *Infancy* 5, 341–353.

Holloway, Charles E. (1997) *Dialect death. The case of Brule Spanish*. Amsterdam: Benjamins.

Hong, Sung-Eun (2001) Empirische Erhebung zu Klassifikatoren in Koreanischer Gebärdensprache. Doctoral dissertation, University of Hamburg.

Hopper, Paul and Elizabeth Closs Traugott (2003 [1993]) *Grammaticalization*. 2nd edn. Cambridge: Cambridge University Press.

Hout, Roeland van and Pieter Muysken (1994) Modelling lexical borrowability. *Language Variation and Change* 6, 39–62.

Hudson, Richard (2000) Grammar without functional categories. In Borsley (ed.), pp. 7–36.

Hutchisson, Don (1985) Sursurunga pronouns and the special uses of quadral number. In Ursula Wiesemann (ed.) *Pronominal systems*. Tübingen: Gunter Narr Verlag, pp. 1–21.

Huwaë, Rosita (1992) Tweetaligheid in Wierden: het taalgebruik van jongeren uit een Molukse gemeenschap. M.A. thesis in linguistics, Universiteit van Amsterdam.

Inkelas, Sharon and Draga Zec (eds.) (1990) *The phonology-syntax connection*. Chicago: The University of Chicago Press.

Inkelas, Sharon and Draga Zec (1995) Syntax-phonology interface. In Goldsmith (ed.) pp. 535–549.

Jackendoff, Ray S. (2002) *Foundations of language*. Oxford: Oxford University Press.

Jacubowicz, Celia, Lea Nash, Cathérine Rigaut, and Christophe Gérard (1998) Determiners and clitic pronouns in French-speaking children with SLI. *Language Acquisition* 7, 113–160.

Jakobson, Roman (1971a) *Studies in child language and aphasia*. The Hague: Mouton.

Jakobson, Roman (1971b) [1957] Shifters, verbal categories, and the Russian verb. *Selected Writings II*, The Hague: Mouton, pp. 130–147.

Jansen, Bert, Hilda Koopman, and Pieter Muysken (1978) Serial verbs in the creole languages. *Amsterdam Creole Studies* II, pp. 125–159.

Jarema, Gonia and Danuta Kdzielawa (1990) Agrammatism in Polish: a case study. In Menn and Obler (eds.), pp. 817–894.

Jong, Jan de (1999) Specific language impairment in Dutch: inflectional morphology and argument structure. Doctoral dissertation, University of Groningen.

Jordens, Peter, Kees de Bot, and Henk Trapman (1989) Linguistic aspects of regression in German case marking. *Studies of Second language Acquisition* 11, 179–204.

Joshi, Aravind (1985) Processing sentences with intra-sentential code-switching. In David Dowty, Lauri Karttunen and Arnold Zwicky (eds.) *Natural language parsing*. New York: Academic Press, pp. 190–205.

Josselin de Jong, J.P.B. de (1926) Het huidige Negerhollandsch (Teksten en woordenlijst). Verhandelingen der Koninklijke Academie der Wetenschappen te Amsterdam. Nieuwe Reeks, 26, 1.

Juczyk, Peter and R. Aslin (1995) Infants' detection of the sound patterns of words in fluent speech. *Cognitive Psychology* 21, 1–23.

Julien, Marit (2002) *Syntactic heads and word formation*. New York: Oxford University Press.

Katz, J.T. (1977) Foreigner talk. Input in child second language acquisition: its form and function over time. In C.A. Henning (ed.) *Proceedings of the Los Angeles Second Language Research Forum*. UCLA.

Kayne, Richard S. (2005) *Movement and silence*. Oxford studies in comparative syntax. Oxford: Oxford University Press.

Kean, Mary Louise (1977) The linguistic interpretation of aphasic syndromes: agrammatism in Broca's aphasia, an example. *Cognition* 5, 9–46.

Keesing, Roger M. (1988) *Melanesian pidgin and the Oceanic substrate*. Palo Alto, CA: Stanford University Press.

Kirtchuk, Pablo Isaac (2000) Deixis and noun classification in Pilagá and beyond. In Ellen Contini-Morava and Yishai Tobin (eds.) *Between grammar and lexicon*. Amsterdam: Benjamins, pp. 31–58.

Kiss, Katalin É. (1995) (ed.) *Discourse configurational languages*. New York and Oxford: Oxford University Press.

Klamer, Marian (2002) Semantically motivated lexical patterns: a study of Dutch and Kambera expressives. *Language* 78, 258–286.

Klavans, Judith L. (1985) The independence of syntax and phonology in cliticization. *Language* 61, 95–120.

Klein, Wolfganf and Clive Perdue (1997) The basic variety (or: Couldn't natural languages be much simpler?). *Second Language Research* 13, 301–347.

Kok, Peter, Herman Kolk, and Marco Haverkort (2006) Agrammatic sentence production. Is verb second impaired in Dutch? *Brain and Language* 96, 243–254.

Kolk, Herman (1998) Disorders of syntax in aphasia: linguistic descriptive and processing approaches. In Brigitte Stemmer and Harry A. Whitaker (eds.) *Handbook of neurolinguistics*. San Diego: Academic Press, pp. 249–260.

Kolk, Herman, Geert Heling, and Antoine Keyser (1990) Agrammatism in Dutch: two case studies. In Menn and Obler (eds.), pp. 179–280.

Kortlandt, Frits (1995) General linguistics and Indo-European reconstruction. *RASK* 2, 91 109.

Kouwenberg, Silvia (2003) *Twice as meaningful. Reduplication in Pidgins, Creoles, and other contact languages*. London: Battlebridge Publications.

Labov, William (1990) [1971] The adequacy of natural language I: the development of tense. In John V. Singler (ed.) *Pidgin and Creole tense-mood-aspect systems*. Amsterdam: Benjamins, pp. 1–58.

Lambert, Richard D. and Sarah J. Moore (1986) Problem areas in the study of language attrition. In Bert Weltens, Kees de Bot, and Theo van Els (eds.) *Language attrition in progress*. Dordrecht: Foris, pp. 177–186.

Langacker, Ronald W. (1991) *Concept, image, and symbol. The cognitive basis of grammar*. Berlin: Mouton de Gruyter.

Lardiere, Donna (1998) Case and tense in the 'fossilized' steady state. *Second Language Research* 14, 1–26.

Larsen-Freeman, Diane E. (1975) The acquisition of grammatical morphemes by adult ESL Students. *TESOL Quarterly* 9, 409–419.

Lefebvre, Claire (1998) *Creole genesis and the acquisition of grammar: the case of Haitian creole*. Cambridge: Cambridge University Press.

Lehmann, Christian (1982) Thoughts on grammaticalization: a programmatic sketch. *Akup* 48. Cologne: Institut für Sprachwissenschaft der Universität zu Köln.

Lehmann, Christian (1988) Towards a typology of clause linkage. In John Haiman and Sandra A. Thompson (eds.) *Clause combining in grammar and discourse*. Amsterdam: Benjamins, pp. 181–225.

Lehtinen, Meri K.T. (1966) An analysis of a Finnish/English bilingual corpus. Doctoral dissertation, Indiana University, Bloomington.

Lely, Heather K.J. van der (1994) Canonical linking rules: forward versus reverse linking in normally developing and specifically language impaired children. *Cognition* 51, 29–72.

Leonard, Laurence B. (1995) Functional categories in the grammars of children with specific language impairment. *Journal of speech and hearing research* 38, 1270–1283.

Leonard, Laurence B. (1998) *Children with specific language impairment*. Cambridge, MA: MIT Press.

Leonard, Laurence B., Kristina Hansson, Ulrike Nettelbladt, and Patricia Deevy (2004) Specific language impairment: a comparison of English and Swedish. *Language Acquisition* 12, 219–246.

Levelt, Willem J.M. (1989) *Speaking. From intention to articulation*, Cambridge, MA: MIT Press.

Levelt, Willem J.M. (1999) Producing spoken language: a blueprint for the speaker. In Brown and Hagoort (eds.), pp. 83–122.

Levelt, Willem J.M., Ardi Roelofs, and Antje S. Meyer (1999) A theory of lexical access in speech production. *Behavioral and Brain Sciences* 22, 1–75.

Liddell, Scott K. (2000) Indicating verbs and pronouns: pointing away from agreement. In Karen Emorey and Harlan Lane (eds.) *The signs of language revisited: an anthology to honor Ursula Bellugi and Edward Klima*. Mahwah, NJ: Lawrence Erlbaum Associates, pp. 303–320.

Lightfoot, David (1979) *Principles of diachronic syntax*. Cambridge: Cambridge University Press.

Lillo-Martin, Diane (2002) Where are all the modality effects? In Meier, Cormier, and Quinto-Pozos (eds.), pp. 241–263.

Lipski, John M. (1978) Code-switching and the problem of bilingual competence. In Michel Paradis (ed.) *Aspects of bilingualism*. Columbia, SC: Hornbeam, pp. 250–264.

Lloyd McBurney, Susan (2002) Pronominal reference in signed and spoken language: are grammatical categories modality-dependent? In Meier, Cormier, and Quinto-Pozos (eds.), 329–369.

Longworth, C.E., W.D. Marslen-Wilson, B. Randall, and L.K. Tyler (2005) Getting the meaning of the regular past tense: evidence from neuro-psychology. *Journal of Cognitive Neuroscience* 17, 1087–1097.

Loos, Eugene (1969) *The phonology of Capanahua and its grammatical basis*. Norman, OK: Summer Institute of Linguistics.

Luján, Marta, Liliana Minaya, and David Sankoff (1984) The Universal Consistency hypothesis and the prediction of word order acquisition stages of bilingual children. *Language* 60, 343–372.

Lynch, John, Malcolm Ross, and Terry Crowley (eds.) (2002) *The Oceanic languages*. Richmond, Curzon.

Lyons, John (1968) *Introduction to theoretical linguistics*. Cambridge: Cambridge University Press.

McCarthy, John (1982) *Formal problems in Semitic phonology and morphology*. New York: Garland Publishers.

McConvell, Patrick (2001) Mix-im-up speech and emergent mixed languages in indigenous Australia. *Texas Linguistics Forum* 44, 328–349.

Magnúsdóttir, Sigríður and Höskuldur Thráinsson (1990) Agrammatism in Icelandic: two case studies. In Menn and Obler (eds.) (1990a), pp. 443–545.

Mallory, J.P. and D.Q. Adams (2006) *The Oxford introduction to Proto-Indo-European and the Proto-Indo-European world*. Oxford: Oxford University Press.

Manning, Chris and Hinrich Schütze (1999) *Foundations of statistical natural language processing*. Cambridge, MA: MIT Press.

Marslen-Wilson W.D. and L.K. Tyler (2003) Capturing underlying differentiation in the human language system. *Trends in Cognitive Sciences* 6, 465–472.

Matras, Yaron and Peter Bakker (eds.) (2003a) *The mixed language debate. Theoretical and empirical advances*. Berlin and New York: Mouton de Gruyter.

Matras, Yaron and Peter Bakker (2003b) The study of mixed languages. In Matras and Bakker (2003a), pp. 1–20.

Meier, Richard P., Keasy Cormier, and David Quinto-Pozos (eds.) (2002) *Modality and structure in signed and spoken languages*. Cambridge: Cambridge University Press.

Meillet, Antoine (1912) L'évolution des formes grammaticales. *Scientia* 12, 384–400. Cited from Antoine Meillet (1921) *Linguistique historique et linguistique générale*. Paris: Champion, pp. 130–148.

Meillet, Antoine and J. Vendryes (1927) *Traité de grammaire comparée des langues classiques*. Paris: Champion, [ch. 8.].

Meisel, Jürgen (1975) Ausländerdeutsch und Deutsch ausländischer Arbeiter. *Zeitschrift für Linguistik und Literatuurwissenschaft* [Sprache Ausländischer Arbeiter] 18, 9–53.

Meisel, Jürgen (1977) Linguistic simplification: a study of immigrant worker's speech and foreigner talk. In Stephen P. Corder and Eddy Roulet (eds.) *The notion of simplification, interlanguages and pidgins and their relation to second language pedagogy*. Genève-Neuchâtel: Droz-Faculté des Lettres de l'Université de Neuchâtel, pp. 88–113. Also published as Meisel (1980) in Sascha W. Felix (ed.) *Second language development: trends and issues*. Tübingen: Narr, pp. 13–40.

Meisel, Jürgen (1989) Early differentiation of languages in bilingual children. In K. Hyltenstam and L. Obler (eds.) *Bilingualism across the lifespan: aspects of acquisition, maturity and loss*. Cambridge: Cambridge University Press, pp. 13–40.

Meisel, Jürgen (ed.) (1992) *The acquisition of verb placement. Functional categories and V2 phenomena in language acquisition.* Dordrecht: Kluwer Academic.

Meisel, Jürgen (ed.) (1994a) *Bilingual first language acquisition: French and German grammatical development.* Amsterdam: Benjamins.

Meisel, Jürgen (1994b) Getting FAT: Finiteness, Agreement, and Tense in early grammars. In Meisel (ed.), pp. 89–130.

Menn, Lisa (1990) Agrammatism in English: two case studies. In Menn and Obler (eds.), pp. 117–178.

Menn, Lisa and Loraine K. Obler (eds.) (1990a) *Agrammatic aphasia: a cross-language narrative source book.* 3 vols. Amsterdam: Benjamins.

Menn, Lisa and Loraine K. Obler (1990b) Theoretical motivations for the cross-language study of agrammatism. In Menn and Obler (eds.), 3–12.

Menn, Lisa and Loraine K. Obler (1990c) Cross-language data and theories of agrammatism. In Lisa Menn and Obler (eds.), pp. 1369–1389.

Miceli, Gabriele, M.C. Silveri, C. Romani, and Alfonso Caramazza (1989) Variation in the pattern of omissions and substitutions of grammatical morphemes in the spontaneous speech of so-called a-grammatic patients. *Brain and Language* 36, 447–492.

Miceli, Gabriele and Anna Mazuchi (1990) Agrammatism in Italian: two case studies. In Menn and Obler (eds.), pp. 717–816.

Mifsud, Manwel (1995) *Loan verbs in Maltese: a descriptive and comparative study.* Leiden: Brill.

Migge, Bettina (2003a) *Creole formation as language contact. The case of the Suriname Creoles.* Amsterdam: Benjamins.

Migge, Bettina (2003b) The origin of predicate reduplication in Suriname Eastern Maroon Creole. In Kouwenberg (ed.), pp. 61–71.

Moravcsik, Edith (1978) Language contact. In Joseph E. Greenberg (ed.) *Universals of human language 1.* Stanford: Stanford University Press, pp. 95–122.

Mühlhäusler, Peter (1975) *Pidginization and simplification of language.* Pacific Linguistics B-26. Canberra: Australian National University.

Mühlhäusler, Peter (2001a) Universals and typology of space. In Haspelmath *et al.* (eds.), pp. 568–574.

Mühlhäusler, Peter (2001b) Personal pronouns. In Haspelmath *et al.* (eds.), pp. 741–747.

Mühlhäusler, Peter (2003) Sociohistorical and grammatical aspects of Tok Pisin. In Peter Mühlhäusler, Thomas E. Dutton, and Suzanne Romaine (eds.) *Tok Pisin texts: from the beginning to the present.* Amsterdam: Benjamins, pp. 1–34.

Müller, Natascha and Aafke Hulk (2001) Crosslinguistic influence in bilingual language acquisition: Italian and French as recipient languages. *Bilingualism: Language and Cognition* 4, 1–22.

Musgrave, Simon (in prep.) Functional categories in the syntax and semantics of Malay. Ms., Monash University.

Muysken, Pieter (1978) Three types of fronting constructions in Papiamentu. In Frank Jansen (ed.) *Studies on Fronting.* Lisse: Peter de Ridder, pp. 65–79.

Muysken, Pieter (1979) La mezcla del quechua y castellano: el caso de la 'media lengua' en el Ecuador. *Lexis* 3, 41–56 Lima: PUCP.

Muysken, Pieter (1981) Halfway between Quechua and Spanish: the case for relexification. In A. Highfield and A. Valdman (eds.) *Historicity and variation in creole studies*. Ann Arbor, MI: Karoma, pp. 52–78.

Muysken, Pieter (1987) Prepositions and postpositions in Saramaccan. In M.C. Alleyne (ed.) *Studies in Saramaccan Clause Structure*. Caribbean Culture Studies 2, 89–101.

Muysken, Pieter (1988a) Affix order and interpretation: Quechua. In Martin Everaert, Arnold Evers, Riny Huybregts, and Mieke Trommelen (eds.) *Morphology and modularity*. Dordrecht: Foris, pp. 259–279.

Muysken, Pieter (1988b) Lexical restructuring and creole genesis. In Norbert Boretzky, Werner Enninger, and Thomas Stolz (eds.) *Beiträge zum 4. Essener Kolloquium über 'Sprachkontakt, Sprachwandel, Sprachwechsel, Sprachtod' vom 9.10.–10.10.1987 an der Universität Essen*. Bochum: Studienverlag Dr. N. Brockmeyer, pp. 193–210.

Muysken, Pieter (1989) Media Lengua and linguistic theory. *Canadian Journal of Linguistics* 33, 409–422.

Muysken, Pieter (1996) Media Lengua. In Sarah G. Thomason (ed.) *Non-Indo-European-based pidgins and creoles*, Amsterdam: Benjamins, pp. 365–426.

Muysken, Pieter (2000) Bilingual speech. A typology of code-mixing. Cambridge: Cambridge University Press.

Muysken, Pieter (2001) Spanish grammatical elements in Bolivian Quechua: The Transcripciones Quechuas corpus. In Klaus Zimmermann and Thomas Stolz (eds.) *Lo propio y lo ajeno en las lenguas autronésicas y amerindias*. Frankfurt/Madrid: Vervuert-Iberoamericana, pp. 59–82.

Muysken, Pieter (2002) La categoría del plural en el quechua boliviano. In Norma Díaz, Ralph Ludwig, and Stephan Pfänder (eds.) *La Romania americana. Procesos lingüísticos en situaciones de contacto*. Frankfurt/Madrid: Vervuert-Iberoamericana, pp. 209–217.

Muysken, Pieter (2005) Quechua P-soup. In Hans Broekhuis, Norbert Corver, Riny Huybregts, Ursula Kleinhenz, and Jan Koster (eds.) *Festschrift for Henk van Riemsdijk*. Berlin: Mouton de Gruyter, pp. 434–438.

Muysken, Pieter and Norval Smith (1990) Question words in pidgin and creole languages. *Linguistics* 28, 883–903.

Myers-Scotton, Carol (1993) *Duelling languages. Grammatical structure in codeswitching*, Oxford: Oxford University Press.

Myers-Scotton, Carol and Janice L. Jake (2000) Four types of morpheme: evidence from code-switching. Broca's aphasia. and second language acquisition. *Linguistics* 34, 1053–1100.

Myers-Scotton, Carol (2002) *Contact linguistics. Bilingual encounters and grammatical outcomes*. Oxford: Oxford University Press.

Nait M'Barek, Mohamed and David Sankoff (1988) Le discours mixte arabe/français: des emprunts ou alternances de langue? *Canadian Journal of Linguistics/Revue canadienne de linguistique* 33, 143–54.

Neidle, Carol, Judy Kegl, Dawn MacLauglin, Benjamin Bahan, and Robert G. Lee (2000) *The syntax of American Sign Language. Functional categories and hierarchical structure*. Cambridge, MA: MIT Press.

Nespor, Marina and Irene Vogel (1986) *Prosodic phonology.* Dordrecht: Foris.

Nespoulous, Jean-Luc, Monique Dordain, Cécile Perron, Gonia Jarema, and Marianne Chazal (1990) Agrammatism in French: two case studies. In Menn and Obler (eds.), pp. 623–716.

Neville, H.J., D.J. Mills, and D. Slawson (1992) Fractionating language: different neural subsystems with different sensitive periods. *Cerebral Cortex* 2, 244–258.

Newman, Aaron J., Michael T. Ullmann, Roumyana Pancheva, Dianne L. Waligura, and Helen J. Neville (2007) An ERP study of regular and irregular English past tense inflection. *Neuroimage* 34, 435–445.

Newman, Paul (1995) Hausa tonology: complexities in an 'easy' tone language. In Goldsmith (ed.), pp. 762–781.

Newmeyer, Frederick J. (1998) *Language form and language function.* Cambridge, MA: MIT Press.

Newmeyer, Frederick J. (2005) *Possible and probable languages. A generative perspective on linguistic typology.* Oxford: Oxford University Press.

Niemi, Jussi, Matti Laine, Ritva Hänninen, and Päivi Koivuselkä-Sallinen (1990) Agrammatism in Finnish: two case studies. In Menn and Obler (eds.), pp. 1013–1086.

Nieuweboer, Rogier (1998) The Altai dialect of Plautdiitsch (West-Siberian Mennonite Low German). Doctoral dissertation, Groningen University.

Nishimura, Miwa (1986) Intra-sentential code-switching: the case of language assignment. In J. Vaid (ed.) *Language processing in bilinguals: psycholinguistic and neuropsychological perspectives.* Hillsdale, NJ: Lawrence Erlbaum Associates, pp. 124–143.

Nordlinger, Rachel and Louisa Sadler (2004) Nominal tense in cross-linguistic perspective. *Language* 80, 776–806.

Nortier, Jacomien (1990) *Dutch/Moroccan Arabic code-switching among young Moroccans in the Netherlands.* Dordrecht: Foris.

Nortier, Jacomien and Henriette Schatz (1992) From one-word switch to loan: a comparison of between language-pairs. *Multilingua* 11, 173–194.

Nowak, M.A., J.B., Plotkin, and V.A., Jansen (2000) The evolution of syntactic communication. *Nature* 404, 495–498.

Nyst, Victoria (2007) A descriptive analysis of Adamorobe Sign Language (Ghana). Doctoral dissertation, University of Amsterdam.

O'Shanessy, Carmel (2005) Light Warlpiri: a new language. *Australian Journal of Linguistics* 25, 31–57.

Osawa, Fuyo (2003) Syntactic parallels between ontogeny and phylogeny. *Lingua* 113, 3–47.

Osterhout, Lee, M.Bersick, and R. McKinnon (1997) Brain potentials elicited by words: word length and frequency predict the latency of an early negativity. *Biological Psychology* 46, 143–168.

Osterhout, Lee, Mark Allen, and Judith McLaughlin (2002) Words in the brain: lexical determinants of word-induced brain activity. *Journal of Neurolinguistics* 15, 171–187.

Ouhalla, Jamal (1993) Functional categories, agrammatism, and language acquisition. *Linguistische Berichte* 143, 3–36.

Ouhalla, Jamal (1994) *Transformational grammar*. London: Edward Arnold.

Packard, Jerome L. (1990) Agrammatism in Chinese: a case study. In Menn and Obler (eds.), pp. 1191–1224.

Packard, Jerome L. (2006) The manifestation of aphasic syndromes in Chinese. In Ping Li *et al.* (eds.), pp. 330–345.

Park, Tschang-Zin (1970) The acquisition of German syntax. Unpublished paper, Institute of Psychology, University of Bern.

Pfau, Roland (in prep.), *Features and categories in language production. A distributed morphology account of spontaneous speech errors*. Amsterdam: Benjamins.

Pfau, Ronald and Marcus Steinbach (2006) Modality-independent and modality-specific aspects of grammaticalization in sign languages. *Linguistik in Potsdam* 24, 5–94.

Pilot-Raichoor, Christiane (2006) The Dravidian zero negative : conceptualisation and diachronic context of its morphogenesis. Paper presented at Rara & Rarissima. Collecting and interpreting unusual characteristics of human languages. Leipzig, Germany, 29 March – 1 April 2006.

Ping Li, Li Hai Tan, Elizabeth Bates, and Ovid J.L. Teng (eds.) *The handbook of East Asian psycholinguistics. vol. 1, Chinese*. Cambridge: Cambridge University Press.

Plank, Frans (1984) 24 grundsätzliche Bemerkungen zur Wortarten-Frage. *Leuvense Bijdragen* 73, 489–520.

Poplack, Shana (1980) Sometimes I'll start a sentence in Spanish Y TERMINO EN ESPAÑOL. *Linguistics* 18, 581–618.

Poplack, Shana, Susan Wheeler, and Anneli Westwood (1987) Distinguishing language contact phenomena: evidence from English/Finnish bilingualism. In Pirkko Lilius and Mirja Saari (eds.) *The Nordic languages and modern linguistics* 6, Proceedings of the Sixth International Conference of Nordic and General Linguistics, pp. 33–56.

Poplack, Shana, David Sankoff, and Christopher Miller (1988) The social correlates and linguistic processes of lexical borrowing and assimilation. *Linguistics* 26, 47–104.

Prévost, Philippe and Lydia White (2000) Missing surface inflection or impairment in second language acquisition? Evidence from tense and agreement. *Second Language Research* 16, 103–133.

Prins, Ronald S. (1987) Afasie: classificatie, behandeling en herstelverloop. Doctoral dissertation, Universiteit van Amsterdam.

Pulvermüller, Franz (1995) Agrammatism: behavioral description and neurobiological explanation. *Journal of Cognitive Neuroscience* 7, 165–181.

Radford, Andrew (1990) *Syntactic theory and the acquisition of English syntax*. Oxford: Blackwell.

Radford, Andrew (1993) Head-hunting: on the trail of the nominal Janus. In Greville G. Corbett, N. Malcolm Fraser, and Scott McGlashan (eds.) *Heads in grammatical theory*. Cambridge: Cambridge University Press, pp. 73–113.

Raun, Alo (1988) Proto-Uralic comparative historical morphosyntax. In Sinor (ed.), pp. 555–571.

Rendón, Jorge Gómez (2005) La media lengua de Imbabura. In Hella Olbertz and Pieter Muysken (eds.) *Encuentros y conflictos: bilingüismo y contacto de lenguas en el mundo andino*. Frankfurt: Vervuert, pp. 39–58.

Reuland, Eric (1986) A feature system for the set of categorical heads. In Pieter Muysken and Henk van Riemsdijk (eds.) *Features and projections*. Dordrecht: Foris, 41–88.

Riemsdijk, Henk van (1978) *A case study in markedness*. Dordrecht: Foris.

Riemsdijk, Henk van (1990) Functional prepositions. In Harm Pinkster and Inge Genée (eds.) *Unity in diversity: Papers presented to Simon Dik on his 50th birthday*. Dordrecht: Foris, pp. 229–241.

Rijkhoff, Jan (2002) *The noun phrase*. Oxford: Oxford University Press.

Rizzi, Luigi (1997) The fine structure of the left periphery. In L. Haegeman (ed.) *Elements of grammar*. Dordrecht: Kluwer, pp. 281–387.

Rizzi, Luigi (ed.) (2004a) *The structure of CP and IP. The cartography of syntactic structures*. Vol. 2. Oxford: Oxford University Press.

Rizzi, Luigi (2004b) On the cartography of syntactic structures. In Rizzi (ed.), pp. 3–15.

Roberts, Ian and Anna Roussou (2003) *Syntactic change. A minimalist approach to grammaticalization*. Cambridge: Cambridge University Press.

Roo, Esther M. de (1999) *Agrammatic grammar. Functional categories in agrammatic speech*. Doctoral dissertation, Leiden University. Utrecht: LOT series.

Rooij, Vincent de (1996) *Cohesion through contrast. French/Swahili code-switching and Swahili style shifting in Shaba Swahili*. Doctoral dissertation, Universiteit van Amsterdam. IFOTT dissertation series.

Ross, John R. (1972) Endstation Hauptwort: the category squish. In P.M. Peranteau, J.N. levi, and G.C. Phares (eds.) *Papers of the Eighth Regional Meeting of the Chicago Linguistics Society*, University of Chicago, pp. 316–328.

Ross, Malcolm (2005) Pronouns as a preliminary diagnostic for grouping Papuan languages. In Andrew Pawley, Robert Attenborough, Jack Golson, and Robin Hide (eds.) *Papuan pasts: cultural, linguistic and biological histories of Papuan-speaking peoples*. Canberra: Australian National University, Pacific Linguistics, pp. 15–65.

Rossem, Cefas van and Hein G.A. van der Voort (1996) *Die Creol Taal. 250 years of Negerhollands texts*. Amsterdam: Amsterdam University Press.

Sadock, Jerold M. (1991) *Autolexical syntax: a theory of parallel grammatical representations*. Chicago: Chicago University Press.

Sánchez, Liliana (2003) *Quechua-Spanish bilingualism. Interference and convergence in functional categories*. Amsterdam: Benjamins.

Sandler, Wendy and Diane Lillo-Martin (2006) *Sign language and linguistic universals*. Cambridge: Cambridge University Press.

Sankoff, Gillian (1980) *The social life of language*. Philadelphia: University of Pennsylvania Press.

Sankoff, Gillian and Suzanne Laberge (1973) On the acquisition of native speakers by a language. *Kivung* 6, 32–47. Reprinted in G. Sankoff (ed.), pp. 195–209.

Sapir, Edward (1921) *Language. An introduction to the study of speech*. New York: Hartcourt, Brace and World.

Sapir, Edward and Morris Swadesh (1964) [1946] American Indian grammatical categories. *Word* 2, 103–112.

Sasanuma, Sumiko, Akio Kamio, and Masahito Kubota (1990a) Agrammatism in Japanese: two case studies. In Menn and Obler (eds.), pp. 1225–1308.

Sasanuma, Sumiko, Akio Kamio, and Masahito Kubota (1990b) Crossed agrammatism in Japanese: a case study. In Menn and Obler (eds.), pp. 1309–1353.

Sasse, Hans-Jürgen (1992a) Theory of language death. In M. Brenzinger (ed.) *Language death*. Berlin: Mouton de Gruyter, pp. 7–30.

Sasse, Hans-Jürgen (1992b) Language decay and contact-induced change: similarities and differences. In M. Brenzinger (ed.) *Language death*. Berlin: Mouton de Gruyter, pp. 57–79.

Sasse, Hans-Jürgen (2001a) Scales of nouniness and verbiness. In Haspelmath *et al.* (eds.) I, pp. 495–509.

Sasse, Hans-Jürgen (2001b) Typological changes in language obsolescence. In Haspelmath *et al.* (eds.) II, pp. 1668–1677.

Schachter, Paul (1985) Parts-of-speech sytems. In Timothy Shopen (ed.) *Language typology and language description, Vol. 1*. Cambridge: Cambridge University Press, pp. 3–61.

Schaerlaekens, Anne Marie (1977) *De taalontwikkeling van het kind*. Groningen: Wolters-Noordhoff.

Schembri, Adam (2003) Rethinking 'classifiers' in signed languages. In Emmorey (ed.), 3–34.

Schiffrin, Deborah (1987) *Discourse markers*. Cambridge: Cambridge University Press.

Schmid, Monika S. (2002) *First language attrition, use, and maintenance. The case of German Jews in Anglophone countries*. Amsterdam: Benjamins.

Schmidt, Annette (1985) *Young people's Dyirbal. An example of language death from Australia*. Cambridge: Cambridge University Press.

Schmidt, Peter (2006) Agreeing adverbials: rare but (mostly) areal. Paper presented at Rara & Rarissima. Collecting and interpreting unusual characteristics of human languages. Leipzig, Germany, 29 March – 1 April 2006.

Schuchardt, Hugo (1909) Die Lingua Franca. *Zeitschrift für Romanische Philologie* 33, 441–61.

Schuchardt, Hugo (1921) *Die Sprache der Saramakkaneger in Surinam*. Verhandelingen der Koninklijke Akademie van Wetenschappen te Amsterdam, Afdeling Letteren, Letterkunde N.R. 14, 6.

Schumann, John F. (1978) *The pidginization hypothesis: a model for second language acquisition*. Rowley, MA: Newbury House.

Schwartz, Bonnie D. and Richard A. Sprouse (1996) L2 cognitive status and the full transfer, full access model. *Second Language Research* 12, 40–72.

Seifart, Frank (2005) The structure and use of shape-based noun classes in Miraña (North West Amazon). Doctoral dissertation, Radboud University Nijmegen. MPI *Series in psycholinguistics* 31.

Sekerina, Irina (1994) Copper Island (Mednyj) Aleut: a mixed language. *Languages of the World* 8, 14–31.

Selkirk, Elisabeth (2004) The prosodic structure of function words. In John McCarthy (ed.) Optimality theory in phonology. [Originally in Jill Beckmann, Laura Walsh Dickey, and Suzanne Urbancyk (eds.) *Papers in optimality theory*. Amherst, MA: GLSA Publications 439–470.]

Selkirk, Elisabeth and Tong Shen (1990) Prosodic domains in Shanghai Chinese. In Inkelas and Zec (eds.), pp. 313–337.

Seuren, Pieter and Herman Wekker (1986) Semantic transparency as a factor in Creole genesis. In Pieter Muysken and Norval Smith (eds.) *Substrata versus universals in Creole genesis*. Amsterdam: Benjamins, pp. 57–70.

Shapiro, Kevin and Alfonso Caramazza (2003) The representation of grammatical categories in the brain. *Trends in Cognitive Sciences* 7, 201–206.

Shapiro, Kevin, Lauren R. Moo, and Alfonso Caramazza (2006) Cortical signatures of noun and verb production. In *Proceedings of the National Academy of Sciences*, 31 January, 103, pp. 1644–1649.

Shi, Rushen (2006) Basic syntactic categories in early language development. In Ping Li *et al.* (eds.), 90–102.

Shi, Rushen, Ann Cutler, and Janet Werker (2003) Function words in early speech perception. In *Proceedings of the 15th International Conference of Phonological Sciences*, pp. 3009–3012. Autonomous University of Barcelona.

Shi, Rushen, Janet Werker, and J. Morgan (1999) Newborn infants' sensitivity to perceptual cues to lexical and grammatical words. *Cognition* 72, 11–21.

Shillcock, Richard C. and Ellen G. Bard (1993) Modularity and the processing of closed-class words. In Gerry Altmann and Richard Shillock (eds.) *Cognitive models of speech processing: the second Sperlonga meeting*. Hillsdale, NJ: Lawrence Erlbaum Associates, pp. 163–185.

Sinor, Denis (1988) The problem of the Ural-Altaic relationship. In Denis Sinor (ed.) *The Uralic languages: description, history and foreign influences*. Handbuch der Orientalistik 8: Handbook of Uralic studies 1; Leiden: E.J. Brill. 706–714.

Sloan Berndt, Rita (1990) Preface. In Menn and Obler (eds.), pp. xxv–xxvii.

Smith, Geoff P. (2002) *Growing up with Tok Pisin. Contact, creolization, and change in Papua New Guinea's national language*. London: Battlebridge.

Smith, Neil V. and Ianthe M. Tsimpli (1995) *The mind of a savant: language learning and modularity*. Oxford: Blackwells.

Smith, Norval S.H. and Hugo Cardoso (2004) A new look at the Portuguese element in Saramaccan. *Journal of Portuguese Linguistics* 3, 115–147.

Smits, Caroline (1996) *Disintegration of inflection. The case of Iowa Dutch*. Doctoral dissertation, Vrije Universiteit Amsterdam.

Smout, Kary D. (1988) A missionary English from Japan. *American Speech* 63, 137–149.

Snow, Catherine E., Pieter Muysken, and Roos van Eeden (1981) The interactional origins of foreigner talk: municipal employees and foreign workers. *International Journal of the Sociology of Language* 28, 81–91.

Spencer, Andrew (1991) *Morphological theory*. Oxford: Blackwell.

Spencer, Andrew and Arnold Zwicky (eds.) (1998) *The handbook of morphology*. Oxford: Blackwell.

Stark, Jacqueline Ann and Wolfgang U. Dressler (1990) Agrammatism in German: two case studies. In Menn and Obler (eds.), pp. 281–441.

Steele, Susan, with Adrian Akmajian, Richard Demers, Eloise Jellinek, Chisato Kitagawa, Richard Oehrle, and Thomas Wasow (1981) *An encyclopedia of AUX. A study of cross-linguistic equivalence*. Cambridge, MA: MIT Press.

Stein, Peter (ed.) (1996) *Christian Georg Andres Oldendorp: Criolisches Wörterbuch, sowie das anonyme J.C. Kingo zugeschriebene Vestindisk Glossarium.* (Lexicographica Series Maior, 69) Tübingen: Niemeyer Verlag.

Stolz, Thomas (1986) *Gibt es das kreolische Sprachwandelmodell? Vergleichende Grammatik des Negerholländischen.* Frankfurt am Main: Peter Lang.

Stolz, Thomas (2003) Not quite the right mixture: Chamorro and Malti as candidates for the status of mixed language. In Matras and Bakker (eds.), pp. 271–316.

Strömqvist, Sven, Hrafnhildur Ragnarsdóttir, and Ulla Richthof (2001) Input and production in the early development of function words. In Jürgen Weissenborn and Barbara Höhle (eds.) *Approaches to bootstrapping: phonological, lexical, syntactic and neurophysiological aspects of early language acquisition.* Amsterdam: Benjamins, pp. 157–177.

Supalla, Ted (1982) Structure and acquisition of verbs of motion and location in American Sign Language. Doctoral dissertation, University of California at San Diego.

Talmy, Leonard (2001a) *Toward a cognitive semantics. I. Concept structuring systems.* Cambridge, MA: MIT Press.

Talmy, Leonard (2001b) *Toward a cognitive semantics. II. Typology and process in concept structuring.* Cambridge, MA: MIT Press.

Testelets, Jakov G. (2001) Russian works on linguistic typology in the 1960–1990s. In Haspelmath *et al.* (eds.), pp. 306–232.

Thráinsson, Höskuldur (1996) On the (non)universality of functional categories. In Werner Abraham, Samuel David Epstein, Höskuldur Thráinsson, and C. Jan-Wouter Zwart (eds.) *Minimal ideas. Syntactic studies in the minimalist framework.* Amsterdam: Benjamins, pp. 253–281.

Tjon, S. (1988) Conversationele Codewisseling bij Chinese jongeren. Seminar paper, Chinese Department, Rijksuniversiteit Leiden.

Traugott, Elizabeth Closs (1982) From propositional to textual and expressive meanings: some semantic-pragmatic aspects of grammaticalization. In Winfred P. Lehmann and Yakov Malkiel (eds.) *Perspectives on historical linguistics.* Amsterdam: Benjamins, pp. 245–271.

Trefossa [H.F. de Ziel] (1957) Trotji. Puëma. Met een stilistische studie over het gedicht Kopenhage, vertalingen en verklarende aantekeningen door J. Voorhoeve. Amsterdam. Cited from J. Voorhoeve and U. Lichtveld (eds.) *Creole drum. An anthology of creole literature in Surinam.* New Haven, CT: Yale University Press.

Tremblay, Mireille, Fernande Dupuis, and Monique Dufresne (2005) The reanalysis of the French prepositional system: A case of grammaticalization in competing grammars. In Batllori *et al.* (eds.), pp. 109–132.

Tsimpli, Ianthe M. (1996) *The prefunctional stage of first language acquisition: a crosslinguistic study.* New York: Garland.

Urioste, Jorge (1964) Transcripciones quechuas. La Paz: Instituto de Cultura Indígena.

Valdman, Albert (1977) L'effet de modèles culturels sur l'élaboration du langage simplifié (foreigner talk). In Stephen P. Corder and Eddy Roulet (eds.) *The notion of simplification, interlanguages and pidgins and their relation to second language pedagogy.* Genève-Neuchâtel: Droz-Faculté des Lettres de l'Université de Neuchâtel, pp. 114–131.

Veenstra, Tonjes (1994) The acquisition of functional categories: the Creole way. In Dany Adone and Ingo Plag (eds.) *Creolization and language change*. Tübingen: Niemeyer, pp. 99–116.

Veenstra, Tonjes (1996) *Serial verbs in Saramaccan*. Dissertation, University of Amsterdam. Leiden: Holland Institute of Generative Linguistics dissertation series.

Verrips, Maaike and Jürgen Weissenborn (1992) Routes to verb placement in early German and French: the independence of finiteness and agreement. In Meisel (ed.), pp. 283–331.

Vila i Moreno, Xavier (1996) When classes are over. Language choice and language contact in bilingual education in Catalonia. Doctoral dissertation, Vrije Universiteit Brussel.

Vincent, Nigel (1993) Head- versus dependent-marking: the case of the clause. In G. Corbett *et al.* (eds.) *Heads in grammatical theory*. Cambridge: Cambridge University Press, pp. 140–163.

Voeltz, F.K. Erhard and Christa Kilian-Hatz (eds.) (2001) *Ideophones*. Amsterdam: Benjamins.

Voort, Hein G.A. van der (1996) Vestindisk Glossarium. In Stein (ed.) pp. 165–187.

Yakpo, Kofi (in prep.) A grammar of Pichi, the creole of Malabo. Doctoral dissertation, Radboud University Nijmegen.

Weber-Fox, Christine, Laura J. Hart, and John E. Spruill III (2006) Effects of grammatical categories on children's visual processing. Evidence from event-related brain potentials. *Brain and Language* 98, 26–39.

Wenzlaff, Michaela and Harald Clahsen (2004) Tense and agreement in German agrammatism. *Brain and Language* 89, 57–68.

Werkgroep Taal Buitenlandse Werknemers (1978) *Nederlands tegen buitenlanders*. Publikaties van het Instituut voor Algemene Taalwetenschap 18. University of Amsterdam.

Wexler, Kenneth (1994) Optional infinitives, head movement, and the economy of derivations. In David Lightfoot and Norbert Hornstein (eds.) *Verb movement*. Cambridge: Cambridge University Press, pp. 305–350.

Wexler, Kenneth (2003) Lenneberg's dream: learning, normal language development, and specific language impairment. In Y. Levy and J. Schaefer (eds.) *Language competence across populations: towards a definition of specific language impairment*. Mahwah, NJ: Lawrence Erlbaum Associates, pp. 11–61.

Whitney, William D. (1881) On mixture in language. *Transactions of the American Philosophical Association* 12, 1–26.

Winford, Donald (2003) *An introduction to contact linguistics*. Oxford: Blackwell.

Zei, Branka and Neven Šikić (1990) Agrammatism in Serbo-Croatian: two case studies. In Menn and Obler (eds.), 895–794.

Zeller, Jochen (2005) Universal principles and parametric variation: remarks on formal linguistics and the grammar of Zulu. Ingede – *Journal of African Scholarship*. University of KwaZulu-Natal.

Zimmer, June and Cynthia Patschke (1990) A class of determiners in ASL. In Ceil Lucas (ed.) *Sign language research: theoretical issues*. Washington DC: Gallaudet University Press, pp. 201–210.

Zipf, George K. (1949) *Human behavior and the principle of least effort*. Cambridge, MA: Addison-Wesley.

Zobl, Helmut and Juana Liceras (1994) Functional categories and acquisition orders. *Language Learning* 44, 159–180.

Zwarts, Joost (1995) Lexical and functional direction in Dutch. In Marcel den Dikken and Kees Hengeveld (eds.) *Linguistics in the Netherlands 1995*. Amsterdam: Benjamins, pp. 227–238.

Zwarts, Joost (1997) Complex prepositions and P-stranding in Dutch. *Linguistics* 35, 1091–1111.

Zwicky, Arnold M.(1977) *On clitics*. Bloomington, IN: Indiana University Linguistics Club.

Zwicky, Arnold M. (1990) Syntactic representations and phonological shapes. In Inkelas and Zec (eds.), pp. 379–397.

Zwitserlood, Inge (2003) Classifying hand configurations in Nederlandse Gebarentaal. Doctoral dissertation, University of Utrecht. Utrecht: LOT.

Author index

Subject index

Language index